Trading Cards TO COMIC STRIPS

POPULAR CULTURE TEXTS AND LITERACY LEARNING IN GRADES K-8

Shelley Hong Xu
California State University—Long Beach
Long Beach, California, USA

With

Rachael Sawyer Perkins
Dolores Street Elementary School
Carson, California, USA

Lark O. Zunich
Long Beach City College
Long Beach, California, USA

INTERNATIONAL
Reading Association
800 BARKSDALE ROAD, PO BOX 8139
NEWARK, DE 19714-8139, USA
www.reading.org

The International Reading Association attempts, through its publications, to provide a forum for a wide spectrum of opinions on reading. This policy permits divergent viewpoints without implying the endorsement of the Association.

Director of Publications   Dan Mangan
Editorial Director, Books and Special Projects   Teresa Curto
Managing Editor, Books   Shannon T. Fortner
Acquisitions and Developmental Editor   Corinne M. Mooney
Associate Editor   Charlene M. Nichols
Associate Editor   Elizabeth C. Hunt
Production Editor   Amy Messick
Books and Inventory Assistant   Rebecca A. Zell
Permissions Editor   Janet S. Parrack
Assistant Permissions Editor   Tyanna L. Collins
Production Department Manager   Iona Muscella
Supervisor, Electronic Publishing   Anette Schütz
Senior Electronic Publishing Specialist   R. Lynn Harrison
Electronic Publishing Specialist   Lisa M. Kochel
Proofreader   Stacey Lynn Sharp

Project Editor   Amy Messick

Cover   Design, Linda Steere; Illustrations, Celina Villanueva

Web addresses in this book were correct as of the publication date but may have become inactive or otherwise modified since that time. If you notice a deactivated or changed Web address, please e-mail books@reading.org with the words "Website Update" in the subject line. In your message, specify the Web link, the book title, and the page number on which the link appears.

Library of Congress Cataloging-in-Publication Data
Xu, Shelley Hong, 1964-
  Trading cards to comic strips : popular culture texts and literacy learning in grades K-8
/ Shelley Hong Xu with Rachael Sawyer Perkins and Lark O. Zunich.
      p. cm.
  Includes bibliographical references and index.
  ISBN 0-87207-570-2
  1. Reading. 2. Comic books, strips, etc. in education. 3. Popular culture. I. Perkins, Rachael Sawyer, 1972- II. Zunich, Lark O., 1959- III. Title.
  LB1050.Z82 2005
  372.41'2--dc22

2005013829

CONTENTS

FOREWORD

Drawing from her experiences as a literacy teacher educator, Shelley Hong Xu has written an inviting and important book—one that offers readers numerous opportunities to explore firsthand a variety of popular culture texts for the purpose of making connections between students' interests in these texts and the literacy practices common to school curricula. The message that emerges is one no classroom teacher, administrator, parent, or teacher educator can afford to ignore in the media-saturated world in which we live and communicate on a daily basis. It is a message rich with implications for policymakers as well in that it clearly illustrates the impact of popular culture on students' lives and the potential for turning what some would deem a distraction into a focused and worthwhile learning experience.

Trading Cards to Comic Strips: Popular Culture Texts and Literacy Learning in Grades K–8 is unique in many respects. To my knowledge, it is the first book to show (not simply tell) how actual classroom teachers are capitalizing on students' interests in popular culture to bridge home and school literacy learning. In their own words, Rachael Sawyer Perkins and Lark O. Zunich, two former students of Xu, have written chapters that concretely capture their experiences in integrating popular culture texts into their regular, standards-based curricula. As practical as these two chapters are, they do not slight in any way the research and theoretical framework on which the book is based. In fact, it is Xu's long-term research involvement with classroom teachers such as Perkins and Zunich that makes this book a perfect blend of theory and practice.

Finally, even the most seasoned of popular culture enthusiasts are likely to find the book's annotated list of print, audiovisual, and digital resources for teachers a valuable asset and one worth keeping for future reference. For it is in this list and the chapters at large that readers are introduced to a world that students know well—a world deserving of our attention and respect as literacy educators, parents, and policymakers.

Donna E. Alvermann
University of Georgia
Athens, Georgia, USA

ACKNOWLEDGMENTS

This book would have been only a dream without support from many people. I first thank Donna Alvermann for her inspiring book *Popular Culture in the Classroom: Teaching and Researching Critical Media Literacy* (Alvermann, Moon, & Hagood, 1999), which sparked my interests in exploring a relationship between students' outside school experiences with popular culture texts and their literacy knowledge, and possible, promising opportunities for teachers to integrate students' popular culture texts into a literacy curriculum. I am also grateful to her for providing constructive and insightful feedback on my work and for opportunities to collaborate with her in research on popular culture texts.

Much appreciation goes to teachers and their students in California and Texas who welcomed me to their classrooms. The teachers took a risk in striking a balance between teaching a mandated literacy curriculum and integrating popular culture texts. I thank them for generously sharing their work, much of which is featured in this book. In particular, I owe a heartfelt thank-you to Rachael Sawyer Perkins and Lark O. Zunich, two remarkably outstanding teachers in California. Their innovative teaching with an integration of popular culture texts, which they wrote about, respectively, in chapters 3 and 4, was an eye-opening experience for me!

I am grateful to the International Reading Association for supporting my research via an Elva Knight Research Grant and to Texas Tech University for its research funds. The findings and opinions expressed herein, however, are solely mine.

Amy Messick, production editor at the International Reading Association, deserves my special thanks for her patience, guidance, and, most of all, for her excellent organizational skills and careful readings of the book manuscript. Without her, this book would not have been a reality. I am also appreciative of anonymous reviewers for their suggestions to improve the book manuscript.

Finally, I thank my colleagues, friends, and students who supported me in varied ways. As always, I am deeply indebted to my family: to Charlie, my son, who patiently explained to me popular culture texts (for his age group) that were unfamiliar to me, and to Spencer, my husband, who took the full responsibility of being the father and the mother to my son so that I could devote my time and energy to this book.

Shelley Hong Xu

VIGNETTE I.1

On one November morning, Maria, an English-speaking Latina kindergartner who is still unable to recite the English alphabet, surprises her teacher and class. During a show-and-tell, she shares every page of her Blue's Clues notebook where she has scribbled all over. (*Blue's Clues* [Kessler, Twomey, Johnson, & Santomero, 1996–2004] is a television show on Nickelodeon [a United States cable television channel] in which the characters use various clues to solve a problem.) While she is turning the pages of the notebook, she starts talking about one episode of the show in which a dog named Blue needs to use different clues to find out her birthday gift from Steve, a character in the show:

> Once upon a time, there is a dog. Her name is Blue. Blue has to find many, many clues. So she can find that birthday present from Steve. Blue found one clue on bananas on the table. Blue's clue is her paw print, just like this. [Maria is pointing at the blue paw print on the cover of her notebook.] Her paw print is on bananas. So bananas is a clue. Got it?

VIGNETTE I.2

During a recess on one January morning, Jamal, an African American third grader who, according to his teacher, has trouble with writing a story "in an interesting way," is entertaining on the playground a group of preservice teachers from a nearby university. He is singing to the tune of "Who Let the Dogs Out?"—a song by the Baha Men (Prosper, 2000), a band from the Bahamas:

> Who let the dogs out?
> Woof, Woof, Woof, Woof, Woof
> Who let the kids out? Who? Who? Who?
> Teachers let the kids out. Teachers, teachers, teachers.
> Why let the kids out? Why? Why? Why?
> Kids are good today. Yes, Yes, Yes. (Adapted from the original song lyrics by the Baha Men; Prosper, 2000)

VIGNETTE I.3

One day in September during lunchtime, Jing, a Chinese American fifth grader who arrived in the United States from China a few weeks ago, is sitting by himself eating his lunch and enjoying his Yu-Gi-Oh! trading cards written in Chinese characters. (*Yu-Gi-Oh!* [Takahashi, 1996] is a Japanese animation in which characters fight against one another by using cards on which the monsters come alive to participate in actual fighting.) That day is the first day that Jing is allowed to bring these cards to school and play with them only during recess and lunchtime. His parents and teacher think that these cards would make him feel less lonely and anxious at school because he cannot communicate much with his peers in English, a subject that he hated at school in China. Very soon, other fifth graders start gathering around Jing, curiously examining the cards with strange symbols. One boy named Ming, from another fifth-grade class, yells with excitement, "I know some of these characters [in Chinese]!" Ever since that day, Ming and Jing have become good friends. Ming secretively brings his Yu-Gi-Oh! cards written in English to share with Jing and to explain to Jing the English equivalents for the Chinese characters on Jing's cards. A few weeks later, Jing's parents are surprised to find during a teacher–parent conference that Jing has started showing some interest in English words.

The events in these vignettes take place at different school settings, with or without a teacher's presence, and the students and the genres of popular culture texts involved are varied. Emerging from these events, however, is an important common theme: The presence of popular culture texts offers these students an *alternative* or *additional* opportunity to demonstrate their literacy knowledge and skills and to engage in meaningful literacy practices. Such an opportunity otherwise may not have occurred with the presence of only some traditional school texts (e.g., prescribed basal readers).

In Maria's case, her show-and-tell with a Blue's Clues notebook presents an opportunity for her to demonstrate her listening comprehension through retelling one episode of the *Blue's Clues* show and an opportunity for her teacher to learn about Maria's strength in listening comprehension, as well as her need for assistance in mastering the English alphabet. Maria's teacher has created both opportunities through making show-and-tell truly a time for her students to show and tell things that matter in their lives.

Jamal creatively substitutes words in the song lyrics of "Who Let the Dogs Out?" to describe part of his school experience. He also conveys a subtle message—students may not get recess if they do not behave in the classroom. If Jamal's teacher had heard his song, perhaps she would have had a chance to learn more about Jamal's writing ability and then find a way to capitalize on his creativity to address his need—writing a story "in an interesting way." After all, Jamal does know how to compose a message in an interesting (and a subtle) way, as evident in his song.

For Jing, an English-language learner, Yu-Gi-Oh! trading cards help to instill a sense of self and relative security in an English-speaking environment and later to develop a friendship with an English–Chinese bilingual student. Most important, the trading cards become a catalyst for Jing to grow interested in the English language. In Jing's case, Yu-Gi-Oh! trading cards are seemingly a more useful common language for him to communicate with his friend, although both speak Chinese. If Jing's teacher had witnessed the discussions on Yu-Gi-Oh! cards between Jing and his friend, she could have seen a possibility to take Jing's interests in English from the level of words up to that of text through encouraging Jing to read books related to Yu-Gi-Oh!

Students' Experiences With Popular Culture Texts

Vignettes like these may have also occurred in your classroom, and Maria, Jamal, and Jing may look quite familiar to you. These three students are among a young generation of the 21st century who have been saturated and bombarded with media made up of various popular culture texts. Pulitzer Prize–winner David Shaw (2003) wrote in a *Los Angeles Times* article that "Individually and collectively, we spend more time with more media than ever before—an average of 10.5 hours a day, about 25% of that time using two media simultaneously...." According to the TV Turnoff Network (2004), the average time per week that the American child ages 2–17 spends watching television is 19 hours, 40 minutes. Students' interactions with popular culture texts are further evident in the information from the U.S. Bureau of the Census (U.S. Department of Commerce, 2003): For 65.8% of the elementary and secondary students who use computers at home, the predominant application is playing games (90.9%). Other applications include surfing the Internet (68.6%), doing school assignments (68.4%), sending e-mails (51.5%), and using word processing programs (48.7%). Students' immersion in multimedia texts provides them with multiple opportunities to interact with popular culture texts. In the next section, "What Is Text?" I (Shelley Hong Xu) will explain the concepts of text, popular culture, and popular culture text.

What Is Text?

Readers have traditionally and narrowly perceived *text* as words (i.e., print) with meanings, and its interpreted meanings may vary across readers, depending on their life experiences and knowledge about the text content. From a perspective of multiple sign systems (i.e., semiotics) in which each sign or symbol carries meaning, a text includes both print (i.e., words) and nonprint elements (e.g., images, sounds, symbols, and animations; Berghoff & Harste, 2002). Consider how you may have enjoyed the humor from a conversation between two main characters, Frasier and Niles, both of whom are well-educated, at times snobbish, professionals in the television comedy *Frasier* (Casey & Lee, 1993–2004). While watching the show, you, the viewer, would interpret not just their verbal exchanges but also their facial expressions and body language. At times, these nonprint texts would play a far more important role than the words themselves in making you laugh. In a similar nature, you would be less tempted to buy a new burger meal from McDonald's if the image of a delicious, fresh-looking burger was not presented along with words that describe this new product.

Furthermore, from a new literacies perspective, which views literacy beyond merely reading and writing printed words (see chapter 1), a text is never neutral, and its meaning always is embedded in "specific places and at specific times" (Gee, Hull, & Lankshear, 1996, p. 3). For example, when a low-fat diet is the fad, an image of a big slice of beef (a visual text) can exemplify part of an unhealthy diet to viewers. However, when a low-carbohydrate diet is the trend, this same image can exemplify an excellent choice for a healthy diet.

What Is Popular Culture?

Popular culture is a term that often is subject to multiple interpretations; it is hard to define, "like nailing gelatin to a wall" (Alvermann & Xu, 2003, p. 148). Generally speaking, "popular culture is often defined as the large-scale acceptance of and pleasure in a particular text produced for audience consumption" (Hagood, 2002, p. 440). Some examples of what is considered to be popular culture (at the time of publication) are *The Polar Express* (Zemeckis, 2004; an animated movie adapted from a children's book with the same name in which a boy who believes in Christmas and Santa Claus takes a polar express to the North Pole to feel the magic of Christmas) and *The Incredibles* (Bird, 2004; an animated movie in which a family of superheroes saves the world). In *Media Literacies: Varied but Distinguishable*, Hagood (2001) describes three different ways to view popular culture: (1) mass culture, (2) folk culture, and (3) everyday culture.

POPULAR CULTURE AS MASS CULTURE. When popular culture is viewed as *mass culture*, it is at the opposite spectrum from the high culture of the elite, and it is produced for the general public. The general public shares similar meanings interpreted from popular culture—those that are intended by producers of popular culture (Storey, 1996). One with a mass culture view, for example, may think that the television show *Yu-Gi-Oh!* has a negative impact on young viewers because the show is about a group of friends who play a card game of Duel Monsters, in which monsters on the cards come alive and fight against one another. The show is, thus, too violent. In addition, the show may promote commercialism by implicitly and explicitly persuading viewers to purchase commodities associated with the show, from trading cards to videos to toys.

POPULAR CULTURE AS FOLK CULTURE. A *folk culture* view of popular culture recognizes and celebrates popular culture of the general public. Unlike those who consider popular culture as mass culture, people with a folk culture view believe that consumers of popular culture, not producers of popular culture, hold the power to interpret popular culture. Consumers derive the meanings of a popular culture text from their own readings of the text (Jenkins, 1992; Storey, 1996). For example, viewers of the *Yu-Gi-Oh!* show may not consider it a marketing tool from a producing company. Rather, the show may serve as a medium of entertainment for some viewers and as a tool for others to learn about the history, geography, and culture of ancient Egypt, a setting for the show.

POPULAR CULTURE AS EVERYDAY CULTURE. A third view of popular culture is *everyday culture*, which acknowledges that the popular culture producers have a power to convey meanings, and consumers of popular culture also possess abilities to analyze critically the messages in popular culture (Alvermann, Moon, & Hagood, 1999; Buckingham, 1998; Luke & Freebody, 1997). People with an everyday culture view may enjoy the animation in *Yu-Gi-Oh!* and also try to resist the messages from the show (conveyed either implicitly or explicitly) that it is cool to have the trading cards like those that the characters have and to play the Duel Monsters game just as the characters do. The view of popular culture as everyday culture is the one that we, the authors of this book, hold and that this book reflects.

What Is Popular Culture Text?

A *popular culture text* often is made of print and nonprint text. The popular culture text genres (see chapter 5) may include, but are not limited to,

- televisual and film texts, such as in television shows, films, videos, and DVDs (digital video discs);
- hypermedia texts, such as on the Internet;
- musical texts, such as on musical CDs (compact discs) and on music television channels;
- comic book texts, such as in comic books, comic strips, and mangas (Japanese comic books);
- trading card texts, such as in DragonBall Z, Pokémon, and Yu-Gi-Oh! trading cards;
- game texts, such as in games on the platform of personal computers (PCs), Sony PlayStation 2, Nintendo, GameCube, Xbox, Game Boy, or handhelds (e.g., Palm Pilots, pocket PCs); and
- zine texts, which are "either commercially published or self-published magazines," a term "commonly used among early and late adolescents" (Guzzetti, 2002, p. 699), or e-zines (the electronic version of a zine).

Each genre does not often stand alone. For example, a hyperlink in a hypertext about a musical band can lead an Internet user to a video clip of the band's performance—a televisual text—and the user later goes back to the original hypertext to read the rest of the text. The user thus navigates from one genre to another during his or her reading of the hypertext. This hypertext is an example of a text with print and nonprint text. Not all genres of popular culture texts contain print and nonprint text. Some popular culture texts, such as toys or clothing, may have only nonprint text. The absence of print in such a popular culture text does not diminish its function of conveying meaning in a similar way that a text with print and nonprint conveys meaning. For example, a Barbie doll with a slim body shape, golden hair, and blue eyes may communicate well with its players about which type of body is considered beautiful by a society.

The Interplay of Popular Culture Texts With Literacy Teaching and Learning

While interacting with popular culture texts, students demonstrate their literacy knowledge. For example, students need to become familiar with story grammar (i.e., characters, setting, problem(s), problem solutions, and theme) in a television show (Buckingham, 1993) or in comic books and cartoons (Mahiri, 1998) in order to enjoy these popular culture texts. An ability to read critically a popular culture text would allow students to identify gender bias in a video game (Harste et al., 2003). Students, who are capable of making intertextual and intercontextual connections among popular culture texts—such as *X-Men* (a comic book series), *Spider-man* (a movie [Raimi, 2002] and a comic book series), and *PowerPuff Girls* (McCracken, Miller, & Potamkin, 2005; a cartoon in which girls invented in a lab by a male professor use their special power to defeat villains and keep their town safe)—and the events of firefighters, police officers, airplane passengers, and others who saved people's lives on September 11, 2001, would develop a deeper understanding of a concept of superheroes. That is, they would understand that superheroes exist in fiction and in reality, they are males *and* females, and physical powers may not be the only characteristics of superheroes (Alvermann & Xu, 2003). Students' literacy knowledge also can become evident while playing video games. In *What Video Games Have to Teach Us About Learning and Literacy*, Gee (2003) identifies 36 learning principles that a good video game reflects. For example, the 12th principle is the *practice principle*. Gee explains,

> Learners get lots of practice in a context where the practice is not boring (i.e., in a virtual world that is compelling to learners on their own terms and where the learners experience ongoing success). They spend lots of time on task. (p. 208)

Similar to the vignettes at the opening of this introduction, an emerging body of research has documented that an integration of popular culture texts into teaching provides students with an *additional* or *alternative* opportunity to learn about literacy and to demonstrate their literacy skills (Alvermann, Hagood, & Williams, 2001; Alvermann & Xu, 2003; Xu, 2002b). Alvermann, Hagood, and Williams's study with an eighth-grade African American student reported that the student's reading, writing, and talking about his favorite band presented him with an opportunity to apply literacy strategies to his interaction with popular culture text. In a similar way, the topic of *Pokémon* (Grossfeld, Kahn, & Kenney, 2005; a Japanese animation in which animals similar to what exist in nature, but with special powers, help their trainers to fight evil) motivated a sixth grader, who often hated writing, to produce a well-written how-to paper on playing a Pokémon game (Alvermann & Xu, 2003).

In this book, we argue for an integration of popular culture texts into literacy teaching and learning. The first base for our argument is the evidence from existing literature that students bring to school a rich source of popular culture texts, whether schools permit them or not. Along with these texts, students also bring to school a wide spectrum of literacy knowledge and skills, some of which may not be easily demonstrated or become evident to teachers if an opportunity for students to interact with a popular culture text does not exist. Consider conversations between Jing and Ming, in Vignette I.3, on Yu-Gi-Oh! cards and on the English and Chinese equivalents on these cards. These conversations would probably never happen in a classroom setting.

Our argument also is supported by existing knowledge about the role that motivation and interests play in students' literacy learning. In her profile of developing readers, Alexander (2003) contends,

> Reading is an emotional domain, not a coldly cognitive enterprise. Reader motivation and affect are powerful forces in this journey toward competence…educators must work to plant the seeds of individual interests early in students' domain journey because their "motivation from within" will ultimately sustain them. (p. 61)

Alexander's view echoes that of other scholars (e.g., Block, Gambrell, & Pressley, 2002; Guthrie et al., 1998) who argue that learners who are learning to read and are becoming fluent readers rely on their interests to stay focused on learning. Alexander further suggests that "one of the goals of effective instruction during this initial stage of development should be to plant and nurture the seeds of individual interests by helping students discover the personal relevance, value, and beauty of reading" (p. 56).

Other strong evidence that supports our argument for an integration of popular culture texts into literacy teaching and learning comes from the International Reading Association (IRA) and the National Council of Teachers of English (NCTE)—two of the largest professional literacy organizations in the United States. In their *Standards for the English Language Arts* (IRA & NCTE, 1996), both print and nonprint texts are listed in several standards as aiding students to develop literacy competencies:

1. Students read a wide range of print and nonprint texts to build an understanding of texts, of themselves, and of the cultures of the United States and the world; to acquire new information; to respond to the needs and demands of society and the workplace; and for personal fulfillment. Among these texts are fiction and nonfiction, classic and contemporary works.

2. Students read a wide range of literature from many periods in many genres to build an understanding of the many dimensions (e.g., philosophical, ethical, aesthetic) of human experience.

3. Students apply a wide range of strategies to comprehend, interpret, evaluate, and appreciate texts. They draw on their prior experience, their interactions with other readers and writers, their knowledge of word meaning and of other texts, their word identification strategies, and their understanding of textual features (e.g., sound–letter correspondence, sentence structure, context, graphics).

4. Students adjust their use of spoken, written, and visual language (e.g., conventions, style, vocabulary) to communicate effectively with a variety of audiences and for different purposes.

5. Students employ a wide range of strategies as they write and use different writing process elements appropriately to communicate with different audiences for a variety of purposes.

6. Students apply knowledge of language structure, language conventions (e.g., spelling and punctuation), media techniques, figurative language, and genre to create, critique, and discuss print and nonprint texts.

7. Students conduct research on issues and interests by generating ideas and questions, and by posing problems. They gather, evaluate, and synthesize data from a variety of sources (e.g., print and nonprint texts, artifacts, people) to communicate their discoveries in ways that suit their purpose and audience.

8. Students use a variety of technological and information resources (e.g., libraries, databases, computer networks, video) to gather and synthesize information and to create and communicate knowledge.

9. Students develop an understanding of and respect for diversity in language use, patterns, and dialects across cultures, ethnic groups, geographic regions, and social roles.

10. Students whose first language is not English make use of their first language to develop competency in the English language arts and to develop understanding of content across the curriculum.

11. Students participate as knowledgeable, reflective, creative, and critical members of a variety of literacy communities.

12. Students use spoken, written, and visual language to accomplish their own purposes (e.g., for learning, enjoyment, persuasion, and the exchange of information). (p. 25)

What Is This Book About?

During the past several years, I (Xu, 2002a, 2002b, 2004) have done research in California and Texas with elementary and secondary classroom teachers and prospective teachers on their experiences of making school–home connections through popular culture texts for students from diverse socioeconomic, linguistic, cultural, and academic backgrounds. Rachael Sawyer Perkins, a fourth-grade teacher, and Lark O. Zunich, a reading instructor, did a project with their students in which they used popular culture texts as a springboard to explore what is important to their students' lives and to guide students to become critical consumers and producers of popular culture texts.

This book draws from research with a focus on classroom teachers' experiences of integrating popular culture texts into literacy teaching for students from diverse socioeconomic, ethnic, linguistic, and academic backgrounds. This book also is written in response to teachers' curiosity about students' experiences with popular culture texts and to teachers' inquiries about how to make popular culture texts a part of a literacy curriculum in order to make school learning more relevant and interesting to all students. Often, various organizations (e.g., U.S. Department of Education, Public Broadcasting Service, and American Pediatric Association) offer parents tips and guidance on making television watching a positive experience for children. Very few professional organizations, however, provide classroom teachers with resources on making a connection between students' school literacy learning and their outside experiences with media texts.

In this book we do not intend to prescribe a program for using popular culture texts, nor do we want to instruct you to follow certain steps in integrating popular culture texts into literacy teaching. Rather, the purpose of this book is threefold. The first is to inform you of students' experiences with popular culture texts, and of their literacy knowledge, skills, and practices in relation to their engagement with popular culture texts (Alvermann, Huddleston, & Hagood, 2004; Morrell, 2004; Xu, 2002a, 2002b)—not to promote or denounce popular culture text. The second is to engage you in exploring some promising possibilities of considering popular culture texts as another genre of text—the one that holds personal interests for students—and as a catalyst for creating additional or alternative opportunities to support and enhance students' literacy learning, in particular that of reluctant or struggling readers (Alvermann, Hagood, & Williams, 2001; Alvermann & Heron, 2001; Alvermann & Xu, 2003; Xu, 2002a, 2002b). The third is to further your understanding of multiple roles that print-based literacy taught in school continues to play in a media-saturated society such as the United States' and in students' reading all types of texts, including popular culture texts as discussed in detail in chapter 5 (Bruce, 2003; Smolin & Lawless, 2003). Thus, teachers need to capitalize on students' rich experiences with multimedia texts to assist them in becoming aware of a similar process between reading a print-based text and a multimedia text.

This book is organized into two parts. Part 1, Learning From Research and Classroom Teachers, discusses research and describes teachers' experiences of infusing popular culture texts into a literacy curriculum. Part 2, Integrating Popular Culture Texts in Your Classroom, focuses on specific information on how to integrate popular culture texts into literacy teaching. You may choose to read part 2 first and then part 1. Each chapter begins with a vignette (or vignettes), followed by a brief discussion of the vignettes in relation to the focus of the chapter.

Chapter 1 presents research and theoretical foundations on popular culture texts in relation to students' lives, their literacy experiences, and their school learning. Chapters 2, 3, and 4 describe classroom teachers' experiences of integrating popular culture texts into teaching at various grade levels (i.e., first–fourth and sixth–eighth grades) and for students from diverse backgrounds. Chapter 2 focuses on the experiences of a first-grade teacher, a primary-grade reading teacher, and a third-grade teacher. These teachers' experiences resulted from a course assignment they completed while they were enrolled in a graduate literacy course taught by Shelley. Their experiences of connecting popular culture texts with a literacy curriculum provide readers with a broad view of what an integration looks like at different grade levels and in different teaching contexts. All chapters are written by Shelley, except for chapters 3 and 4, written by Rachael Sawyer Perkins and Lark O. Zunich, respectively. These chapters are different in organization from chapter 2; they allow readers to take an in-depth look at a complete process of making popular culture texts part of literacy teaching, from a teacher's surveying students' interests to making a connection between a popular culture text and children's literature. While reading chapters 2, 3, and 4, please keep in mind that one unit or a lesson that a teacher successfully implemented in her class may need to be modified for your students' academic needs and according to your students' interests in popular culture. The teaching examples, which are intended to illustrate what an integration might look like, cannot be a perfect fit for all classes.

Chapter 5 offers suggestions on how teachers can gain knowledge about popular culture texts through learning from students; it also describes the similarities and differences between some commonly read popular culture texts and the texts students are learning at school. Chapter 6 presents some specific ways of bringing popular culture texts into the classroom, ranging from sharing students' and teachers' pleasure derived from reading popular culture texts to engaging students in critical literacy practices with popular culture texts. Chapter 7 discusses issues involved with using popular culture texts (e.g., time management, addressing standards, censorship, and school administrators' support) and presents possible ways for teachers to address each issue.

This book concludes with two appendixes: Appendix A includes annotated resources on popular culture texts, and Appendix B presents reproducible forms for readers' use with popular culture texts in the classroom.

With this overview of the book, you, as a teacher, may be wondering how classroom teachers have used popular culture texts to enhance their students' literacy learning. If you are eager to find out what a Blue's Clues notebook looks like, who the Baha Men are, and what Yu-Gi-Oh! trading cards are, you are invited to participate in exploring popular culture texts and in thinking about alternative or additional ways to use popular culture texts in the classroom. It is time for you to turn the page and begin your journey to your students' world surrounded by popular culture texts.

PART 1

Learning From Research and Classroom Teachers

CHAPTER 1

New Literacy Studies and Popular Culture Texts

VIGNETTE 1.1

In the department of video games at a Wal-Mart store (the largest U.S. discount retail store), five boys are gathering around John, an 8-year-old Caucasian boy who is playing the demo version of a Nintendo game, *Mario vs. Donkey Kong* (Nintendo, 2004; a video game in which Mario, a plumber, goes through various obstacles to defeat the bad guy, Donkey Kong). Although John is the one playing, the other five boys are not passive viewers of the game. After the group figures out that John is not quite skillful at playing this particular game, they offer him specific advice so that he can finish the game and the other boys will get their turns sooner. José, a 10-year-old Latino boy, shouts out, "Make Mario jump to get that help square (where a player learns what to do next), and you'll know what you are supposed to do. Quickly! quickly!" Adam, an 11-year-old Caucasian boy, offers his tip, "Use the *A* button to make Mario jump onto Shyguy [an enemy], press the *B* button to make him pick up Shyguy, and press the *B* button again, and Mario will throw this Shyguy at another Shyguy. You will knock two Shyguys off the path." Morgan, a 12-year-old African American boy, says, "That's what I did when playing *Super Mario 2*" (Nintendo, 1988; another video game with the same character). Dong, a 7-year-old Chinese American boy, agrees with Morgan, "Yeah." Later, Morgan helps John finish the level and gets his turn, during which he completes three levels.

VIGNETTE 1.2

In a third-grade classroom, the students, who are Caucasians, Asian Americans, and Latinos, are having a discussion on *A Fine, Fine School* (Creech, 2001) in small groups, and the teacher is participating as a group member in the discussion by sharing her response to the book. Later, the students are engaged in an activity in which they compare and contrast two characters from the book, Tillie (the student who asks the principal to give weekends and holidays back to students) and Mr. Keene (the principal who wants the students to go to school all year around so that they can learn more things).

Vignettes 1.1 and 1.2 offer us a point of entry into a discussion on what literacy is, how it has been changing, and how people use literacy. From a traditional perspective of literacy, what the six boys are doing in the department of video games in Vignette 1.1 seems to have nothing to do with literacy; they are merely playing a video game—either as a way of entertaining themselves or as a way of wasting time. In contrast, the teacher in Vignette 1.2 engages her third graders in meaningful and purposeful literacy learning through responding to literature and a follow-up compare-and-contrast activity related to the book they read. From a New Literacy Studies (NLS) perspective, both the children in the Wal-Mart store and the third-grade classroom are learning, and they are involved with different types of literacy for different purposes.

In this chapter, I (Shelley) discuss, from an NLS perspective, research on literacy learning inside and outside school settings, which serves as a theoretical foundation for this book. Related to this discussion, I talk about the role that motivation plays in students' literacy engagement. This chapter concludes with an overview of research on students' interaction with popular culture texts and on teachers' experiences with exploring possibilities of integrating popular culture texts. I also present a discussion of four approaches to using popular culture texts in literacy teaching.

New Literacy Studies

Two United Kingdom scholars, David Barton and Mary Hamilton (1998), highlighted the social nature of literacy in an introduction to their work investigating different types of literacy (e.g., vernacular literacies such as cooking literacy and community literacy) with which people were involved in daily life:

> Literacy is primarily something people do; it is an activity, located in the space between thought and text. Literacy does not just reside in people's heads as a set of skills to be learned, and it does not just reside on paper, captured as texts to be analyzed. Like all human activity, literacy is essentially social, and it is located in the interaction between people. (p. 3)

Barton and Hamilton's work was part of the NLS movement, which began in the early 1980s. Researchers with an NLS perspective were interested in what literacy looks like in settings outside of school, such as in the home, community, and workplace, and in how people used literacy in daily life. For example, Shirley Brice Heath (1983) discovered through her ethnographic study of the people of the Piedmont Carolinas that literacy practices in Roadville (a Caucasian working-class community) were very different from those in Trackton (an African American working-class community), and that literacy practices in each community were valued differently by their schools. Roadville children's experience with being read bedtime stories enabled them to have a better chance to be successful at school, while Trackton children's participation in collaborating on a story with other storytellers did not seem to help the children with school literacy tasks.

In a similar way, Street (1984, 1995) documented three types of literacy with which children and youth in an Iranian village engaged: *maktab* literacy (related to Islamic religion and taught in local Qur'anic schools), *commercial* literacy (related to reading and writing that occurred in fruit sales in a village), and *school* literacy (taught in state schools). *Maktab* literacy, though unrecognized from a perspective of Western literacy, involved children in meaningful and active discussion of religious texts and later prepared them well for jobs.

A common theme underlying these examples of NLS is that a wide range of literacy practices exists outside school settings and that these practices often do not fit into the traditional notion of literacy (which is often print based) promoted and valued by school institutions. In the rest of this section, using Vignette 1.1, I explain the concepts central to an NLS perspective: meaningfulness in social contexts, domains and Discourse, social institutions and power relationship, critical literacy practices, multiliteracies, and changing literacy. Although I discuss each concept separately, all concepts are interrelated, which you would easily note through a discussion. A discussion of each concept focuses on an explanation of the concept and on an application of the concept to the event described in Vignette 1.1.

Meaningfulness in Social Contexts

One important concept of literacy as social practice is meaningfulness and purposefulness in a particular social context. Reading and writing are not merely cognitive and psychological processes. Rather, they become meaningful only when situated in specific contexts (Barton & Hamilton, 1998; Gee, 1996, 2003; Heath, 1983; Street, 1984, 1995). It is a meaningful and purposeful literacy practice when a person reads a recipe with the purpose of learning how to cook a new meal. Asking students to learn how to read and spell the words of their favorite food has a meaningful purpose for them; their ability to read and spell the food-related words would be useful when they go grocery shopping with their parents. On the other hand, asking students to repeatedly copy labels for food (some of which students seldom eat) just for the purpose of memorizing these words seems to be less meaningful and purposeful.

In Vignette 1.1, 8-year-old John and the boys around him are not involved in a traditional way of reading—that is, reading words. They, however, try to make sense of the text on the screen (i.e., images, animations, sound effects, colors, and words) by judging the spatial relationship among different images and using appropriate strategies, such as clicking the help button on the screen to obtain hints. This game-playing event is reflective of a literacy practice familiar to this group of boys with game literacy. The text on the screen makes sense to them, and they enjoy the pleasure derived from completing one level and from being challenged constantly at the next, more advanced level. Their motivation is high enough to enable them not to easily give up the game (e.g., in the case of John). Anyone who has not developed game literacy will not know how to start the game, not to mention finishing the first level. Furthermore, images and words, for example, would become meaningless to a game illiterate, who would not know how to interpret them in relation to each other. Thus, meaningfulness and purposefulness of game playing seem to exist among this group of boys.

Domains and Discourse

Other concepts related to literacy as social practice are *domains* and *Discourse*. Barton and Hamilton (1998) define *domains* as "structured, patterned contexts within which literacy is used and learned…. There are particular configurations of literacy practices and there are regular ways in which people act in many literacy events in particular contexts" (p. 10). Each domain has its own structures and ways of doing things. School and home are two different domains, although they share some commonalities. For example, students use literacy skills and texts in both domains, but the types of literacy skills and texts and the frequency of each skill and text differ to a greater extent across the two domains. Students read televisual texts, for instance, more often at home than at school; skills associated with reading televisual texts (e.g., using facial expressions and sound effects for meaning making) are different from those used for reading books at school. School is more structured than home, as teachers follow a set of daily routines and standards in their teaching, and teachers expect students to master skills and concepts appropriate to their grade levels.

In a similar way, Gee (1996) describes *Discourse* as "ways of behaving, interacting, valuing, thinking, believing, speaking, and often reading and writing that are accepted as instantiations of particular roles (or 'types of people') by specific *groups of people*" (p. viii). Gee uses *Discourse* (which focuses on a social aspect of how people use language) with a capital *D* to differentiate it from *discourse* with a lowercase *d*, which refers to connected linguistic units (e.g., words, sentences, and paragraphs). Different Discourse communities value different types of literacy. When shouting out the name of a winning team you support during a sports game, the name is just a discourse. But while shouting, you are also waving your arms, singing, jumping, or clapping. Thus you are behaving in the ways that are recognizable to people from a Discourse community of spectators of a sports game. Because each Discourse community has its own ways of using language and expressing ideas, when people from one Discourse community want to communicate with people from another Discourse community, they need to modify their ways with words. For example, when communicating with parents (who belong to another Discourse group) during a teacher–parent conference, teachers often have to use terms understandable by parents (and the general public) rather than educational jargon. In addition, people can belong to different Discourse communities. A teacher can be a mother or a father, a daughter or a son, a neighbor, and a game player.

In Vignette 1.1, the boys behave differently when in the domain of game playing, which contrasts with the students' domain of reading a book in Vignette 1.2. While playing a game, the boy (John) in Vignette 1.1 is engaged in reading words and other nonword text and in constantly pressing buttons to carry out actions. The boys belong to a Discourse community of game players who know how to play a game, which includes making an intercontextual connection while choosing strategies, that is, applying strategies they used or learned in playing a similar, previous game. Another characteristic of this Discourse community includes a support system. It is common for observers of game playing in a public place, who are initially strangers to one another, to offer support to the game player. People in this community are also very familiar with how to locate resources for practicing their game-playing skills, such as where to get free demo play of a newly released game.

Social Institutions and a Power Relationship

Literacy is never neutral and is often reflective of a power relationship between individuals and social institutions (e.g., students and schools). Some types of literacy, such as print-based literacy, have been dominant forms of literacy taught at school for some time. They thus are more visible, and schools have highly valued them (Barton & Hamilton, 1998; Gee, 1996; Lankshear & Knobel, 2003; Luke & Freebody, 1997). In contrast, teachers do not teach and promote other forms of literacy, such as game literacy, as shown in Vignette 1.1, and these literacies are thus less visible. Print-based literacy is more influential than game literacy because a student's progress from one grade to another in school depends on how well the student can pass standardized (print-based) reading and writing tests. Another example illustrative of visibility and dominance of one particular form of literacy is when a student uses a language at school other than the native language he or she speaks at home. As an only or a predominant medium of instruction, English becomes more visible and valued by schools, while a student's native language tends to be less visible and, in some cases, devalued by schools.

Another layer of a power relationship is associated with who owns what types of knowledge. For example, in an outside of school setting, the boys in Vignette 1.1 hold the power of knowledge related to game playing, a domain in which their teachers are most likely powerless because the teachers possess little or no knowledge of game playing. In this scenario, the boys become teachers of their teachers. When it comes to a school setting, the power relationship is reversed with teachers as knowledgeable authorities and students as less knowledgeable learners.

Critical Literacy Practices

Because literacy is not neutral but is reflective of a power relationship, texts (print, nonprint, or a combination of both) produced by those who hold power may convey messages that mirror their beliefs, perspectives, and ideologies. Readers of texts that are engaged in critical literacy practices would (1) go beyond the surface text and at times beyond the pleasure derived from reading the text, (2) situate the text in a broad social and cultural context, and (3) explore what the text means to a reader and how the text positions a reader (Fairclough, 1989; Freire, 1970; Luke & Freebody, 1997; Vasquez, 2003, 2004). For example, a television show, a print and nonprint text that is familiar to a student, positions him or her as a knowledgeable viewer of the show. By contrast, this same show can position a teacher who is not familiar with it as a less knowledgeable viewer of the show. When a television commercial promotes a fast-food chain's burger (in response to the fad of a low-carbohydrate diet), its image of a big, juicy beef patty, crispy and fresh vegetables, and half a bun (instead of one bun) tells the television viewers that this new burger is healthier than other fast-food burgers, and viewers who want to follow a low-carbohydrate diet should eat this burger. This commercial illuminates this food chain's belief that customers tend to follow what is in fashion (in this case, the diet) and that customers would buy this burger if they followed a low-carbohydrate diet. A closer look at this commercial reveals that it positions all television viewers as followers of a low-carbohydrate diet, and they exclude those viewers who are on another diet (such as a low-fat diet) or those viewers who do not believe in a low-carbohydrate diet.

In Vignette 1.1, if we (as readers, game players, or educators) go beyond the entertainment that a free demo of a newly released video game offers, we easily can sense the commercialism associated with the free demo. Although the demo provides a source of pleasure for the boys at no cost at the time of playing, the demo also serves as a powerful and effective way to advertise this particular game. So eventually Nintendo (the company that produces the game) gains some profit by just making this demo available for Wal-Mart shoppers (and shoppers in other retail, department, and electronic stores). With that said, the boys are positioned as potential buyers of this new game. Another way to look critically at the game playing and the free demo is to explore a gender and linguistic bias. For example, we may question why no girls seem to be interested in playing a demo game. If the game is designed in response to boys' interests, the girl population is excluded. When the linguistic units in the game are written only in English, people speaking another language also are deprived of an opportunity to play and enjoy this game.

Multiliteracies

Another key concept associated with literacy as social practice is multiliteracies. That is, literacy is not limited only to printed words. Rather, literacy involves other modes of meanings, besides the meanings from linguistic units (words) (Gee, 2003; Kress, 2003; New London Group, 1996). New London Group reminds us of various modes of meaning that exist in today's environment: "visual meanings (images, page layouts, screen formats); audio meanings (music, sound effects); gestural meanings (body language, sensuality); spatial meanings (the meaning of environmental spaces, architectural spaces); and multimodal meanings" (p. 80). Even in a print-dominant newspaper, the designers couple visual representations with linguistic units to convey messages. For example, an important piece of story will appear on the front page with a title written in bigger type and with several eye-catching pictures.

In Vignette 1.1, while playing a video game, John deals with linguistic meanings, visual meanings, audio meanings, and spatial meanings. To some extent, he is working with multimodal meanings. The other boys, who are watching John, have read John's body language, which manifests a possible struggle or frustration. During their observation, they deal with gestural meanings as they respond to John's inability to successfully complete a level by offering him specific advice.

Changing Literacy

A last crucial NLS concept is related to the changing nature of literacy. Because literacy is social and cultural, and society and culture constantly change, literacy practices accordingly change (Lankshear & Knobel, 2003). People acquire new forms of literacy "through processes of informal learning and sense making as well as formal education and training" (Barton & Hamilton, 1998, p. 12). Computer literacy, for example, is one example of a new form of literacy that has occurred with the advancement and widespread use of technology in the world. Computer literacy, which not many people possessed 10 or 20 years ago, has become an important qualification in the 21st century that many employers seek in their potential employees.

The boys in Vignette 1.1 are observing, playing, and exchanging advice, all of which are part of informal learning and sense making. It seems that they have acquired or are acquiring game literacy related to playing Nintendo games. When more people can afford an Internet connection at home, those interested in game playing can play games online and search for cheats (hints that help a game player win a video game faster or do things that are not written in the game manual) and strategies online. When this time comes, a new form of literacy related to game playing *online* would emerge.

Key Points of New Literacy Studies

To sum up this section, the social nature of literacy includes the following concepts:

- Literacy carries meaning only in its specific context.
- Each domain has its own structures and ways of doing things, and different Discourse groups use literacy in different ways.
- Some forms of literacy are more influential and powerful than others because they are supported by some social institutions.
- One who practices critical literacy becomes a critical consumer of literacy text.
- Literacy involves not only linguistic units but also other modes of meanings, such as visual, audio, gestural, spatial, and multimodal meanings.
- Literacy changes with the society, and new forms of literacy come into being with such changes.

By now you have probably developed some understandings of the key concepts in NLS. I invite you to apply these concepts related to literacy as social practice to Vignette 1.2 (Figure 1.1; see also Reproducible A.1 in Appendix B). I also encourage

Figure 1.1   Literacy as Social Practice

Vignette 1.2
In a third-grade classroom, the students, who are Caucasians, Asian Americans, and Latinos, are having a discussion on *A Fine, Fine School* (Creech, 2001) in small groups, and the teacher is participating as a group member in the discussion by sharing her response to the book. Later, the students are engaged in an activity in which they compare and contrast two characters from the book, Tillie (the student who asks the principal to give weekends and holidays back to students) and Mr. Keene (the principal who wants the students to go to school all year around so that they can learn more things).

Key Concepts of Literacy as Social Practice	Your Understanding
Meaningfulness in Social Contexts	The book is related to students' school experiences. The teacher checks their comprehension through their responses to the book.
Domains and Discourse	Students share their knowledge about their life gained in the outside-school domain. The teacher joins the class discourse community.
Social Institutions and Power Relationship	The teacher negotiates a power relationship between herself and the class through giving them a power to share their response.
Critical Literacy Practices	In the compare and comtrast activity, the students explore Tillie as a strong female character who speaks out about a critical issue at school.
Multiliteracies	During the discussion, the teacher and the students interact with print and illustrations in the book and other modes for meaning (e.g. body language).
Changing Literacy	Literature discussion itself manifests a change in literacy teaching. In the near future, a literature discussion can be done via performing on media.

you to apply these concepts to anything you have observed in your life at home, in your community, and at your workplace.

Motivation and Students' Literacy Engagement

An NLS perspective may not have been directly reflected in research on a relationship between student motivation and students' literacy engagement, but what research has to say about the role of motivation in students' literacy learning supports an argument for an integration of popular culture texts, a type of alternative text that holds personal connection and pleasure for students. Many scholars (e.g., Block, Gambrell, & Pressley, 2002; Guthrie, 2004) have considered promoting students' intrinsic motivation to read as an important goal of successful reading instruction. In Allington and Johnston's (2002) book on exemplary fourth-grade classrooms, they document that many teachers provide interesting materials for instruction.

Guthrie (2004), a leading scholar on motivation, has called for teaching to develop engaged readers. Engaged readers, Guthrie argues, have intrinsic motivation and powerful purposes for literacy tasks. Intrinsic motivation has "such attributes as curiosity, involvement, preference for challenge, and desire to read," and it helps students to increase "the amount of reading" and thus "contributes to achievement more strongly than extrinsic motivation" (p. 4). In a similar manner, powerful purposes "compel an individual to read a certain type of text for certain types of cognitive goals" and help him or her become an expert on this type of text (p. 5). Guthrie also argues that instructional materials should have content that has an "optimal level of familiarity,...connections to students' experience, and the presence of interesting features" (p. 9).

Although research related to popular culture does not generally focus on examining the role of motivation, some findings associated with motivation to read popular culture texts can provide some insights into a relationship between motivation and students' engagement with literacy tasks. A study by Alvermann (2001) reports on an African American adolescent, Grady, who disliked reading at school and in an after-school media club. This same young man, however, was eager to participate in e-mail communications with Alvermann and was very much interested in reading a Pokémon trainer's manual. In a similar manner, how intrinsic motivation plays in students' learning is well illustrated in Morrell's (2004) own experience of linking popular culture texts (e.g., hip-hop songs) to classic literature (e.g., Shakespeare's "Sonnet 29" [1938] and Whitman's "Oh Me! O Life!" [1937]) in his secondary English classes. Both Alvermann's observation and Morrell's experience echo the insights from New London Group (1996): "There is ample evidence that people do not learn anything well unless they are both motivated to learn and believe that they will be able to use and function with what they are learning in some way that is in their interest" (p. 85). Besides the fact that interesting materials play a role in motivation, Gee (2003) discovered, through his own experiences of playing different types of video games and through his observations of children and adolescents playing games, that being challenged to play a game with increasing difficulty and being constantly rewarded for a successful completion of a level excite and motivate game players who sustain their engagement with a game for a longer period of time than with another literacy task (e.g., reading books).

Research on Popular Culture Texts

Students' Engagement With Popular Culture Texts

Scholars have conducted research from an NLS perspective since the late 1990s, focusing on students' interaction with popular culture outside of a school setting. Researchers have been interested in finding out the roles that popular culture texts play in students' lives and literacy knowledge and the skills that students demonstrate while interacting with popular culture texts. Even though the population on which a majority of research has focused continues to be limited to preadolescents and adolescents, the findings from the research have shown important insights into a complex set of relationships among popular culture interests, students' lives, and literacy practices.

Research has indicated that besides the benefit of pleasure and enjoyment that students obtain through their interactions with popular culture texts, students develop and practice schooled literacy—mostly print literacy—and acquire new forms of literacy that they do not learn from school. In a study of his 6-year-old son's experience with Pokémon video games, Sefton-Green (as cited in Vasquez, 2003) notes that his son interacted with a Pokémon-related text in different forms, such as a Pokémon movie and a Pokémon toy. The boy's easy access to a text across different platforms—an intertextual connection—allowed him to obtain more Pokémon-related information than if he could only have read a print text on Pokémon. In a similar manner, a popular culture text offered some students an alternative opportunity to practice and demonstrate their literacy knowledge and skills. In an after-school media club, Ned, an African American adolescent male with below-average reading ability, had the freedom to read, write, and talk about his favorite band (Alvermann, Hagood, & Williams, 2001). If teachers forced Ned to read something in which he was not interested, the researchers contend, his ability to use literacy strategies would never have been visible to them.

Students' engagement with popular culture texts not only makes their literacy skills and knowledge (some of which are related to school-based print literacy) more visible but also helps challenge a common misconception about students passively consuming popular culture without critically analyzing the possible impact popular culture might have on their thinking and their lives. Research on students' interaction with popular culture has shown that students, if guided, can become critical consumers and producers. Working with a class of second, fourth, and eighth graders, Alvermann and colleagues (1999) scaffolded the students in the process of looking at multimedia texts from different perspectives (without discounting their pleasure derived from the texts). For example, Hagood asked the fourth graders first to share why they liked their two favorite bands, Backstreet Boys and Puff Daddy & the Family, and then to analyze the similarities and differences between the messages that the image on the CD jacket of each band tried to pass on to the listeners and fans. The discussion led the students to design a new CD jacket on which they shared an image of "cool and tough" that mirrored their perspective.

In England, Evans (2005) engaged 10- and 11-year-olds in discussing their likes for Beanie Babies (bean-stuffed animals). To Evans's surprise, the children seemed to be more critical than adults thought they were, as the children discussed what collecting Beanie Babies meant. For example, some children recognized the advertising strategies of the Ty company (which manufactures Beanie Babies), such as making a newly released Beanie Baby a rare version and making some Beanie Babies retire earlier so that more people would buy them. Other children attributed a fad of collecting Beanie Babies to adults' involvement. More adults than children, as the children in Evans's study observed, were buying these toys (as presents for their own and others' children).

Four Approaches to Using Popular Culture Texts

In *Popular Culture in the Classroom*, Alvermann and colleagues (1999) describe four approaches to using popular culture texts based on existing research on popular culture. In the first approach (I call it an *approach of banning popular culture*), teachers view students' popular culture texts as *low culture* as opposed to *high culture* (e.g., canonical texts, such as classic children's literature). In this view, popular culture is harmful to students' mental and moral development, and thus teachers have a responsibility to keep popular culture texts out of an official school setting, including talks of popular culture interests and any commodities associated with popular culture (e.g., a T-shirt with a picture of Spiderman).

The second approach (I call it an *approach of critically analyzing popular culture*) allows for the presence of popular culture texts in school but for an educational purpose. Teachers with the second approach would permit students to bring popular culture texts into the classroom and would then engage them in critically reading and analyzing popular culture texts without inviting students to share their pleasure derived from the texts. Popular culture texts thus become an object of critical analysis rather than a source of pleasure as they are for students in an outside of school setting. For example, if students expressed their love for a rap artist and started performing a rap song, teachers would seize this teachable moment to ask students to critically examine some negative messages in the song lyrics and in the performance.

The third approach (I call it an *approach of celebrating popular culture*) focuses on celebrating students' enjoyment with popular culture texts. Teachers with this approach tend to overlook a responsibility to guide students to critically analyze the texts. Teachers, for example, may allow students to write about the Spider-man character from the movie *Spider-man* (Raimi, 2002), but do not ask students to discuss and compare how this character is similar to or different from strong female characters in other movies, such as *Charlie's Angels* (Barrymore, Goldberg, Juvonen, & Nichol, 2000; three women detectives use their martial arts skills, knowledge of technology, and sex appeal in solving a case of stolen high-tech software) and *Catwoman* (Fottrell, Melniker, Uslan, & Pitof, 2004; a woman who is bullied by others subsequently acquires catlike abilities—speed and reflexes—and takes revenge).

In the fourth approach (I call it *celebrating and critically analyzing popular culture*), teachers provide students with opportunities to express their pleasure derived from popular culture texts, possibly through sharing why they like one particular popular culture text. In the meantime, teachers engage students in discussing various issues (e.g., gender, ethnicity, and multiple perspectives) related to the texts. Teachers, for example, would ask students to share their pleasure by discussing questions such as why they like the movies *Spider-man* and *Spider-man 2* (Raimi, 2004), or which actor has the best performance in each movie. Later, teachers would guide students to explore issues associated with the movies, such as gender. Teachers could ask students to compare and contrast the Spiderman character with other strong male and female characters in children's literature (e.g., Juice in *Just Juice* [Hess, 1999]) and in other movies (e.g., *Charlie's Angels* and *Catwoman*). The fourth approach is the one we prefer to use, and many examples in this book are reflective of this approach to some extent.

The framework of the four approaches has provided a valid and useful tool to analyze teachers' thinking on using popular culture texts. These four approaches of using popular culture texts have been used in my work (Xu, 2004) with 15 female teachers. The findings of this study have suggested that teachers predominantly used the third approach of celebrating popular culture, and those who employed the fourth approach of celebrating and critically analyzing popular culture exhibited differences in how they would engage their students in critically reading and analyzing a popular culture text (without discounting students' pleasure). A few teachers alternated between the second and third approaches.

Now that you have gained some understandings of the four approaches, you may want to try exploring with a peer the use of these four approaches (see Figure 1.2; see also Reproducible A.2 in Appendix B). Choose the same piece of popular culture text (e.g., the *Spider-man 2* movie), think about how you might view and use it, and then assign an approach to it based on the description of each approach I have explained. Finally, discuss with your partner the similarities and differences in the approach(es) to using popular culture texts.

Figure 1.2   Four Approaches to Using Popular Culture Text

1. Popular Culture Text: *PowerPuff Girls TV show*

2. How You Might View and Use It:

The girls in the show have girl power! To some extent, they are good role models for female students.

I would use this TV show along with other children's books that have strong female characters (e.f., Ed Young's Lon Po Po)

2. How Your Partner Might View and Use It:

Yes, the girls are powerful, cute, and funny. But there is too much violence. The girls are always fighting.

I don't think I would use this show in my teaching. My principal and parents would have a problem with it.

3. Your Approach(es)

a combination of 3rd and 4th approach

3. Your Partner's Approach(es):

1st approach

Similarities in Approach(es) Between You and Your Partner:

Both are familiar with the show. But our approaches don't share anything in common.

Differences in Approach(es) Between You and Your Partner:

I try to bring to class a text that interests my students and that has some connections to what we are learning.

My partner seems to have some reservations about a popular culture text and doesn't see its use in teaching.

Exploring an Integration of Popular Culture Texts

In comparison to a growing body of research on students' engagement with popular culture, there is only an emerging line of research on teachers' experiences with learning about students' popular culture interests and with trying an integration of popular culture texts into a literacy curriculum. The research, though limited and emerging, generally is promising.

Research on the learning experiences of classroom teachers and literacy teacher educators has focused on the process of how to learn about students' popular culture interests and on what educators have learned (Alvermann & Heron, 2001; Gee, 2003; Mahar, 2003; Norton, 2003; Vasquez, 2003). In an outside school setting, Vasquez became familiar with Pokémon after talking with her nephew and observing his design of a new Pokémon trading card. Similarly, Gee, through observing his own son and other children play video games and through his own experience of playing, identified 36 learning principles that applied to playing a well-designed video game. In an after-school media club, Alvermann and Heron became students of a high school student who was a fan of a Japanese animé (Japanese animated cartoons), *DragonBall Z* (Fukunga, Fukunga, Watson, & Fukengama, 1996–2003; characters fight against villains and evil people to prevent them from possessing magic Dragon Balls). In a school setting, Norton read and listened to her students talk about Archie comic books (about life and friendship of a teenage boy) and came to realize many literacy skills and strategies that her students employed during their engagement with *Archie* comic books (e.g., critical thinking skills). Like Norton's students, Mahar's middle school students from an animé club taught her about a wide range of Japanese animé.

In the setting of a literacy teacher education course, Harste and colleagues (2003) conducted a study with 20 teachers and future teacher educators who were engaged in playing a first-person shooter game, a subgenre of video games popular among students of various ages which involves "moving through a virtual world in a first-person perspective (you see only what you are holding and move and feel as if you yourself are holding it) using weapons to battle enemies" (Gee, 2003, p. 26). As the study revealed, the teachers and future teacher educators perceived playing a game as "meaningless child's play," voiced their opinion of being positioned as the less knowledgeable ones who did not know how to play the game, and expressed their "moral and ethical concerns" about the game (Harste et al., 2003, p. 227). Given the experiential gap between children and literacy workers Harste and his colleagues had observed, they suggested that educators "study common literacy events in order to better understand our students and to be able to build curriculum from that point of reference" (p. 226), and to "keep our curricula current and our teaching relevant" (p. 228). In doing so, teachers make their school literacy-learning experience more personally meaningful and engaging to students.

In the United Kingdom, Marsh (2003) worked with future teachers who expressed positive attitudes toward integrating students' popular culture interests. But Marsh's observation of these teachers during their field experiences proved to her that teachers' actual use of students' popular culture texts was minimal. In the United States, I (Xu, 2002a, 2002b, 2004) conducted research with preservice and inservice teachers to examine their experiences of using popular culture texts.

Findings have indicated that teachers believe popular culture has a positive influence on students' motivation (judged by students' engagement and changed attitudes toward school work) and learning (judged by the reading or language arts standards addressed). My studies also have shed some light on why teachers tended to hesitate to integrate popular culture into a literacy curriculum. Some examples of possible reasons were teachers' limited knowledge of students' popular culture texts, time and curriculum constraints that allowed for little divergence from a scripted curriculum, a lack of school administrators' understanding and support, censorship, and issues associated with popular culture (e.g., violence, gender, and racial biases).

What educators have learned from exploring students' popular culture texts helps them challenge their stereotypical, negative views of the texts and begin developing an understanding of why popular culture texts are important to their students. To some educators, their experiences of exploring popular culture texts (as in Harste and his colleagues' study) have reinforced, to some extent, their negative and resistant view about popular culture texts. Additionally, educators have also come to realize that while interacting with popular culture texts, students do have some levels of engagement with school-like literacy practices and, in the meantime, have an opportunity to develop other forms of literacy (e.g., game literacy). The experiences have allowed educators to witness the social nature of students' literacy practices with popular culture texts. That is, students belong to various Discourse communities into which educators may find it hard to belong, not to mention maintain a status of a knowledgeable authority, a role that educators often assume.

Concluding Thoughts

This chapter discusses how literacy is defined differently from an NLS perspective, how literacy practices have become more of a sociocultural process rather than only a cognitive process, and how meaning making relies not only on linguistic units but also on nonlinguistic units. These new ways of looking at literacy practices provide a useful and unique lens from which we discern and understand students' engagement with popular culture texts. Alvermann and colleagues' (1999) four approaches to using popular culture texts in teaching offer classroom teachers a useful guide for infusing popular culture text into teaching to support students' literacy learning. Finally, research on teachers' learning experiences of integration, though limited, has shown some promising possibilities. In the rest of the book, you will read many examples of teachers' integration of popular culture texts, and I hope that these examples provide you with a starting point to consider bringing these texts into teaching as another way to enhance students' literacy learning.

CHAPTER 2

Integrating Popular Culture Texts in Primary Grades

VIGNETTE 2.1

In a first-grade classroom with predominantly Latino children, Anna, a teacher, is reviewing different types of nouns with her students. When she gets to the proper noun category, she says, "I know you know many proper nouns, like SpongeBob (a character in the television animation *SpongeBob SquarePants* [Hillenburg, 2005], which is about friendship among various sea animals), Ash (a human character in the television animation *Pokémon* [Grossfeld, Kahn, & Kenney, 2005])...." Before she is able to finish her examples, the 20 students in her class start giving out examples of proper nouns (Xu, 2004, p. 417).

This vignette illustrates a possible way that teachers may capitalize on students' familiarity with popular culture to enhance students' literacy learning. In this chapter, I (Shelley) showcase three teachers' different ways of making popular culture texts part of their teaching in a primary grade. All three teachers took a graduate literacy course that I taught. One of the required course assignments was to do a project that explored the use of popular culture texts in relation to literacy teaching and learning. Once they had finished the project, the teachers wrote a paper that detailed the process of their exploration and reflected on their experience. How each of the teachers infused popular culture texts into literacy curriculum varied—there seems to be no one fixed, perfect way to build on students' interests. (This point also will be evident in Rachael's chapter 3 and Lark's chapter 4.) In this chapter, you will learn how each teacher gained knowledge of students' popular culture interests, seized teachable moments of linking popular culture texts with children's literature, and guided the students in different literacy activities with popular culture texts. (Note that pseudonyms are used for teachers and students throughout the chapter.)

Superheroes Are Not Just Boys and Big: Jean's Unit on Superheroes

Jean was a middle class Caucasian who had been teaching for 10 years when she conducted this project. Her 20 first-grade students were mainly from European American middle and upper middle class families, and most of them academically were at the first-grade level. The 400 students in her school were mainly middle class; about 5% were English-language learners. Jean's daily literacy instruction included minilessons on phonic skills and concepts, comprehension, and vocabulary; read-alouds; and guided readings. Her students often were engaged in journal writing, independent reading, and literature discussion. Jean was aware of her limited knowledge of students' popular culture interests but felt that she knew a little bit about them through her 8-year-old son.

Learning About Students' Popular Culture Interests

Initially, Jean did not know how to connect students' popular culture interests with her teaching, in particular with addressing reading and language arts standards (see IRA & NCTE, 1996). One teachable moment occurred in a literature discussion during which her students' fascination with superheroes gave Jean an idea of how to take advantage of her students' expert knowledge of superheroes. In a small-group literature discussion on *Little Red Riding Hood* (McPhail, 1995), Jean heard the following conversation:

James: The huntsman is a superhero. He saved the Little Red Riding Hood and her grandma.

Charlie: Yeah, he saved two people at one time.

José: He is a superhero. But Captain Underpants [a character from Dav Pilkey's *Captain Underpants* series] is a superhero. He saved the world.

At this moment, Jean joined the group and started an interesting discussion with the group about who is a superhero in books the students had read.

Jean: Who else in the books we have read is a superhero?

John: Muriel in *World Famous Muriel and the Scary Dragon* [Alexander, 1985]. But she is a girl.

Jean: What do you mean she is a girl?

John: You know, superheroes are boys and men.

Jean: Not always.

Mary: Yes, not always. In *Lon Po Po* [Young, 1989; a Chinese folk tale with a plot similar to *Little Red Riding Hood*], the sisters are truly superheroes. They saved themselves without boys' help.

Jean: Looks likely we can have a unit on superheroes so that we all can learn more about superheroes.

Students' interests in superheroes and an emerging stereotypical understanding of gender related to superheroes gave Jean an idea of using students' knowledge of superheroes as a springboard to guide her students in learning more about superheroes. She decided to tie this learning experience (i.e., exploring superheroes) with addressing one of the reading and language arts standards for first grade—identifying character traits. Admitting that she had some knowledge of superheroes (because of her son), Jean asked her son questions about the superheroes portrayed in television cartoons and comic books and later learned more about superheroes from her students throughout various literacy activities.

Integrating Students' Popular Culture Texts

BRAINSTORMING SUPERHEROES STUDENTS KNEW. Jean began her unit on superheroes by asking her students to brainstorm the superheroes they knew from books, video games, television shows, and movies. Later, she also added comic books after she had learned that some students were quite knowledgeable of comic books through reading with their older siblings. Table 2.1 lists the superheroes that Jean's students identified.

READING BOOKS WITH SUPERHERO CHARACTERS. After reading the list of superheroes that her students identified, Jean realized that she was more familiar with the superheroes in books than those in television shows, movies, comic books, and video games. Jean felt, as she shared with her peers and me in the graduate course, a need to learn about the superheroes that were unfamiliar to her. Jean watched television shows and videotapes, and she read several issues of the *Spider-man*, *Superman*, and *X-Men* comic book series. In addition to her own learning about various kinds of superheroes, Jean gathered all the books with superheroes for her students to read during independent reading time, as she believed that students needed to become familiar with superheroes from varied text genres. (See Table 2.2 for a list of books with superhero characters; also see Field's article "Beyond Superman: Superheroes in Picture Books" [2004] for more recently published books.) She also asked those students who are familiar with the superheroes presented in different media genres to give a brief presentation during a daily oral language activity on their superheroes.

DISCUSSING CHARACTER TRAITS OF SUPERHEROES. During the unit, Jean had planned for a discussion activity, but she did not prepare any discussion questions. Rather, she allowed the discussion to naturally evolve. Once they were on the topic, her students were leading the discussion in which they portrayed a

Name of Superhero	Text	Source of Text				
		Book	Video Game	TV Show	Movie	Comic Book Series
Huntsman	*Little Red Riding Hood*	x				
Captain Underpants	Captain Underpants series	x				
Muriel	*World Famous Muriel and the Scary Dragon*	x				
Spiderman	*Spider-man*	x	x	x	x	x
Superman	*Superman*	x	x	x	x	x
X-Men	*X-Men*		x	x	x	x
PowerPuff Girls	*PowerPuff Girls*	x	x	x	x	
Pikachu	*Pokémon*	x	x	x	x	x
Yami Yu-Gi	*Yu-Gi-Oh!*		x	x	x	x
Austin Powers	Austin Powers series	x	x		x	
Goku, Piccolo	*DragonBall Z*	x	x	x	x	x

relatively complex picture of what a superhero can do and what he or she looked like (or should look like).

Steve: I think Pikachu [a Pokémon character that is an electrical mouse] is a superhero.

Jose: No, he is not. He is so little, and he is an electrical mouse.

Steve: Yes, he is. He has special power, and he always saves Ash, Brock, and Misty [human characters from the animation *Pokémon*].

Jean: So, the size does not matter.

Jose: Yes. One time, I saw on television about a 5-year-old boy who called 911 to save his grandpa. He had a heart attack.

Jean: How interesting. Now we are talking about real superheroes. Jose, what made you say this boy is a superhero?

Jose: He saved his grandpa's life by calling 911. And he is little.

Table 2.2   Books With Superhero Characters

Bennett, W.J. (1997). *The children's book of heroes*. New York: Simon & Schuster.

Derrien, P. (2002). *Super H*. New York: Rouergue.

Fisch, S. (2000). *Batman beyond: No place like home*. New York: Random House.

Graham, B. (2000). *Max*. Cambridge, MA: Candlewick.

Hoffman, E. (1999). *Heroines and heroes/Heroínas y héroes* (Eida de la Vega, Trans.). St. Paul, MN: Redleaf Press.

Isaacs, A. (1994). *Swamp angel*. New York: Dutton Children's Books.

Kellogg, S. (1995). *Sally Ann Thunder Ann Whirlwind Crockett: A tall tale*. New York: Morrow Junior Books.

Lester, J. (1994). *John Henry*. New York: Dial Books for Young Readers.

Mooney, E.S. (2000). *The PowerPuff girls: Snow-off*. New York: Scholastic.

Peterson, S. (2000). *Batman beyond: New hero in town*. New York: Random House.

Pilkey, D. (1997). *The adventures of Captain Underpants*. New York: Blue Sky Press.

Pilkey, D. (2000a). *Captain Underpants and the perilous plot of Professor Poopypants*. New York: Blue Sky Press.

Pilkey, D. (2000b). *Ricky Ricotta's giant robot: An adventure novel*. New York: Blue Sky Press.

Pilkey, D. (2000c). *Ricky Ricotta's giant robot vs. the mutant mosquitoes from Mercury*. New York: Blue Sky Press.

Pilkey, D. (2001a). *Captain Underpants and the wrath of the wicked Wedgie Woman*. New York: Blue Sky Press.

Pilkey, D. (2001b). *Ricky Ricotta's giant robot vs. the voodoo vultures from Venus*. New York: Blue Sky Press.

Pilkey, D. (2002a). *Ricky Ricotta's mighty robot vs. the Jurassic jackrabbits from Jupiter*. New York: Blue Sky Press.

Pilkey, D. (2002b). *Ricky Ricotta's mighty robot vs. the mecha-monkeys from Mars*. New York: Blue Sky Press.

Pilkey, D. (2003a). *Captain Underpants and the big, bad, battle of the Bionic Booger Boy, part 1: The night of the nasty nostril nuggets*. New York: Blue Sky Press.

Pilkey, D. (2003b). *Captain Underpants and the big, bad, battle of the Bionic Booger Boy, part 2: The revenge of the ridiculous Robo-Boogers*. New York: Blue Sky Press.

Pinkney, B. (1997). *The adventures of Sparrowboy*. New York: Simon & Schuster.

Schanzer, R. (2001). *Davy Crockett saves the world*. New York: HarperCollins.

Whatley, B. (1999). *Captain Pajamas*. New York: HarperCollins.

Wisniewski, D. (2002). *Sumo mouse*. San Francisco: Chronicle.

Jean: So a superhero needs to know how to use the brain. Who else in our life do you know is a superhero?

Brooke: Those soldiers who fight in another country. They are so strong, and brave.

Jean: [smiling] You just mentioned another character trait for a superhero—bravery.

At the conclusion of the small-group discussion, Jean gathered her students and started a large-group discussion on why a person is a superhero and what makes a superhero do what he or she has done. Jean documented her students' responses in Table 2.3.

Lessons From Jean's Experience

Jean did not plan this unit on superheroes ahead of time; rather, she let her students' interests guide her in making instructional decisions as to what needed to be included in the unit and how the interests were tied into a mandated literacy curriculum. Table 2.4 lists the literacy activities and IRA and NCTE (1996) Standards for English Language Arts that Jean addressed with her students. Jean viewed this unit as another way to help her students learn about character traits and gain a deeper understanding of the concept of *superheroes*. To some extent, Jean successfully found a balance between her school district's mandated literacy curriculum and her students' interests that motivated her students to participate in critical literacy practices (Vasquez, 2004). Similar to the students in Dyson's (1997) study with 7- to 9-year-old students from middle and working class backgrounds, the first-grade students in Jean's class had their individual superheroes they admired, and such an admiration at times carried some level of biases (e.g., gender). Jean's guidance in encouraging her students to look critically into the role gender played in a portrait of a superhero did not seem to discount students' pleasure of *reading* texts of these superheroes. In so doing, Jean struck a balance between celebrating students' popular culture and critically analyzing popular culture texts.

Table 2.3   Character Traits of Superheroes

Why Is a Person a Superhero?	What Makes a Superhero Do What He or She Has Done?
saves the world, saves a neighbor's cat, saves his family, defeats evil, defeats bad guys	brave, strong, nice, smart, having muscles, having special power (e.g., electrical shock attack as Pikachu does)

Table 2.4   Literacy Activities in Jean's Unit on Superheroes and IRA and NCTE Standards

Literacy Activities in the Unit on Superheroes	IRA and NCTE Standards
1. Brainstorming Superheroes Students Knew	Standard 1 Standard 3 Standard 8 Standard 12
2. Reading Books With Superhero Characters	Standard 2 Standard 3 Standard 5
3. Discussing Traits of Superheroes	Standard 6 Standard 11 Standard 12

The IRA and NCTE Standards are enumerated in this book's Introduction, pages 7–8.

These Two Bands Celebrate Their Own Culture: Sherry's Unit on Musical Bands

Sherry was a middle class Caucasian who had been teaching for 15 years when she conducted this project. Sherry worked in an early reading intervention program with twenty 5- to 8-year-old students in a Title I school (the U.S. federal government's compensatory education program) with a student population of 350 in a rural school district. Most of her students were from upper working class and lower middle class families. Some students were Spanish–English bilingual; others were native English speakers with reading difficulties. Sherry provided the students with additional assistance in reading and writing 30 minutes per day for several days in each week.

Sherry's daily literacy instruction included minilessons on phonic skills and concepts (including phonemic awareness activities), comprehension strategies and vocabulary development, read-alouds, and guided readings. Her students were often engaged in journal writing, making words (students use letters from a given list to create words), and independent reading and literature discussion. Sherry was aware of her limited knowledge about her students' engagement with popular culture but expressed a great interest in learning about her students' experiences and in seeking ways to incorporate students' interests into teaching. I have written in my other work about Sherry's experience with integrating popular culture interests into her teaching (Alvermann & Xu, 2003; Barone, Mallette, & Xu, 2005; Xu, 2001). I wanted to write about her experience again because it was illustrative of the additional learning experiences that popular culture texts could offer students who were not generally motivated to be engaged in literacy learning at school.

Learning About Students' Popular Culture Interests

In her popular culture project, a scheduling issue permitted Sherry to work only with a group of five third-grade students that included three Latinos, one African American, and one European American. Sherry described this group of students as "reading below grade level and needing a 'boost' in motivation" (Xu, 2001, ¶ 48). Thus she began her project with a survey in which she asked her students about their favorite television shows, movies, videos, video games, music, magazines, books, websites, and other things that interested them. The survey showed that the dominant popular culture text genres were Latino music and rap music. Similar to Jean, Sherry let her students have a say in planning activities of the unit on music. The following discussion of Sherry's unit on musical bands describes its components.

Integrating Popular Culture Texts

SELECTING A COMMON INTEREST FOR THE UNIT. After Sherry and her students voted on the choice of two songs as the focus of the unit, "Who Let the Dogs Out?" by the Baha Men (Prosper, 2000) and "Azucar" by A.B. Quintanilla and Los Kumbia Kings (1999), the students showed their motivation for the unit. Sherry noted, "a high level of excitement and anticipation prevailed" (Xu, 2001, ¶ 50). Sherry was happy to witness that "the culturally diverse group wanted to use music as a springboard for literacy" (Xu, 2001, ¶ 50). Before planning the unit on bands, Sherry visited the websites of both bands and listened to the songs (although she was familiar with the song "Who Let the Dogs Out?"). After her own exploration of the bands, Sherry thought that both bands "represented two different cultures and different styles of using music as a tool to convey messages" (Xu, 2003, p. 10), and she discovered educational values in the songs by both bands. The songs of the Baha Men, who were from the Bahamas, reflect a blend of music genres such as the indigenous junkanoo music (music of the Bahamas that is played mostly with drums and some European instruments), funk, rhythm and blues, hip-hop, and dancehall. The songs of A.B. Quintanilla and Los Kumbia Kings, led by A.B. Quintanilla, III, the brother of the late Latina pop artist Selena, are in the Tejano style, a Tex-Mex blend of traditional, rock, and country music.

READING THE LYRICS. Sherry had heard about the song "Who Let the Dogs Out?" everywhere, including on the school playground. She was surprised to learn that her students had never read the lyrics of both songs. Feeling the importance of learning more about the songs and using this teachable moment for a short comprehension lesson, Sherry led her students to visit the websites of the Baha

Men (www.bahamen.com) and Asklyrics (www.asklyrics.com/songs/Kumbia_ kings_lyrics/2.htm) for the Baha Men's and A.B. Quintanilla and Los Kumbia Kings' lyrics. Sherry printed out the lyrics and let her students follow along while they were listening to the songs—some of them even hummed along. While they listened, Sherry observed that her students were more involved in the rhythm and beats of each song than they were interested in the actual meanings of the song lyrics. Not to discount students' pleasure derived from listening to the songs, but to encourage students beyond just enjoying the music, Sherry decided to guide her students to learn more about the recording artists and the stories behind their success.

LEARNING ABOUT THE ARTISTS. Sherry and her students again took advantage of the Internet and located information about the two musical bands. The difficulty level of the texts from the websites did not make Sherry's students lose any interest in reading them. Sherry provided each student with a copy of the texts from the websites and then read and explained the text paragraph by paragraph. Several students decided to keep the text to show their friends "the coolest thing they got at school" (Xu, 2001, ¶ 52) that day. After learning more about the artists, Sherry and her students found that "these two groups were decent role models" (Xu, 2001, ¶ 52). In addition, they found that the two groups shared their cultures through music—the Baha Men communicated to listeners the culture of the Bahamas through junkanoo music, and A.B. Quintanilla and Los Kumbia Kings played Tejano to share the Latin American culture.

LEARNING TO DANCE LA CUMBIA. One more activity that Sherry's students initiated was learning how to dance La Cumbia, a traditional dance A.B. Quintanilla and Los Kumbia Kings performed while singing, which some students had seen on a music television station. Sherry at first was worried about how her students were going to learn this dance, as she herself did not know about it at all. She also was concerned about a possible disconnection between learning to dance and her students' literacy learning. After a talk with me during one graduate course session in which I asked her to try her students' idea, she decided to let her students learn how to dance La Cumbia. Sherry tapped into her students' community funds of knowledge (resources of a community) by inviting two parents she knew to teach the group and herself La Cumbia dance. To Sherry's surprise, her students were able to practice the skills of following instructions while learning the dance from the two parents.

COMPARING AND CONTRASTING TWO SONGS. To conclude the unit, Sherry engaged her students in two literacy activities that the students suggested, which seemed to be authentic and purposeful. One literacy task was for the students to compare and contrast "Azucar" and "Who Let the Dogs Out?" Sherry and the students discussed the similarities and differences between the two songs, and then the students copied down the key points in their own Venn diagrams (Figure 2.1) or in

**Figure 2.1   Sample of a Student's Venn Diagram of "Azucar"
and "Who Let the Dogs Out?"**

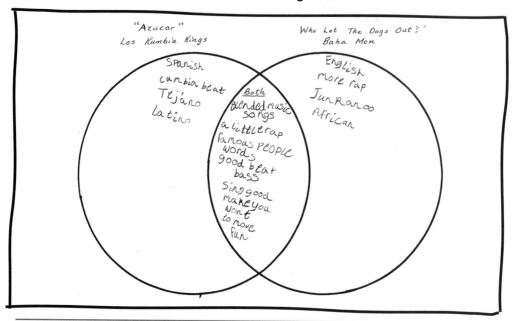

From Xu, S.H. (2001). Exploring diversity issues in teacher education. *Reading Online, 5*(1), 1–17.
Retrieved February 7, 2005, from http://www.readingonline.org/newliteracies/action/xu

a paragraph format (Figure 2.2) and added their own thoughts. In another literacy
activity, each student wrote a thank-you letter to the parents who had taught them La
Cumbia after Sherry reviewed with the students the format of a letter (Figure 2.3).

Lessons From Sherry's Experience

Unlike Jean, Sherry purposefully planned to do a unit based on her students'
popular culture interests. Similar to Jean, Sherry let her students' interests guide
her in making instructional decisions as to what they needed to include in the unit.
As Sherry reflected later in her paper for the graduate course, "The activities grew
according to students' interest and needs. It sort of took on a life of its own" (Xu,
2001, ¶ 56). Table 2.5 lists the literacy activities that Sherry did with her students
and the IRA and NCTE (1996) Standards for the English Language Arts she
addressed. In this unit, Sherry offered her students an opportunity to read print
and nonprint texts. More important, Sherry capitalized on her students' community
fund of knowledge (Moll & Gonzalez, 1994) to make this unit part of culturally
responsive teaching in which she made learning about other cultures not
separated from students' interests and their own culture. Another seemingly
nonliteracy-related benefit Sherry and her students gained through this unit was a

Figure 2.2 Sample of a Student's Paragraph on "Azucar" and "Who Let the Dogs Out?"

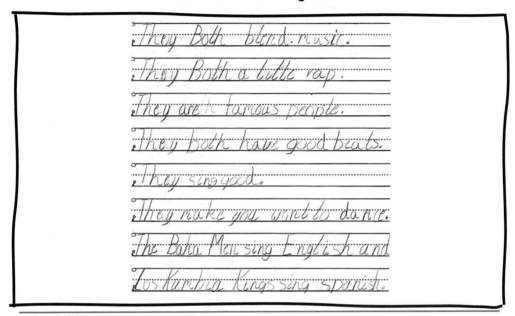

They Both blend music.
They Both a little rap.
They are famous people.
They both have good beats.
They sing good.
They make you want to dance.
The Baha Men sing English and
Los Rumba Kings sing spanish.

From Xu, S.H. (2001). Exploring diversity issues in teacher education. *Reading Online*, 5(1), 1–17. Retrieved February 7, 2005, from http://www.readingonline.org/newliteracies/action/xu

Figure 2.3 Sample of a Student's Thank-You Letter

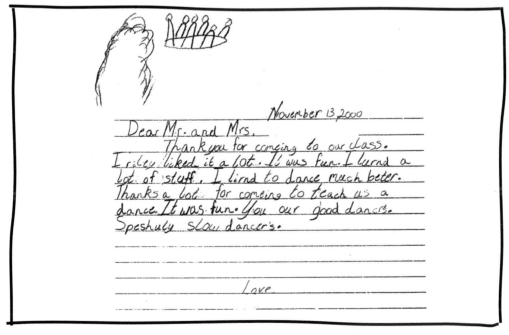

November 13, 2000

Dear Mr. and Mrs.
    Thank you for coming to our class.
I riley liked it a lot. It was fun. I lurnd a
lot of stuff. I lirnd to dance much beter.
Thanks a lot for coming to teach us a
dance. It was fun. You our good dancers.
Speshuly slow dancers.

                    Love

Table 2.5   Literacy Activities in the Unit on Musical Bands and IRA and NCTE Standards

Literacy Activities in the Unit on Musical Bands	IRA and NCTE Standards
1. Selecting a Common Interest for the Lesson	Standard 1 Standard 3 Standard 8 Standard 11 Standard 12
2. Reading the Lyrics	Standard 1 Standard 3 Standard 8 Standard 9
3. Learning About the Artists	Standard 1 Standard 3 Standard 8 Standard 9 Standard 11
4. Learning to Dance La Cumbia	Standard 9 Standard 12
5. Comparing and Contrasting Two Songs	Standard 4 Standard 5 Standard 9 Standard 12

The IRA and NCTE Standards are enumerated in this book's Introduction, pages 7–8.

closer relationship between Sherry and her students. Sherry considered this unit as a way to show her students that she "cared and valued their interests and cultures. I learned La Cumbia right along with them" (Xu, 2001, ¶ 58). Teachers' knowledge of students and a closer connection with students, as Nieto (2004) argued, are key to becoming an effective educator in the 21st century.

Scooby-Doo Can Teach Us About Contextual Clues: April's Unit on Scooby-Doo

April was a middle class European American who had been teaching for five years when she conducted this project. April worked with 20 third-grade students in a Title I school with a student population of 300 in a rural school district. Most of

April's students were from migrant families, and they were heterogeneous in terms of academic performance. April's daily literacy instruction included minilessons on comprehension strategies and vocabulary development. Her students were often engaged in journal writing, making words, independent reading, and literature discussion. The instructional materials included fiction and nonfiction books and local newspapers.

Learning About Students' Popular Culture Interests

April confessed that although she was in her late 20s, she did not know much about her students' popular culture. As she put it, "They are in a popular culture world, and I am in a teacher's world" (Xu, 2003, p. 6). Like both Jean and Sherry, April had an interest in learning about her students' experiences with popular culture. Unlike Jean and Sherry, April chose to develop a unit based on a popular culture text that was familiar to her and her students. April's justification for her text choice was that "*Scooby-Doo* [Hanna & Barbera, 1978; a television animation in which a dog named Scooby-Doo helps his owner and owner's friends to solve mysteries, some of which involve fighting against bad guys] was a television show, movie, and best seller that was mentioned several times in a student survey" (Xu, 2003, p. 6). Another reason for April's choice was that she wanted to see if her students enjoyed the show in a way similar to the way she did. April seemed to have played a major role in developing this unit on Scooby-Doo, but she did take her students' input into consideration. In order to keep herself up with the latest episodes of the show, April started watching the show. Visiting the show's website (which she admitted did not exist when she was growing up) offered April more information on Scooby-Doo of which she was not aware (e.g., the information on the cast, the merchandise).

Integrating Students' Popular Culture Texts

COMPARING AND CONTRASTING SCOOBY-DOO WITH INSPECTOR GADGET. The first activity that April's students did was to compare and contrast one episode of *Scooby-Doo* with *Inspector Gadget Saves Christmas* (Patton, 2001), a short video suggested by some students. After viewing both tapes and having had a review on how to use a Venn diagram, the students discussed in small groups the similarities and differences between the two stories. The students noted how Scooby-Doo and his gang solved a mystery in both a similar and a different way from Inspector Gadget. Some students commented that the techniques used by the creators of the show were very similar to those used by authors of children's books.

ENGAGING IN CREATIVE WRITING. A second activity was to have students complete a story after April read only the first seven pages of *Scooby-Doo and the Weird Water Park* (McCann, 2000). According to April, "the students were thrilled" (Xu, 2003, p. 8) about doing a creative writing assignment related to the show. The students went through the writing process and had their peers edit their drafts, and later the students did their final drafts on a computer. April was amazed at the writings done by some students who often did not enjoy writing and who usually did not produce much in a piece of writing (Xu, 2003; Figure 2.4).

IDENTIFYING CHARACTER TRAITS. A third activity in the unit was for the students to study in depth the character traits in one episode of the show *Scooby-Doo and the Weird Water Park.* For this activity, April had her students watch the show and read the book based on the show. Through providing her students with an opportunity to read multiple versions of a text (e.g., a Scooby-Doo television show and a Scooby-Doo book), April helped some of her struggling readers better comprehend the text with assistance of various contextual clues (e.g., words heard in a read-aloud of a book and in a show, factual expressions seen in a show). Before asking her students to complete a character cluster on one of the characters in the show, April asked her students to discuss the character traits of their classmates. Then, working in groups, the students completed a cluster on the characters from the show—Shaggy, Fred, Velma, Daphne, or a sea creature. In addition, the students were required to write a few sentences about the characters based on the characters' traits or why the students felt that one particular character had the described traits.

WRITING RECIPES. In a fourth activity, April and the students used a Scooby-Doo recipe downloaded from the Scooby-Doo website (www.cartoonnetwork.com/tv_shows/scooby/index.html) to make Scooby-Doo snacks. To encourage her students to tap into their community resources and to tie this unit into their lives, April asked them to write up their favorite recipes (Figure 2.5), all of which were later compiled into a third graders' cookbook. While visiting the Scooby-Doo website, April asked her students to note some reading skills and strategies that they had not noticed or had not used while reading books. For example, she asked her students to think about how icons on the screen actually served as headings or subheadings like those in an informational book. Helping students note a function of icons made literacy learning during this unit go beyond the limit of the show; that is, April was teaching her students how to read an Internet text.

Lessons From April's Experience

In this Scooby-Doo unit, April focused heavily on teaching literacy skills and concepts through multimedia texts and through tapping into students' community funds of knowledge (Table 2.6). During this unit, her students had multiple opportunities to read or write different genres of texts (e.g., movie, book, and Internet text) for authentic purposes, which otherwise would have been impossible for them. These opportunities were especially valuable for the students, given that their interactions with multimedia texts were possible only during a weekly one-hour visit to a computer lab. April's choice of Scooby-Doo, which seemed to be a relatively safe (or less controversial) and familiar topic from

Figure 2.4   Sample of a Student's Scooby-Doo Story

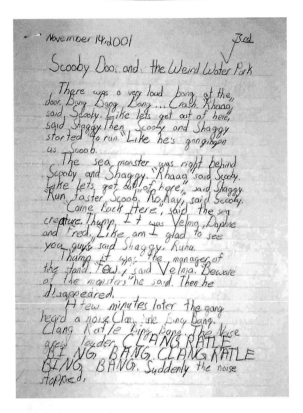

November 14, 2001   3rd

Scooby Doo, and the Weird Water Park

There was a very loud bang, at the door, Bang Bang Bang...Crash. Rhaaa, said Scooby. Like lets get out of here, said Shaggy. Then Scooby and Shaggy started to run. "Like he's gonging on us Scoob.

The sea monster was right behind Scooby and Shaggy. "Rhaaa said Scooby. Like lets get out of here," said Shaggy. "Run faster Scoob, Ro,hay, said Scooby.

Come Back Here", said the sea creature. Thump, It was Velma, Daphne and Fred. "Like am I glad to see you guys" said Shaggy. Runu.

Thump it was the manager of the stand. "Few, said Velma. Beware of the monsters" he said. Then he disappeared.

A few minutes later the gang heard a noise Clang, ttle Bing Bang. Clang Rattle Bing Bang. The Noise grew louder, CLANG RATLE BING BANG. CLANG RATLE BING BANG. Suddenly the noise stopped.

Then they turned around. "AHHAH," the gang found the monster. "RUN," Fred screamed at the top of his lungs. "Like lets get out of here", said Shaggy.

A few minutes later the gang set up an old trap that they had known for a long time. Then finally the monster came. "Now" said Fred then a giant net fell on top of the monster. "Yes" said Shaggy "All Right" said Fred. "We Got em" said Velma. They took off the mask. "It's the man from the stands" said Fred.

So you were the one the whole time. "Yha you got a problem with that"? "No" said Daphne. Then they were in the van and the police had taken the man from the stands to jail.

41

Figure 2.5   Sample of a Student's Favorite Recipe

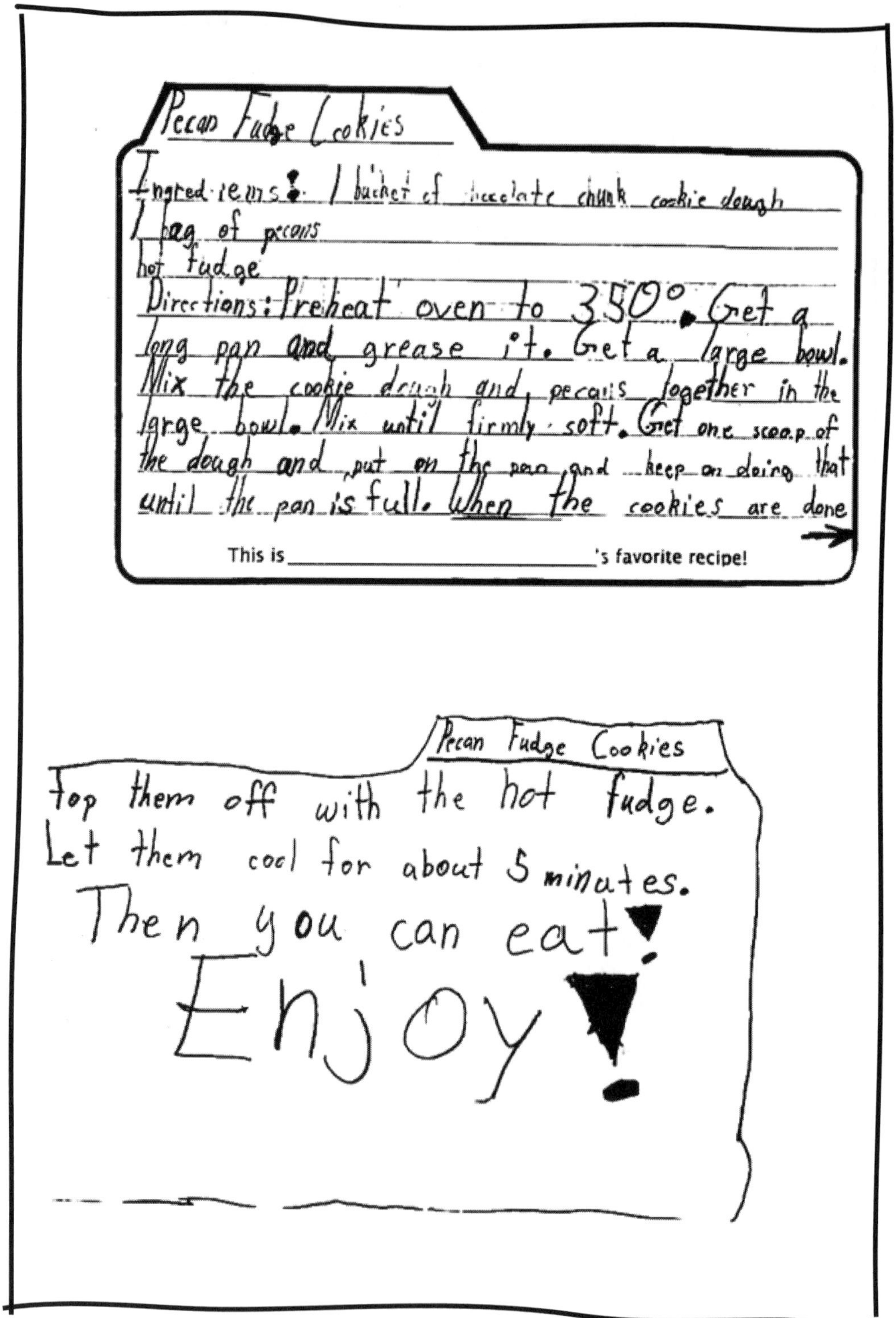

Pecan Fudge Cookies

Ingredients: 1 bucket of chocolate chunk cookie dough
1 bag of pecans
hot fudge

Directions: Preheat oven to 350°. Get a long pan and grease it. Get a large bowl. Mix the cookie dough and pecans together in the large bowl. Mix until firmly soft. Get one scoop of the dough and put on the pan and keep on doing that until the pan is full. When the cookies are done

This is _____'s favorite recipe!

Pecan Fudge Cookies

top them off with the hot fudge.
Let them cool for about 5 minutes.
Then you can eat!
Enjoy!

Table 2.6   Literacy Activities in the Unit on Scooby-Doo and IRA and NCTE Standards

Literacy Activities in the Unit on Scooby-Doo	IRA & NCTE Standards
1. Comparing and Contrast Scooby-Doo With Inspector Gadget	Standard 1
	Standard 3
	Standard 8
	Standard 11
	Standard 12
2. Creative Writing	Standard 5
	Standard 12
3. Identifying Character Traits	Standard 2
	Standard 3
	Standard 8
4. Writing Recipes	Standard 5
	Standard 11
	Standard 12

The IRA and NCTE Standards are enumerated in this book's Introduction, pages 7–8.

which a unit can be developed, may indicate April's hidden reluctance to venture into using students' popular culture texts unfamiliar to her.

Concluding Thoughts

In this chapter, I described the three teachers' experiences with incorporating students' popular culture interests into literacy teaching. Although they did these projects as part of a graduate course assignment, their experiences have showed that it was possible to use popular culture texts as alternative or additional texts to traditional children's literature. The three units allowed the teachers to address various literacy curriculum standards in a way that had a connection to students' interests and personal life. More important, many crucial parts of students' literacy learning at school would not have happened without these units. For example, Jean's students would not have had an opportunity to become aware of their biases about superheroes and then to challenge these biases through discussion. It would have been less motivating for students in Sherry's class to learn about Bahamian and Hispanic cultures, not to mention learning to dance La Cumbia. April's students would never have had a cookbook featuring their favorite recipes that reflect the life and culture of the community in which they are living.

CHAPTER 3

Integrating Popular Culture Texts in a Fourth-Grade Class

VIGNETTE 3.1

After the unit Dreams to Jobs (SRA/McGraw-Hill, 2000), my (Rachael's) students have been able to link their popular culture interests to other areas of the curriculum. For example, during social studies, most students are unfamiliar with the concept of *founding* a new town or city. David, a student, explains to the class that Jebediah Springfield, a character in the television show *The Simpsons* (Collier & Anderson, 1996), is based on a historic figure that was responsible for the start and development of the Simpsons' hometown, Springfield. The students accept David's explanation and are able to understand the concept as it appears in the social studies lessons. Occasionally a student brings in a comic book that reminds the class of something that has been discussed in class. Once Sean, another student, brings in a comic book, pointing out the difference between a narrative text and a dialogue. He is using this visual format to help the class understand and remember to use quotation marks when a person is speaking. Moreover, he is reminding the class of the importance of describing an event while writing a narrative text, in addition to dramatizing the text with dialogue. Each time this happens, it brings a smile to my face because I know the students are conceptualizing what I am teaching enough to link curriculum content to a part of their reality—popular culture texts.

This vignette illustrates the impact that my unit, Dreams to Jobs—in which I (Rachael) capitalized on students' interests in cartoons, comic books, and comic strips—has made on my students' learning. In this chapter, I share my current practices in literacy instruction and how I used the students' interests to drive my instruction while still adhering to the constraints of a reading program. I describe my experiences (and struggles) in learning about my students' interests in popular culture, and how I guided them to make a connection between their interests and the reading unit theme. In particular, I share how I created a unit project that allowed the students to explore reading, writing, and their own community, all within the comfort zone of their popular culture interest.

Instructional Setting

My Teaching Experience

I began teaching in 1996, and like many new teachers, I found myself changing grade levels every year. In my first five years of teaching, I taught five different grade levels ranging from kindergarten to fifth grade. Although changing grade levels is no teacher's ideal situation, I found that it has given me a realistic education in students' reading development. Reading and writing instruction quickly became my main focus, especially when I moved to the fourth and fifth grades from the primary grades. I noted that the students who had a firm grasp on reading functioned well in every subject, while those who struggled with reading seemed to have difficulty in all of their subjects. Once I recognized this pattern, I began to study for a reading specialist credential and a master's degree in reading and language arts at a nearby university. My main goal in this program was to improve my practices within the classroom. As a general education teacher in a self-contained classroom (i.e., a classroom in which all subjects are taught to a single group of students), I was faced with following a paced, rigorous basal reading program, Open Court Reading (Science Research Associates/McGraw-Hill, 2000), which presents a spiraling curriculum of skills within thematic units of study.

Students who grasp new concepts easily and embrace every new literature selection with enthusiasm are excited to begin a new unit, as it means they will have a new set of ideas to mull over. Others, who have mastered the skills in the spiraling curriculum, are bored but tolerate the instruction. They are not being challenged, which is reflected in their classroom demeanor. Still other students, who have reading and writing difficulties, respond to the new unit differently. Initially, they are thrilled to start the new unit, simply because they are so glad to be rid of the last torturous unit. Quickly, however, they realize that the new unit holds a set of tasks perhaps even more insurmountable than the ones they found in the previous unit. As teachers, we can identify these students in every classroom. The trick is to meet the needs of the students we have identified while simultaneously meeting the demands of the state standards and district-adopted reading programs, which often allow little room for deviation.

My Students

When I was implementing this unit with an integration of students' popular culture interests, I was teaching fourth grade in an urban elementary school in a large school district in California. My school had fewer than 1,000 students, ranging

45

from prekindergarten to fifth grade. My fourth-grade class consisted of 32 students who represented an extremely diverse range of cultural, linguistic, and socioeconomic backgrounds and academic abilities. The students were Filipino American, Samoan American, Latino, and European American. Most of the students sounded fluent in English when they were chatting with their friends at school but spoke another language at home. In fact, a portion of the parents and grandparents of these students spoke no English at all, and the students were often the translators for their families. The literacy areas in which some of my students struggle the most are vocabulary development, fluency and reading comprehension, and writing.

The academic abilities in my class were greatly varied. I had the gifted students, who accounted for about one fourth of the class. I had several students who attended classes in the Resource Specialist Program, a special education services program for students with accommodations in their individualized education plans. I also had two English-language learners (ELLs) who were nearing redesignation into the English Only category. The majority of my students were average students who were representative of the school's population.

The Instructional Program

Daily instruction with this group of students could be challenging because the range of abilities in the classroom was wide. Open Court Reading, the mandated basal program, though comprehensive and spiraling in nature, in practice is often used to teach to the middle ability level. The program, implemented fully every day, takes well in excess of two hours, which leaves little time to be devoted to differentiated instruction. Several of my students were beyond the target skill level for the program, while others were struggling with the most fundamental skills set forth in each unit. The focus of my instruction, therefore, was to strike a balance between teaching a mandated program and supplementing that program with teaching practices that served to augment and enhance student growth.

One daily supplemental activity I did with my students was fluency and comprehension practice. Using leveled passages from Johns's *Basic Reading Inventory* (2001), as a group, we read the passage aloud in unison. I led so the students could practice breaking words into syllables for decoding and practice reading the passage aloud with correct phrasing, intonation, and pacing. We then discussed the passage. Throughout the week, we used the same passage for one-minute fluency practice during which the students were trained to listen to their partner read for one minute, marking any errors that were made to help the reader understand the errors he or she made, and to generate a word count (total words read – errors = words per minute).

Daily instruction also included directed lessons in comprehension strategies. The basal stories, social studies texts, and supplemental literature were all a basis for strategies instruction in my classroom. We discussed literature in large and small groups and focused on using vocabulary and comprehension strategies, which included visualizing, asking questions, and summarizing after reading. These techniques, consistently applied, had worked well, and my students were showing great improvements in both fluency and comprehension.

Integrating Popular Culture Texts Into the Unit Dreams to Jobs

While studying for a master's degree, I enrolled in Shelley's graduate literacy course, during which I was presented with a challenge of using print and nonprint texts based on my students' popular culture interests in my literacy instruction. I had the dual challenge of creating activities that not only coincided with the students' interests and the California Reading and Language Arts Standards but also connected the activities to the current Open Court Reading unit (California Department of Education, 1999). The students were in the first few weeks of a new fourth-grade unit, Dreams to Jobs. The stories were appropriate for the unit of study, and the students were diligently following along through the unit, but there was no spark of interest. Worse yet, there was little or no sense that the students understood what they were reading and what relevance it had in their lives.

I began to have brief dialogues with my students during the first few weeks of the unit to learn what they knew about starting and running a business. A few of the students actually had parents who had started their own businesses, and they were quite realistic in their understanding of the work and money involved in running a successful business; others had no knowledge as to the business-related concepts, such as money, profits, and debts.

The students' lack of engagement with the topic was especially unsettling when a culminating project for the unit required them to write an expository (informational) text about creating a business. Not only would the students need to have the background knowledge necessary to write expository text competently, but they would also have to have the ability to write expository text proficiently. It was a daunting task in light of the general disinterest in the unit. I came to realize that if I could find the right venue to awaken their sense of curiosity for this unit, the students would take interest in it. This required learning more about my students and finding out about their interests.

Learning About Students' Popular Culture Interests

I had a great deal of fun learning about my students' popular culture interests, as well as a great deal of headaches. My first clue about fourth graders' interests in popular culture was presented to me daily in the form of student illustrations, many of which were unsolicited. Several of my students were continually drawing in class to the exclusion of doing other activities. The drawings, surprisingly, were quite good for this grade level. Several other students were habitually poring over Yu-Gi-Oh! cards in class, at recess, and essentially whenever they could get away with it. Others could be seen reading cartoons and comics, and there was a never-ending supply of cartoon theme songs to be heard.

I began asking the students about their favorite comics and cartoons, and they were always surprised not only that I asked about their interests but also that I knew about them. In this regard, I am fortunate in that my cartoon-animation artist husband works for major studios that produce animated features for television and movies, which are calculated to attract the interests of students. I began to make subtle comments about comic books and television cartoons. The students would become excited and, of course, naturally change the subject at hand to that of cartoons and comic books. During one of the Open Court Reading Dreams to Jobs stories, a student made a comment that was so apropos that he could not have commented in a more timely way. He said, "Having a job seems like too much work. I am going to draw cartoons when I grow up."

I responded at this chance to launch the unit project that I had been planning. I began a discussion about what it would be like to be a cartoon-animation artist. Many of the students held the opinion that it was easy work, and one commented, "I wouldn't have to read or write. I could just draw whatever I wanted." Others simply had no idea about how comic books and cartoons were actually made. Especially to my advantage was the fact that they had no idea how much reading and writing were involved in this line of work.

I enlisted the help of my husband, Thomas Perkins, who specializes in character designs for television animation, to start the unit. I invited him to the class as a guest speaker to tell about his lifelong dream to be a cartoon-animation artist for cartoons and comics. When I revealed to the students that I had invited to the classroom a cartoon-animation artist who had worked on many of their favorite television shows, they were ecstatic. They immediately began barraging me with questions about cartoons and retelling the plots of their favorite cartoon episodes while I mused over how amazing their comprehension and retelling abilities were when it came to their own pursuits. For the first time during this unit, I had captured their interest.

Planning for the Unit

I considered the task and goals ahead and decided on a series of structured activities, each one having a rationale and a connection within the sequence of activities. These activities had to serve several purposes. First and foremost, they had to captivate the students' interest, hence the link to their popular culture interests. Moreover, the activities had to link back to their own lives so it would be personally meaningful as well as allow the students to capitalize on their own backgrounds to understand the business-related concepts. Finally, the activities had to be scaffolded and varied in nature to include the full spectrum of types of learners in my classroom. I began by introducing a comic strip by one of their favorite authors that illustrated the unit theme, Dreams to Jobs. This provided students with a chance to relate to the topic and begin to explore it in terms of their own enjoyment. Following this activity, I engaged the students in unfamiliar activities, such as interviewing, information organization, and writing information articles. I made these standards-based activities more palatable and interesting to the students by keeping their popular culture interests at the forefront. I incorporated lectures and demonstrations of a cartoon-animation artist who showed the students how he turned his dream to be an artist into a real job. Finally, I linked the business-related concepts back to their own lives, making the new ideas pertinent to their world rather than presenting them as a disconnected set of facts and skills that would be inapplicable in their lives. (See Table 3.1 for a unit overview of literacy activities.)

Table 3.1   Unit Overview of Literacy Activities

Literacy Activity	Description
1. Activating Prior Knowledge	I gave the students a comic strip by Dav Pilkey to read at the onset of the project. This step was crucial as it provided a link between their popular culture interests and learning, a correlation that many of them had never made before.
2. Completing the K-W-L Chart	We used a K-W-L chart to explore and chart their prior knowledge of comics and animation jobs. This became a valuable tool for creating interview questions for the cartoon-animation artist to answer.
3. Sorting Questions	Once the full list of questions was on the K-W-L chart, the students *sorted* the questions into categories. Once we had created categories (which would ultimately become the paragraphs of the informational article), I gave them the opportunity to add more questions to the category to ask during the interview.
4. Conducting the Interview	The students listened, took notes, and asked questions to gather information for their writing. At the end of the interview, the cartoon-animation artist did a demonstration on how to draw a comic strip using layout, narrative text boxes, and different types of dialogue boxes to convey emotion.

(continued)

Table 3.1   Unit Overview of Literacy Activities *(continued)*

Literacy Activity	Description
5. Participating in Guided Writing	This activity had two components. First we used a *graphic organizer* (similar to an outline) from the reading series to organize information. Once the organizer was complete, the students used a *guided writing* activity to turn the organized information into a well-written and organized informational article. Some students completed the task independently, while others felt comfortable following along.
6. Conducting Research	I placed the students into groups according to their interests in different businesses. Once they were in the groups, they were responsible for gathering information about the business. Students used the Internet, magazines, and the interview process to learn about their chosen business.
7. Writing Comic Strips on Starting and Running a Business	The students used the information they gathered to create a comic strip about starting the business they chose. The comic strip was a graphic organizer. Each panel contained text and images to remind them of all the details needed for each paragraph.
8. Writing an Expository Text	The students used their comic strips and the guided writing sample from earlier to write an organized, informational article about the business they chose.
9. Writing Personal Reflections	I gave the students the opportunity to reflect upon their learning. They wrote about what they learned and how they learned.
10. Conducting a Tour	The students gave tours of the class book and website to visiting teachers, parents, and administration. The students were able to share their learning with others and reinforce the idea that they did something fun and learned at the same time.

Learning About Dav Pilkey

With the stage set for this unit and with a group of excited students, I began to prepare with the class for the cartoon-animation artist's visit by introducing the class to a website (www.davpilkey.com) of a much-beloved children's author, Dav

Pilkey. All of the students in my fourth-grade room pored over the Captain Underpants series of books as if they were the only books in the world. Pilkey's website contains a printable autobiography of himself, formatted in text and photographs in a fun-to-read, hilarious comic strip format. When I, before handing out the comic strip, told the students that we were going to read something to help us prepare for our writing assignment, the students had a mixed reaction. Some cheered, while others stared at me in disbelief that I was actually going to let them read a comic strip in class. Within minutes the students were laughing, pointing out funny parts to each other, and acting out the comic strip, which chronicled the events of Pilkey's life leading him to become a professional comic book writer and illustrator.

After I let the students have their fun, I asked them to talk to me about the comic in relation to the Dreams to Jobs unit. I began with the question "What did Mr. Pilkey have to do in order to become successful in this field?" I began charting the students' comments. I was surprised at how much information they had gleaned from such a short, humorous comic strip. Students' responses included that he had to love art, have a dream and a goal to be an artist, go to school and continue through college, and work hard even when he was discouraged to make his dream come true. These wonderful observations paved the way for the first activity.

Learning From a Cartoon-Animation Artist

PREPARING FOR THE INTERVIEW. After reading Pilkey's autobiographical comic strip, the students were extremely excited about having the opportunity to interview a real cartoon-animation artist. One student joked that the class did not want to ask *dumb questions* as the children in the Pilkey comic do. I laughed and agreed, and we set to work in creating questions that would give us information about how Pilkey started with a dream and turned it into a real job. We began by creating a K-W-L chart (Ogle, 1986; a chart where students offer prior knowledge, or what they *know*; generate questions about what they *want* to know; and at the end of the unit, summarize what they *learned*) so we could list what we thought we already knew about cartoon-animation artists, comic books, and cartoons, and then listed as many questions as we could generate about what we wanted to know about these topics. I found out that many of the students did not associate reading and writing with the role of a comic book or television animation artist. Many of the students suggested that the role of a cartoon-animation artist was to draw and color whatever he or she wanted. I recorded all of their ideas, without offering any insight or asking leading questions; I wanted to record what the students knew or assumed about the art and animation jobs.

Upon entering the *W* portion of the K-W-L chart, however, I began to participate more actively in order to encourage more insightful, probing questions that had to do with comic books and creating animation as a job. Many of the students wanted to ask simple questions, such as "What is your favorite superhero?" and "Can you draw Yu-Gi-Oh! characters?" It took quite a bit of time to guide the students to ask questions pertinent to the Dreams to Jobs unit. We discussed the types of questions that would be useful to gather information about the field of animation. I returned to their comments about Pilkey, reminding them that the comments they made about him fell into distinctly different categories, namely how he got the dream to be a writer–illustrator, what kinds of things he had to do to achieve his dream, and what his job was really like. I wrote these categories on the board and suggested that if they could not think of a unit-related question, these categories might be a good place to start.

After this discussion and much modeling of how I wanted the students to formulate interview questions, I allowed them to write as many interview questions as they wanted. I knew that the students needed the opportunity to ask both fun and unit-related questions, so I gave them the rule that for every *fun* question, they also had to make up a question related to the unit. The students, even the reluctant ones, were writing down questions furiously. This rule supported their desire to ask any question they wanted to know, no matter how silly, and also forced them to think about the unit as well. As I peered over students' shoulders while they were writing, I noticed two things: First, my most reluctant writers only asked fun questions, and second, almost all of the fun questions they asked were directly related to the unit. For example, several students asked how many characters Perkins could draw in a single day. This proved to be a good lesson for the students later on, when he explained that he sometimes worked on a single character for days at a time, making revisions until the character he drew matched the style of the show and coincided with the script. The fun questions, such as this one, often proved to be the most informative for the students.

I charted many of the questions on the K-W-L chart for the students to see (Table 3.2). Explaining to the students that the end goal of the interview was to write an informational article about the cartoon-animation artist, I suggested that the students should set up topics that they could write about. I wanted the students to arrange the questions into categories, so I suggested a *question sort* (students write questions on blank 3" x 5" cards, which are sorted into categories according to topic). The students were familiar with doing word sorts (Bear, Invernizzi, Templeton, & Johnston, 2000; students sort words into categories according to spelling pattern or word meaning) and quickly began grouping the questions into four categories, which were (1) how Perkins developed the dream to become a cartoon-animation artist, (2) what his education was like, (3) what his *dream job* was like, and (4) what other goals he has for the future. Because these questions were a recurrent theme among the students, it was decided that these would be the best topics for paragraphs in the articles. The students then worked collaboratively to eliminate duplicate questions and to add additional questions to the categories. This technique helped the students apply critical thinking skills to analyzing and quantifying information, and generate ideas for categories. Just before the interview, the class and I brainstormed interview techniques. We came up with the following techniques:

1. Make good questions that will get us the information we want (who, what, when, where, and why).

Table 3.2   K-W-L Chart

K (What We Think We Know)	W (What We Want to Know)	L (What We Learned)
• Drawing is a fun job. • Some cartoons are funny and some are action. • You have to know how to draw really well. • Cartoons are on TV and comics are in books.	• Does the cartoon-animation artist draw for TV or for comic books? • How long has he been drawing? • Where does he work? • How many characters can he draw in one day? • How long does he work every day? • What kinds of pens and pencils does he use? • How did he become a cartoon-animation artist? • How long has he been an cartoon-animation artist? • Did he have to go to school? For how long?	• Cartoon-animation artists need to read scripts so they know what to draw. • Cartoon-animation artists work hard and draw pictures over and over to get pictures perfect. • Perkins started drawing when he was 4 years old. • Perkins draws for both television and books. • He works anywhere from 10 to 18 hours a day, depending on the schedule. • He uses special pens and pencils that make a nice line. He also uses the computer. • He went to college and got a degree in fine art. • He loves his job. It is his childhood dream fulfilled.

2. Take notes. (But listen, too!)
3. Do not ask the same question twice.
4. Please be polite.
5. Speak clearly and loudly.
6. Debrief after the interview.

THE INTERVIEW. The day for the interview was an exciting one. I informed Perkins that the students were reading a unit about different people, both fictional and nonfictional, who had taken steps to create a career for themselves. He knew that the students were interested in comic books and cartoons, and that they wanted to know how he became a professional artist. He would first talk about his experiences and then allow the students to ask any questions. I had provided the students with a note-taking organizer in which I split the page up into four sections, one for each category of questions, and typed the questions at the top of each section. As the cartoon-animation artist talked, the students took notes in an organizer. At the end of his talk, the students asked many questions and took many notes. I was extremely surprised to see that the students were taking their role as interviewers very seriously, only asking questions that pertained to the four topics, and writing notes energetically. When it was time for them to ask all the fun questions they wanted, their hands began flying in the air, they cited favorite cartoons and comics, and they began to compare favorite artists. The students really enjoyed this opportunity to share their interests with an adult, and to have these interests not only taken seriously but also discussed as if they were truly important, original, and valuable.

Perkins finished up the one-hour visit by giving a brief demonstration of how a comic book is created. Armed with a how-to book on drawing comics, Perkins shared that the biggest secret to writing a truly great comic strip on cartoons was having a well-written, solid script. He pointed out that despite the visual appeal of comics, no one would buy one that was poorly written. While he was writing out a simple script on the board, the students helped to offer details and dialogues they thought would be funny. Once Perkins created the simple script, he brought it to life in a rough, penciled comic strip (Figure 3.1). While drawing, he explained the individual story panels, the narrative text boxes to establish the sequential order of texts, different styles of dialogue text bubbles to convey different emotions, and drawing techniques (e.g., drawing initial establishing shots to let the reader have an idea of the setting, and drawing close-up shots to show character emotions).

After the interview, the students and I listed, based on Perkins's talk, all of the sequential steps needed to create a comic strip.

1. *Gather information.* Gather information that you will need to write your comic strip. Take notes to remind you to put information you need in the comic strip.

2. *Write a script.* Use your notes. Separate your notes into different categories. These will become your comic strip panels. Write your script. Remember, there are two *scripts*: One is the narrative text that tells the sequential events, and the other is the dialogue that your characters say. Use different kinds of dialogue balloons to convey different emotions.

3. *Draw a storyboard.* Once your script is written, draw a storyboard. Make sure your pictures reflect what is happening in the dialogue and in the narrative text.

4. *Lay out your comic panels and place narrative text boxes and dialogue balloons.* Start your final comic strip. Remember to leave the first panel blank for your title. Space out your cartoon panels so panels with a lot of action have more room. Place your narrative text boxes and dialogue balloons in the panels first. This way, you will have room for your drawings.

5. *Draw images.* Once your text is written in each panel, use the rest of the room to draw your images.

6. *Color and ink.* Finally, color your images. Be careful not to color in your narrative text boxes and dialogue balloons. You want these to be clean and

**Figure 3.1   Comic Strip Drawing by Thomas Perkins,
the Visiting Cartoon-Animation Artist**

Used with permission from Thomas Perkins.

easy to read. Once everything is colored, use a thin permanent black marker to trace your drawings and words. This will make sure that everything is clear and easy to read. After inking, use an art gum eraser to erase any stray pencil lines.

I then gave the students time to draw a comic strip using what they had learned from Perkins (Figure 3.2). They applied a new form of text organization in this alternative writing activity. The drawing they had just witnessed looked so easy to do, but it actually was quite difficult for them. While drawing, they had to refer back to their notes for the steps. Many commented that because Perkins had been drawing for a really long time, he was very skillful. I was so glad to see that they were beginning to make connections to the unit—it takes time and hard work to turn a dream into a job. The students had such a wonderful time that most of them asked to stay and keep working on their comics after the bell had rung.

The students were thrilled with this lesson and insisted that the comic be displayed on the classroom door. For weeks after this, they would bring other students to stand by the open door at recess and lunch for an impromptu lesson on how comic books are actually made. They were able to teach other students the steps required to write and illustrate a comic strip.

Figure 3.2   Student Drawing a Comic Strip After Thomas Perkins's Presentation

Writing Expository Text: Shared Writing

The next step was to use the information the students gathered during the interview to create an expository text about how this cartoon-animation artist turned his childhood dream of drawing cartoons into a reality. Because the interview process was a shared experience, I decided this would be the perfect opportunity to have a shared writing experience. I believe that before students can be expected to write a specific kind of text, they have to know what it is and how to go about writing it. We had discussed expository text throughout the year, and I had drawn students' attention to elements of nonfiction. However, this was the first opportunity for the students to write an expository text for a unit this year.

I typically would have taught the structure of an outline at this point. However, I felt it would be too overwhelming for some writers in my class this year to create a structure from scratch. I opted to use a graphic organizer from the Open Court Reading program, which was laid out in a friendly and accessible manner. I guided the students in completing the organizer by offering sentences and phrases if they needed them. This scaffolded approach made the students feel comfortable, and everyone in the room participated in some way.

Once we completed the graphic organizer (Figure 3.3), we moved on to writing our rough draft by using the graphic organizer as a guide. I modeled the writing process on an overhead projector. When I asked how we should start our article, the students all offered that we should begin with an introductory paragraph. I asked for suggestions for an opening sentence. We worked our way through the introduction, taking care to introduce the topics that we would cover in the article, using our graphic organizer as a checklist. Over the next few days, we wrote the main topic paragraphs and the conclusion. As the students grew more comfortable with the process, I began to remove some of the support. Instead of writing down a sentence that the students could copy, I asked for suggestions, and then directed the students to write a sentence in their own words. Gradually, the students became comfortable with the process as many students asked if they could go ahead on their own. Their final drafts reflected all the elements we had previously included in the graphic organizer. Many of the students felt comfortable enough to make creative additions to the group essay that I wrote on the overhead projector, while others copied verbatim. Figure 3.4 is an example of a student's completed expository text.

Independent Research Projects

After we completed our informational articles using the writing process, the students began to think about jobs they wanted to research. I instructed them to write a list of three or four businesses or careers they were interested in. Using these lists, I grouped the students into collaborative research groups based on business types. One group, for example, was interested in doughnut shops, and another wanted to learn about comic book stores. Arranged in these groups, the

Figure 3.3 Completed Expository Text Graphic Organizers

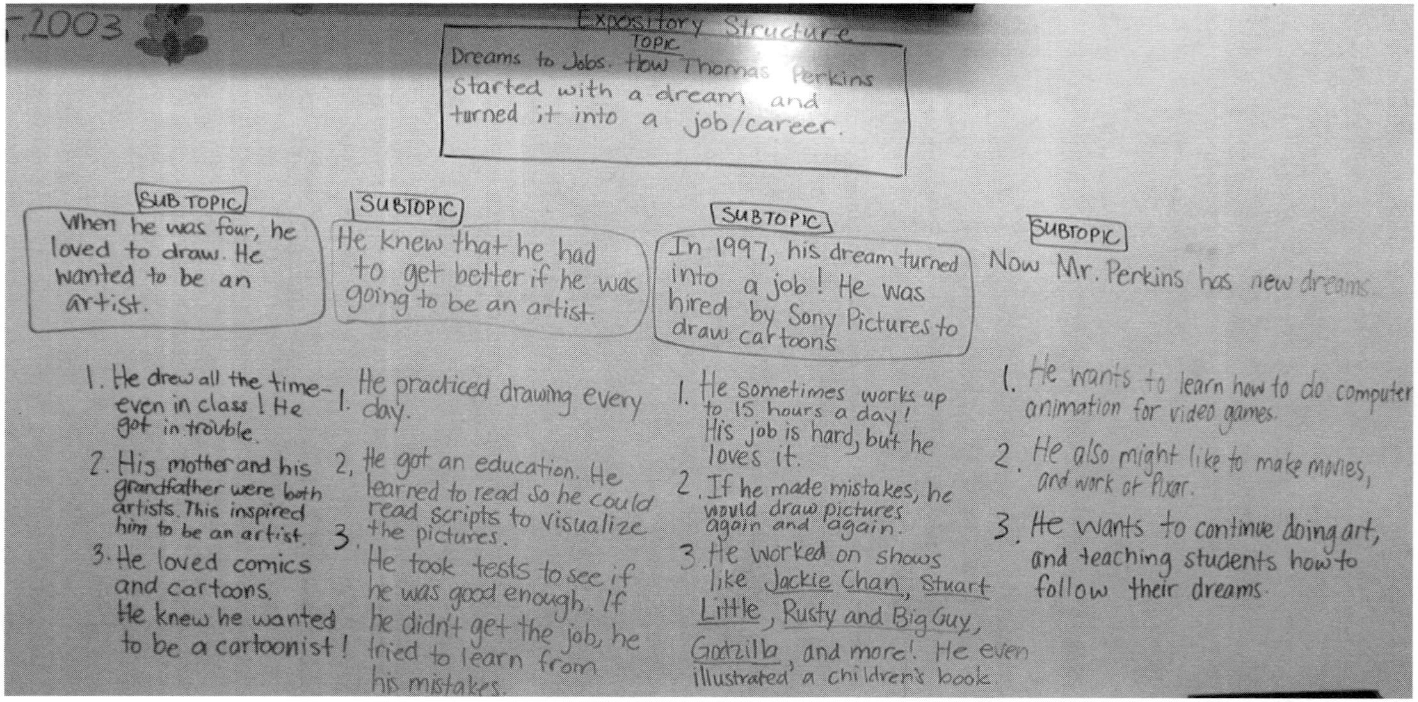

Expository Structure

TOPIC
Dreams to Jobs: How Thomas Perkins Started with a dream and turned it into a job/career.

SUBTOPIC
When he was four, he loved to draw. He wanted to be an artist.

1. He drew all the time—even in class! He got in trouble.
2. His mother and his grandfather were both artists. This inspired him to be an artist.
3. He loved comics and cartoons. He knew he wanted to be a cartoonist!

SUBTOPIC
He knew that he had to get better if he was going to be an artist.

1. He practiced drawing every day.
2. He got an education. He learned to read so he could read scripts to visualize the pictures.
3. He took tests to see if he was good enough. If he didn't get the job, he tried to learn from his mistakes.

SUBTOPIC
In 1997, his dream turned into a job! He was hired by Sony Pictures to draw cartoons

1. He sometimes works up to 15 hours a day! His job is hard, but he loves it.
2. If he made mistakes, he would draw pictures again and again.
3. He worked on shows like Jackie Chan, Stuart Little, Rusty and Big Guy, Godzilla, and more! He even illustrated a children's book.

SUBTOPIC
Now Mr. Perkins has new dreams.

1. He wants to learn how to do computer animation for video games.
2. He also might like to make movies, and work at Pixar.
3. He wants to continue doing art, and teaching students how to follow their dreams.

2003

Figure 3.4   Student's Completed Expository Text About Thomas Perkins

December 3, 2008

Dreams to Jobs, Mr. Perkins

Have you ever had a dream and you turned it into a job? Well Thomas Perkins did. When he was young he dreamt of being an artist. He finally got his dream job, and he still has more dreams!

When he was 4 he loved to draw. He wanted to be an artist. He drew all the time, even in class! His mom and grandpa were artist, this inspired him alot to be an artist. He loved comics and cartoons. He knew he wanted to be a cartoonist.

He knew he had to get better so he practiced every day. For him to get the job he didn't just have to know how to draw he had to know how to read. He went to college for 10 years. He took test to see if he was good enough, if he didn't make it he would learn from his mistakes

His dream came true in 1997. He was hired by Sony Pictures. Sometimes he worked up to 15 hours a day, his job is hard but he still loves it. If he made mistakes he would practice drawing more so he can get much better. He has worked on shows like, Jackie Chan, Stuart Little, Rusty and Big Guy, Godzilla, and more.

Now Mr. Perkins has new dreams like working to be a computer animator. He might like to make movies with Pixar, He wants to continue doing art and teaching students how to follow their dreams.

students could bring their own experiences to the group, as well as share the responsibility of the research.

Before beginning our research, we brainstormed the following topics for research using the unit stories: *the dream*, *about the business*, *business location*, *supplies*, *employees*, and *money* (to start the business). I typed these topics on a note-taking organizer for the students, and they worked together to complete the parts they already knew. Over the course of a week, the students worked individually and collaboratively to learn more about their businesses. The students began with brainstorming questions for interviewing people in the community who ran a business. Students' experience of interviewing Perkins helped prepare them for this interview by formulating interview questions and conducting an actual interview. In addition, I encouraged students to practice with one another in mock interviews so that they would have necessary interviewing skills.

When it was time for an interview, my students tapped into their community's resources. One student's father, who owned a doughnut shop, allowed students to interview him after school. Another student visited a local Krispy Kreme (a donut shop franchise in the United States) with a list of questions for the manager. Still another student, whose aunt worked at Toys "R" Us (a toy store franchise in the United States), interviewed the store manager about running a toy store. The students found clever ways of learning about starting and running their chosen business, and in the process, they also learned more about the people in their community. Most important, they learned how hard their parents worked. Throughout the process of interviewing, I allowed the collaborative groups to meet each day to exchange information that they had learned.

Once all the research was completed, I announced that we were going to do a project. The students groaned, assuming that they had to write another article. I agreed that they eventually would be writing another article, but later. This time, they would be drawing their own comic strip about starting and running a business. I had purchased professional comic book paper from a local comic book store, and I explained that they were going to write their own professional comic strip to be compiled in a Dreams to Jobs class book. The students were excited to get to work. I reviewed the steps of writing a script and laying out a comic script and instructed them to write a script that had both a narrative text box and dialogue or thought balloons to make the strip entertaining and fun to read. I wanted the students to create a comic strip before writing the informational article for two reasons: I wanted them to have fun with writing and with their popular culture interests, and I wanted them to create a visual aid that would help them remember the necessary elements of starting and running a business. At the end of the unit, the students would be held responsible for the unit writing assessment, which would be an expository piece on running a business.

The students worked on their comic strips diligently during our independent work time (Figure 3.5). Each comic strip was divided into eight panels, or pictures: (1) title and author, (2) the dream, (3) about the business, (4) business location, (5) supplies, (6) employees, (7) finances, and (8) the ending. Each panel of the comic

Figure 3.5   Student's Finished Comic Strip

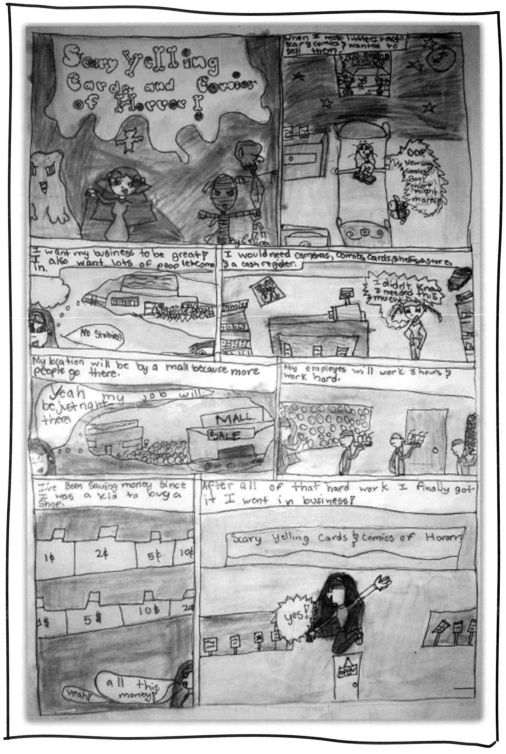

strip was devoted to an area of their research. Each comic strip, whose individual panels are about respective areas of research chosen by the students, had its own unique voice. Even those students who had been the most reluctant to write willingly participated in this project, and many of these students had written more for this assignment than they had all year long.

As the students neared completion of their comic strips, I began to have them write an expository text on starting and running a business. The students followed the same steps for writing their articles about the cartoon-animation artist, using their comic strips to complete the expository text graphic organizer. After reviewing with me the structure of an expository text, the students independently began to write. At independent work time, I called the students back individually for a writing conference during which I helped them with any problems they had and made suggestions. The students wrote so much. They had much personal experience to bring to their writing after having done research. More important, they had enjoyed the projects leading up to this final expository writing and fully understood the subject matter. Whenever they became confused about what to write next, they could look at their comic strip, and they were immediately back on task. Figure 3.6 is a student's expository text on starting and running a business.

Sharing Our Work

After the project was completed, I gave the students the opportunity to reflect upon their learning and make their learning available to the public. Rather than telling them what steps we had taken during the unit, I encouraged them to tell me. They were able to describe the various activities we had done in great detail and what they had learned from these activities. I also encouraged them to share their opinions of their favorite and least favorite activities. At the end of the discussion, I gave each student the opportunity to write about his or her learning. I explained that this was not going to be a piece of writing that I would grade; rather it was a personal expression of what they had learned. I also explained that this reflection would be included in the class book along with their comic strip and final expository text. The students' reflections were surprising. One student wrote about all the activities we did and resources we used, such as business owners and the Internet. This student concluded her reflection by saying, "The most exciting thing I like in this unit was making a comic strip because it was really easy to write the essay. It felt like cheating but you weren't. I also learned how to draw better than I did. It was fun." She summarized her project in a few sentences (Figure 3.7).

As an extension, I created a website (see Figure 3.8, www.tnperkins.com/comicsproject) that explained the steps of the unit so the students could see their work published. Thomas Perkins, as a reward to the students for doing such a great job, offered to draw characters to appear on the website, which I had set up to look like a comic strip. The students were able to access the website from the classroom computers. They had fun for months afterward reading about their projects and the learning objectives they had achieved, and seeing some of the

Figure 3.6   Student's Expository Text

House of Donuts

I have always wished to open up my own donut shop. Donuts were my favorite thing to eat in the morning while I was watching tv. When I was a small boy, my dad would take me to go eat donuts and drink some chocolate milk. It was the most fun I had ever had. I decided to open up my own donut shop, so I can give people food for their breakfast so that they do not have to make it themselves. Thats how my dream began.

Now that know I want to open a donut shop, I will need to get a good business location and I will need to buy supplies. The best location for my store would be near a police station, and also near a Starbucks. I will need many supplies, but the most important supplies I need are dough, chocolate, and other things to make donuts, a cash register, emergency cameras, and tables and chairs for people to sit. I will need a cash register so that people can buy the donuts and eat them, and I will have a place to put my money. I also need emergency cameras so that I can see if anyone is trying to steal anything from my donut store. Last I need tables

(continued)

Figure 3.6   Student's Expository Text *(continued)*

and chairs so my customers can sit peacefully and eat their donuts. I know I lots of supplies.

I need to hire some cashiers, a salesperson, bakers, and a manager. The cashier will count the money and take it to the bank at the end of each day. The salesperson will help the customer find the item they want to purchase. The bakers will make the donuts and my manager will be boss if I am away. I will hire these employees to help out with the business.

I need money for my business because I do not have about $3 million dollars, I can not open up my own donut shop. My investor will give me the money to start my business, but I have to earn the money by working hard for it. If I do not get the money to start my business than that means I should not bother trying to open up a business anyway. I will work hard to open my business up and I will never give up trying to fulfill my dream. I now have everything to start my business. I will do whatever I can to be the best boss I can be. This is the best moment of my life. I will do hard work and make sure everything is ok.

comic strips online. Because the unit was so successful and the students were so proud of their work, I invited parents, other teachers, and school administrators to the classroom to visit. We even received a visit from district administrators and reading coaches. The students prepared *tours* so they could be prepared to explain to visitors exactly what the unit was, what they had learned, and why it was so successful. The students in each group had assigned themselves jobs, and even prepared notecards so they could give a good tour. It was significant that the

Figure 3.7   Student Reflection on the Dreams to Jobs Unit

Dreams to Jobs: Final Reflection

Well the first thing we did in this unit is to write on the Concept and Question Board. After that we interviewed an artist from Warner Brothers. We picked businesses and got into groups and had conversations. The groups looked on the internet and got information to write an essay. Then we made a comic strip so it could be easier to write another essay. In the essay we had to talk about money, investors, location, supplies, and employees. We also made our own website.

The most exiting thing I like in this unit was making a comic strip because it was really easy to write the essay. It felt like cheating but you weren't. I also learned how to draw better than I did. It was fun!

Figure 3.8   The Dreams to Jobs Unit Website

Used with permission from Thomas Perkins.

Figure 3.9   Class Book of Dreams to Jobs

idea of giving tours to visitors came from the students themselves. The students used their independent work time and often their recess and lunch times writing notecards. Finally, I compiled all of the student work, including printed pages of the comic strips, into a class book of Dreams to Jobs (see Figure 3.9). I placed the book in the classroom library, and it was by far the most sought-after book in the classroom. Each student had his or her own page containing his or her comic strip, final expository text, and final reflection.

Reflecting on the Use of Popular Culture in the Unit Dreams to Jobs

Teaching reading to a mixed-ability group of students, who are, on the best of days, disinterested in the subject, is a very difficult thing to do. Frequently the literature selections in basal readers are not compatible with the students' interests, beliefs, or even the reality of their lives. This unit grew out of my concern for teaching a group of students basic skills and, moreover, to challenge my gifted students at the same time. Any student in the class at his or her own ability level could approach the activities I provided at all times. More important, they wanted to participate in the activities because they were interested. Throughout the unit, I was greatly rewarded by students' accomplishment and was also challenged in various ways.

The Challenges of Planning a Unit on Popular Culture

The Challenge of Following California Content Standards and IRA and NCTE Standards

This project was designed specifically to encompass multiple fourth-grade state-mandated content standards (California Department of Education, 1999). With a unit of this magnitude, it was possible to set up miniactivities that covered individual content standards while they were conducive to achieving a larger goal. Moreover, the standards were taught in an authentic setting that allowed students to see a purpose for learning the individual skills. The state content standards embedded into this project included but were not limited to the following:

Structural Features of Informational Materials 2.1 (fourth grade): Identify structural patterns found in informational text (e.g., compare and contrast, cause and effect, sequential or chronological order, proposition and support) to strengthen comprehension.

Writing Strategies 1.0 (fourth grade): Students write clear, coherent sentences and paragraphs that develop a central idea. Their writing shows they consider the audience and purpose. Students progress through the stages of the writing process.

Organization and Focus 1.1 (fourth grade): Select a focus, an organizational structure, and a point of view based upon purpose, audience, length, and format requirements.

Organization and Focus 1.2 (fourth grade): Create multiple-paragraph compositions:

a. Provide introductory paragraph.

b. Establish and support a central idea with a topic sentence at or near the beginning of the first paragraph.

c. Include supporting paragraphs with simple facts, details, and explanations.

d. Conclude with a paragraph that summarizes the points.

e. Use correct indentation.

Research and Technology 1.6 (fourth grade): Locate information in reference texts by using organizational features.

Writing Applications 2.3 (fourth grade): Write information reports:

a. Frame a central question about an issue or situation.

b. Include facts and details for focus.

c. Draw from more than one source of information.

Table 3.3 lists IRA and NCTE (1996) standards I addressed in this unit.

Table 3.3   Literacy Activities and IRA and NCTE Standards Addressed in Dreams to Jobs Unit

Literacy Activities in the Unit Dreams to Jobs	IRA and NCTE Standards
1. Activating Prior Knowledge	Standard 1 Standard 2 Standard 3
2. Completing the K-W-L Chart	Standard 1 Standard 2 Standard 7
3. Sorting Questions	Standard 5
4. Conducting the Interview	Standard 8 Standard 12
5. Participating in Guided Writing	Standard 5 Standard 6 Standard 8
6. Conducting Research	Standard 8
7. Writing Comic Strips on Starting and Running a Business	Standard 12
8. Writing an Expository Text	Standard 5 Standard 6 Standard 12
9. Writing Personal Reflections	Standard 5 Standard 6
10. Conducting a Tour	Standard 11

The IRA and NCTE Standards are enumerated in this book's Introduction, pages 7–8.

The Challenge of Planning

This unit took a great deal of continual planning, as well as a great deal of instructional time, to accomplish. Each activity was part of a sequential set of skills, and some students were ready to move on before others. The activities, therefore, had to be flexible enough to allow students to move ahead if they were comfortable with the skills, while other students could follow along with guided instruction if they needed to. I found that it was much easier to *manage* the students, who were all working at different rates, if I set clear language and content objectives for each step of the project. This ensured that the students knew what I expected them to learn and accomplish, as well as how they were to present their understanding of the content in terms of language structure. I used the Sheltered Instruction Observation Protocol (SIOP) model set forth in *Making Content Comprehensible for English Language Learners* (Echevarria, Vogt, & Short, 2000) to guide my own instructional planning for all components of instruction. The SIOP model helped me in (a) planning a lesson with a focus on building my students' background knowledge on a topic under study and (b) delivering the lesson with careful attention to scaffolding student learning and to engaging active student participation. Despite the fact that my students were not all ELLs, they were all unfamiliar with the concepts and terminology associated with business and management. Before the students could write about loans, profits, debts, and interest, they had to understand those concepts, and a simple vocabulary lesson was not going to be enough. I spent much time lesson planning for supplementary activities to build background knowledge that would enable students to gain an understanding of concepts that was solid enough for them to formulate their own ideas. Ultimately, it was extremely rewarding because the students had both the necessary background knowledge to write about starting a business as well as the writing and organizational skills expected of them.

The Challenge of Balancing

The main struggle I encountered was the ever-present demand of adhering to state, school, and district guidelines of standards and reading programs, and at the same time trying to be creative. Everyone, from the general public to the state administration, expects much of classroom teachers—we are expected to cover all the standards, keep up with district and school pacing plans, and often to remain in step with other classrooms on the grade level so as to ensure that all students on the grade level are receiving the same instruction. This kind of pressure stifles creativity and often leads me to wonder why I go to such great lengths to be creative. During this project, my students received the skills and vocabulary instruction that the other classes did. I presented instruction in an authentic way rather than in a series of activities that would not allow the students to connect the terms and concepts to real life. However, I felt the constant need to be able to justify my instruction, especially when my students were creating comic strips during writing time. I was happy that it was an easy justification to make.

I constantly tried to provide a balance between teaching complex, new ideas to the students and maintaining the appeal to the students' popular culture interests. The students needed to learn about businesses for their reading unit and, ultimately, had to learn how to write an expository text. I discovered that the trick was not merely to use popular culture as an enticement to do something totally unrelated to their interests. Instead, I made a conscious effort to actually use the popular culture interests as a foundation upon which students could build new concepts. The students were interested in comic books and cartoons and would read comics and talk about animation during class. Instead of making these topics taboo, I instead used them as the driving force of my instruction. These popular culture interests are easy to dismiss as unrelated to the educational arena; however, these interests are arguably extremely important. Students bring with them to school what they have learned at home through their cultures and from television and comics. By capitalizing on these *funds of knowledge*, I was able to make learning student centered rather than teacher imposed (Moll, Amanti, Neff, & Gonzalez, 1992). Not only were the students able to use their knowledge of popular culture to learn new concepts, but they also began to connect their interests to real life. Comics and cartoons were no longer as mysterious; the students began to understand that there is a great deal of hard work, revision, time, and money that went into them. For the first time, the students realized that their pastime was someone else's daily reality. This realization was important for them to make on their own, particularly because I wanted them again to make this discovery in the context of local businesses.

The Challenge of Letting Your Students Lead Instruction

I learned that the students were far more capable than I had given them credit for. I had provided them with an example of how to gather and implement information but, up to this point, had never let them attempt it on their own. By stepping back and allowing them to take control of a project, I learned that many of the students were extremely resourceful in gathering information. It is never easy or comfortable to undertake a project where you, as the teacher, are not explicitly in control of the lesson. I ultimately found it to be a great success. I had taken great care to set up very specific rules of classroom and small-group conduct, which we reviewed prior to and following each work session, and which helped tremendously with student conflict or management problems.

The completion of this unit has resulted in students who feel comfortable enough to bring their own interests to school. They know their teacher will not berate them for asking a question about a comic or cartoon, as long as they can justify the correlation to the subject matter at hand. I occasionally have a student who merely wants to talk about cartoons, but I persist in having the student verbalize the connection to the current task. Students are occasionally caught drawing comic strips, but I simply redirect them to their task, acknowledge their desire to draw, and tell them when the next appropriate time to continue their drawing will be.

Concluding Thoughts

I am always pleased that I have gone to great lengths to make learning fun and relevant to my students' lives. Though reading programs have the best of intentions and are based on research, they often lack real-world applicability because they are meant for such a broad audience. The students at my school live in a very different reality than students in another state, or even another part of our city. Good teaching is taking a solid reading program and applying individualized instruction of the program to make the skills accessible and relevant to students. I feel confident that during the course of this project, my students were excited about learning, had fun during the process, and emerged with a mastery of skills.

I will continue to capitalize upon the popular culture interests of my students to make learning enjoyable and meaningful. Even as an adult, I can say that my own learning is purely interest based. I can learn what I need to, but I learn the most about subjects I am interested in or that have an immediate relevance to my own life. Students are no different. A student, however, may not have the ability to understand readily and completely a new concept unless it is correlated with something of interest that resides in his or her own background knowledge. As a teacher, I am willing to find a way to bridge that gap. This project may not work for my class next year. I will have to find out what their popular culture interests are and build a different unit of instruction. Undoubtedly, it once again will be worth the effort.

CHAPTER 4

Integrating Popular Culture Texts in Developmental Reading Classes for Sixth- to Eighth-Grade Students

VIGNETTE 4.1

While I (Lark) implement a unit with a component of rap music and songs, my students come through the door actually eager to participate in each day's activities. They would ask, "Are we reading *Holes* [Sachar, 1998] today?" or "Will we have time to work on a rap about Stanley [a main character in the book] today?" When I answer them with a *yes*, the students actually give me "high fives," pump their fists into the air, and make hoots and grunts of approval.

This vignette is an example of the excitement and enthusiasm that my students displayed throughout the unit on *Holes*. In this chapter, I (Lark) describe my experience of experimenting with capitalizing on my students' popular culture interests to enhance literacy learning. In particular, I share how I (a) learned about my students' popular culture interest in rap music, (b) guided my students to make a connection between rap lyrics and adolescent literature via a theme of bullying, and (c) stimulated my students to explore the issue of bullying that was relevant to their outside of school life. I conclude this chapter with my reflections on this experience and present advice for teachers who are interested in integrating popular culture texts into a literacy curriculum.

Background

My Teaching Experience

I have been teaching middle school since 1995. Like all good teachers, I have a series of teaching techniques that come from ideas that I have seen implemented in other places and then adapted to my needs as a reading teacher for students with low reading scores. As I studied for a reading specialist credential and master's degree in reading and language arts at a nearby university, I was exposed, through books, classes, colleagues, and observations, to theories of and research on reading, as well as practical information on teaching reading. Theorists and practitioners have influenced my teaching. Sometimes I followed their methods carefully, and at other times I freely adapted ideas or practices completely. My use was based on what would be best for my students.

My Students

I teach developmental reading classes for sixth- to eighth-grade students in an urban middle school that is part of a large school district in California. Figure 4.1 shows the student demographics in my school district. About 66% of the students at my school site are bused to school. Over 46% of the students receive free or reduced-cost lunch (Long Beach Unified School District Bulletin, n.d.).

The students in my classes are reading at a minimum of two grade levels below their current grade levels. Two classes, approximately 20 students per class, are filled with students who have not made progress for a year. These students have developed many coping strategies to get by in their content area classes. My tasks are to help them (a) learn to read instead of using their various coping strategies and (b) become motivated to learn.

Figure 4.1   Long Beach Unified School District Demographics

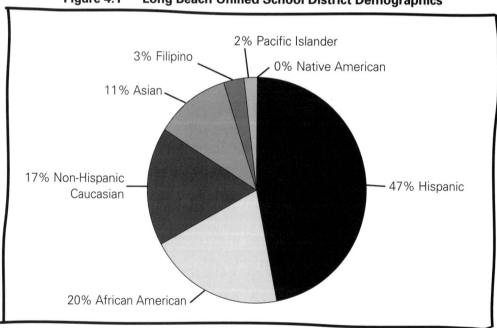

Instructional Routines

My class is a combination of direct instruction on specific reading strategies and an adapted use of literature circles. Each day I begin with a check of the student planners in which the students write the objective and homework for each class. My school district requires that all students in a reading class log a minimum of 100 minutes of homework reading each week. Along with their homework reading, I ask the students to perform a comprehension activity. The comprehension activities include finding the main idea, making predictions, making connections, finding parts of themselves in the characters, summarizing, finding interesting quotations, and asking questions of the author.

The planner check is followed by a warm-up activity. I developed a five-minute fluency exercise (Rasinski, Linek, Sturtevant, & Padak, 1994) that consists of the following three steps: (1) I model correct intonation, phrasing, pacing, and pronunciation of a short passage from a leveled text; (2) the class and I read the same selection aloud again, practicing correct intonation, phrasing, pacing, and pronunciation; and (3) the students read the passage aloud on their own, at their own pace, continuing to practice good fluency habits. The short passages include fiction and nonfiction texts.

The focus of my daily instruction is to help my students master reading strategies. While reading *Comprehension Instruction: Research-Based Best Practices* (Block & Pressley, 2002), I discovered the Collaborative Strategic Reading method developed by Klingner and Vaughn (1999). This method combines the best of direct instruction within context and reciprocal teaching. The reading is divided up into four processes: (1) *preview* (before reading), (2) *click and clunk* (during reading), (3) *get the gist* (during and after reading), and (4) *wrap up or summarize* (after reading).

I select specific strategies to teach during these stages. To determine exactly what to say and how to communicate these strategies with my students, I have relied heavily on Gerald Duffy's book *Explaining Reading: A Resource for Teaching Concepts, Skills, and Strategies* (2003). During the preview stage, I emphasize the strategies of activating schema, scanning, predicting, and visualizing. The idea behind click and clunk is to teach students to self-monitor their comprehension. When they hit a *clunk*—a place where meaning breaks down—they learn to use context clues and strategies of questioning and rereading. To enhance comprehension or get the main point, students learn to clarify, make inferences, summarize, and allow their visualization to grow and change. Along the way, students learn to continually check their predictions and make new predictions. Finally, students engage in a summary of the processes they have used to analyze what they have learned.

The reading strategies students practice are drawing conclusions, evaluating what has been learned, synthesizing the main idea, and completing the visualization of the whole reading passage. While teaching my students each specific strategy at various stages, I ask my students to take notes on the strategy and organize them in their workbook. To apply the strategies in real-life reading, the students read short stories, information text, or novels suggested in Hill, Noe, and King's book *Literature Circles in Middle School: One Teacher's Journey* (2003).

Integrating Popular Culture Texts Into the Unit on *Holes*

When I was enrolled in Shelley's graduate literacy course, one of the assignments was to develop a media text set (with print and nonprint text) based on students' popular culture interests, and to use the text set to address, through several activities, grade-level-appropriate reading and language arts standards. Beyond using the media text set for my students to practice strategies that I had been teaching, I engaged my students in discussing common themes from their favorite rap lyrics: bullying and injustice. This activity helped me become more knowledgeable of my students' academic abilities as well as their lives beyond school.

Learning About Students' Popular Culture Interests

The most challenging aspect of teaching adolescents is gaining their respect and trust. If you, the teacher, can achieve those two things, the students will follow you into a variety of academic adventures. In middle school, children are at a crossroads where they are discovering that their parents are not always correct or perfect. Usually, a distance between parents and their child is beginning as the student starts to carve out a unique self identity. Students now need an adult who is not their parent to take an interest in their lives and act as a guide. Thus, the role of the middle school teacher is born.

Discovering my students' popular culture interests was a challenge. My interests lie in classical music, modern dance, well-written television dramas, independent films, Janet Evanovich mysteries, and spiritual exploration. My interests may not even fit with adult categories of popular culture, much less with adolescent popular culture. My students and I live in two different worlds, so figuring out my students' interests was the first necessary step for me to take.

I began doing my homework by watching the new shows on the WB, Fox, and UPN television channels, which cater to adolescents and specific demographic groups. I listened to music highlighted from those shows and learned the names of characters in movies, such as *X-Men* (Arad, Donner, & Lee, 2000), and the characters on the television shows, such as *The Simpsons* (Groening, Brooks, & Jean, 1989). In addition, I listened carefully to my students' conversations to learn which Saturday morning cartoons they were watching. Then I began watching these cartoons myself. From this exploratory research of mass media, I thought I was familiar with adolescent popular culture. But there is a difference between what is popular for teens nationally and what is acceptable to teens within my school. There is even a difference between what teachers (or parents) think is popular for teens and the reality of what the teens in the class think is popular.

To get more specific information about my students' popular culture interests, I created a game. In the last minute or two before the closing bell rang, we played the *Truth Shuffle*. It was a nonthreatening way for me to learn more about my students. I said, "If what I say is true about you, you must change seats." We began with something directly related to their life experience, such as the following: "Those wearing white socks change seats." "If you're wearing earrings, change seats." "All those who like pepperoni on their pizza change seats." After playing the game once or twice with these nonthreatening revelations, I got more specific. I asked about particular television shows, cartoon characters, and musical taste. Because my students were allowed to move *every time* the statement was true for them, they changed seats several times as I mentioned programs, cartoons, books, and other popular culture concepts they liked. I was able to learn a great deal about popular culture in general, and specifically about their music interests. When I asked who listened to rap music, only three or four students remained in their seats. I knew I had hit a winner. Unfortunately, I did not know anything about rap music. I asked students to write down the names of the rap artists they liked so they could earn some extra credit points. I gathered up a list of names and headed down to a local music store that allowed people to listen to CDs before purchasing them.

I got the surprise of my life. The lyrics from the songs were filled with slang words that were new to me. Those words I could understand advocated violence or were sexually explicit and bordering on pornographic. I was stunned and thought my students had done this on purpose to shock me. I went back and asked for the names of more popular rap artists. I repeated the process with the same result. I decided that MTV (a U.S. music television channel) might show a different side of rap. I was wrong. Now I had images to go with violent and racy lyrics. I was still determined, and I began searching websites that would provide the lyrics for rap songs and information about artists (see Table 4.1 for the websites). I was certain that there had to be some rap music out there that was appropriate (in my opinion) for middle school students and that would help my students explore the content of rap music from a different perspective.

After navigating the websites listed in Table 4.1, and especially after reading H.A. Rhodes's article titled *The Evolution of Rap Music in the United States* (2004) on the website of the Yale-New Haven Teachers Institute, I developed a better appreciation for rap music and those artists who have pursued it. I was able to gain knowledge about themes of rap music, such as injustice, taking action, and living in the moment. I also learned that there are plenty of rap artists who do not use foul language, but actually speak of uplifting life events. The students, in my interactions with them, seemed to be aware of these artists, but they were not their favorite artists, and the students had only moderate appreciation for these rap artists. I thought that perhaps the students memorized the words but had not really *listened* to the message of the songs, so I asked a few students to explain the lyrics to me. I cited my unfamiliarity with slang words as a basis for needing more information from the students. These students were well aware of the

Table 4.1   Websites and Media Resources for Rap Music

www.yale.edu/ynhti/curriculum/units/1993/4/93.04.04.x.html
This is a rap music project on the website of Yale-New Haven Teachers Institute. This website also includes an excellent article by Henry Rhodes, *The Evolution of Rap Music in the United States* (2004).

www.ohhla.com
The Original Hip-Hop Lyrics Archive is a website for finding rap artists and lyrics that are not NC-17 rated (rated not acceptable for children under 17 years of age). Music lovers maintain this website, which does not have connections to any one recording company. Volunteers type in the lyrics they hear. If someone types in a lyric incorrectly, plenty of people will correct it.

www.rapmusic.com
This website features news and information on rap songs and rap artists and even suggestions on how to write rap music.

www.djmaj.com
Maj's website mixes the best of positive hip-hop and rap artists. Some raps contain overt religious messages. Maj is a live performance artist. There are some CDs of his work.

www.bbc.co.uk/education/listenandwrite
This interactive website is for children of any age. Students can write the lyrics for many different styles of music.

violent and sexually explicit messages. Although some students may pretend to their parents that they do not listen to or understand the words and pretend that they were only enjoying the rhythm and beat of the music, it has been my experience that they do pay close attention to the lyrics.

Challenging My Students to Critically Read Rap Music

Once I felt comfortable with rap music, I challenged the students to tell me what their favorite artists wrote about—the theme of the song. Interesting enough, for many of the students, the concept of *theme* was new to them. Although they admitted they had heard the term often in an English class, they were not at all sure what it meant or how they could find it from a text that they had read. So we changed the word *theme* to the term *big picture* or *major message*. Using some song lyrics and short stories, we identified the big picture or major message. It was interesting that a few students, who can rap every word of a song perfectly, did not realize its major message. These students had to talk with a partner to figure out the theme.

Once students understood that the theme was the big picture or major message of a song, and that they personally were able to determine the theme, they were more than eager to find out the theme of their rap song. The students copied or printed lyrics from websites (e.g., the Original Hip-Hop Lyrics Archive, 2002, at www.ohhla.com) with profane words replaced by symbols such as *#$!*?*. The students completed this task with no complaining, and a few students even examined more than one song. Those with computers at home discovered other websites specific to their favorite artists.

After obtaining a copy of song lyrics, the students used a four-box journal (see Table 4.2 for an example of a four-box journal on *Holes*) to identify a theme. The four-box journal is my own creation based on the information from *Literature Circles in Middle School: One Teacher's Journey* by Hill, Noe, and King (2003). Students do not need any special handouts for a four-box journal. The steps for creating this journal are as follows:

Fold a sheet of paper into four parts.

Box 1 is for writing a summary of a text.

Box 2 is for recording interesting words (formally known as self-selected vocabulary).

Box 3 is for formulating discussion questions. The students were taught the Focus, Answers, Thoughts and Feelings (FAT) method of writing discussion

Table 4.2   Sample Four-Box Journal on *Holes*

Summary	Interesting Words
After 2 weeks of digging, Stanley found a gold tube. The initials K.B. were on the tube. Stanley gave the tube to X-Ray. He suggested X-Ray turn it in tomorrow.	1. forbidden—to order not to do or be done or used. 2. intelligence—having or showing intelligence or intellect. 3. perseverance—to keep at something in spite of difficulties. 4. mansion—a large impressive residence.
FAT Discussion Questions 1. Why didn't Stanley say "no" and "if I find it, it's mine; I dug it up, find your own"? 2. How hard was it for great, great, grandfather to be rejected? 3. How does it feel to be at Camp Green Lake?	Making Connections (Text to Self, Text to World, Text to Text, Text to Art) 1. It reminds me of when I read this book about a girl who got bullied by a boy, and then the boy started to like her. (Text to Text) 2. He gets blamed for no reason. He didn't even do that. (Text to Self)

questions: The questions will *focus* on the main themes or ideas; the *answers* may require an inference from the reader or may ask the reader to speculate from what they have known of the characters; and these questions often examine the *thoughts and feelings* of the character. An example of a theme question might be "What is the difference between a leader and a follower?" A question that focuses on a character's thoughts or feelings might be "How do you think the gang members felt when they saw a girl shoving their leader in her locker?"

Box 4 is for making connections: text to self, text to text, text to world, and text to art. (For an explanation of these connections, see *Mosaic of Thought* by Keene and Zimmermann, 1997.)

The four-box journal enhanced students' ability to comprehend characters, a theme, and vocabulary, and to make connections. In my experience, assigning a single job or role to struggling readers during a literature circle only meant that they would stop reading as soon as they fulfilled the role. By having students complete the four boxes, I could reasonably be assured that they had both read and understood the text.

After the students had identified the theme of a rap song through the four-box journal, I asked them to list the theme of their favorite rap song on butcher paper (large white paper that resembles the type of paper used to wrap meat). The themes included being in love, losing love, overcoming bullies and getting justice, being poor or rich, and having life dreams. For my students, the theme of their favorite rap songs leaned heavily in the direction of bullies/oppression/getting justice.

Challenging My Students to Link Rap Music to Other Text Genres

SELECTING TEXTS FOR A MEDIA TEXT SET. Based on the predominant theme of bullying, oppression, and getting justice, I developed the following media text set (a set of educational nonprint materials) that included different text genres.

Movie/DVD and Young Adult Literature—*Holes* (Davis, 2003; Sachar, 1998): An innocent boy is convicted of a crime and sent to a detention camp run by a devious warden.

Nonfiction—*So, You Wanna Be a Rock Star?* (Anderson, 1999): The book profiles 18 professional child or teen bands; provides a guide to breaking into the music business; and offers practical advice on instruments, rehearsing, performing, and planning a budget.

Rap Song—"All for a Purpose" on *The Ringleader, Volume 3* (Maj, 2003): The song mix number 10 speaks about the power of our words. In the rapping portion, Maj makes it clear that words are powerful and should be used to elevate and empower.

Short Story—"Priscilla and the Wimps" (Peck, 2004): A tall girl comes to the rescue of a small boy and punishes the school bully by locking him in a locker.

Website—The Original Hip-Hop Lyrics Archive (2002; www.ohhla.com): This website has the lyrics of rap songs and information about hundreds of artists. This is a great place to find school-appropriate music.

Although my students were not involved directly in developing the media text set, the texts were required reading for my developmental reading class and were popular at that time (i.e., the movie *Holes* [Davis, 2003]). The short story "Priscilla and the Wimps" (Peck, 2004) and the novel *Holes* (Sachar, 1998) were united by a theme of bullying and oppression. The solution to the problem of bullying, however, was resolved very differently by the characters in each story.

Holes, both the book and the movie, was very popular on my campus, but that was not the main reason I selected it. *Holes* is a sophisticated novel that weaves four story lines from three different time periods. Because the images of many movies and rap songs are of a violent warrior type of hero, I took the advice of William Brozo (2002), the author of *To Be a Boy, to Be a Reader: Engaging Teen and Preteen Boys in Active Literacy*. He suggests that we need to show young men that there are many ways to be a man in society. *Holes* is listed in his book under the Jungian archetype of healer. Indeed, the main character in *Holes*, Stanley Yelnats, did heal old family wounds and brought reconciliation of a homeless boy to his mother.

I also included the Original Hip-Hop Lyrics Archive (2002; www.ohhla.com) that listed hundreds of artists, including rap artists and song lyrics. When I was asking students about the themes of their favorite rap songs, I showed respect for their musical taste. But I also wanted to guide them to become familiar with other kinds of rap music and rap artists who conveyed positive messages to young people. I found a rapper named DJ Maj whose song *All for a Purpose* (2003; see www.djmaj.com for the lyrics) told about the need to be true to one's inner voice and to live your life with a purpose. The song touched on one of our major themes related to *Holes*, which was destiny. To make the media text set more related to students, I included a nonfiction book, *So, You Wanna Be a Rock Star? How to Create Music, Get Gigs, and Maybe Even Make It Big!* (Anderson, 1999). I felt the book would provide my students with additional information about professional child or teen bands and about becoming a rock star.

EXPLORING THE THEME OF BULLYING. I engaged my students in exploring the theme of bullying, oppression, and getting justice through four activities with the media text set. In particular, we began by sharing our understandings of bullies who lived around us. We then investigated how characters in children's literature and in rap music deal with bullies and getting justice. Finally, the students produced a text related to the story of *Holes* as a whole or to the main character of the story, Stanley. The text would be in a form of a rap about Stanley (i.e., a rap, a song, or a poem), a persuasive essay, or an artistic collage that represented Stanley's journey toward his destiny. Through these activities, the students became critical readers, consumers, and producers of popular culture texts.

Understanding bullies around us. Working in pairs, students made a bubble map of those who are possible bullies. I took input from all groups and made a bully bubble map on an overhead transparency (see Figure 4.2). Then we talked about what bullies had in common.

Discussing "Priscilla and the Wimps" in small groups. The students wrote out the FAT questions related to the short story, and I made a master list of questions for the whole class (see Table 4.3). Each student acted as a discussion leader for two questions. I walked around the classroom to monitor the discussions and listen to students share their perspectives.

Understanding the events in Holes. The sophisticated nature of the book made it important for students to understand various story lines, including details and the interrelationship among the four story lines. I provided students with an empty flow chart to write down important events after reading several chapters. As a class, we then made a master flow chart of events and discussed these events. In Figure 4.3, for example, we detailed how Elya Yelnats's family curse got started.

Figure 4.2   Bully Bubble Map

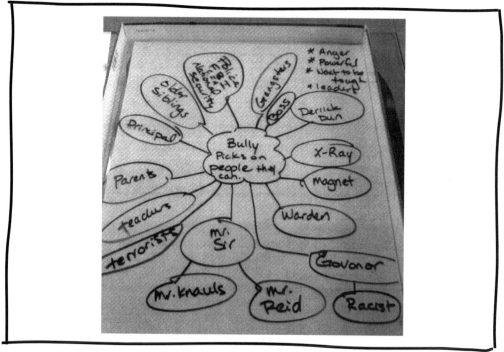

Table 4.3   FAT Questions for Discussing "Priscilla and the Wimps"

FAT QUESTIONS
Directions: When it is your turn to be the leader, choose two questions from the following to ask the group.
If you were Monk, how would you react?
If you were Monk's friends, what would you do?
Do you think people at school will tease Monk about getting beaten up by a girl?
Do you think Priscilla got in trouble for what she did?
What might happen to Priscilla after this incident?
How do you think Priscilla felt after she rescued her best friend?
What did Monk's gang think after Priscilla threw Monk into a locker?
How do you find a true friend that won't turn his or her back on you?
Why didn't the gang help Monk?
How do you think Priscilla felt when she was shoving Monk in her locker?
How do you think the Kobras felt when they saw Priscilla shoving Monk in her locker?
What do you think happened to the Kobras after the Priscilla-and-Monk incident?
Will this incident change Monk's behavior?
What is the difference between a leader and a follower?
How do you know the person is your best friend?
How would you feel being saved by a girl?
How do you think Monk felt when someone bullied him?
Why do the Kobras follow someone who is weaker than they are?
Why is Monk Klutter the leader?
Why do people become bullies?
How do you avoid a bully?

Figure 4.3   Elya Yelnats and the Family Curse

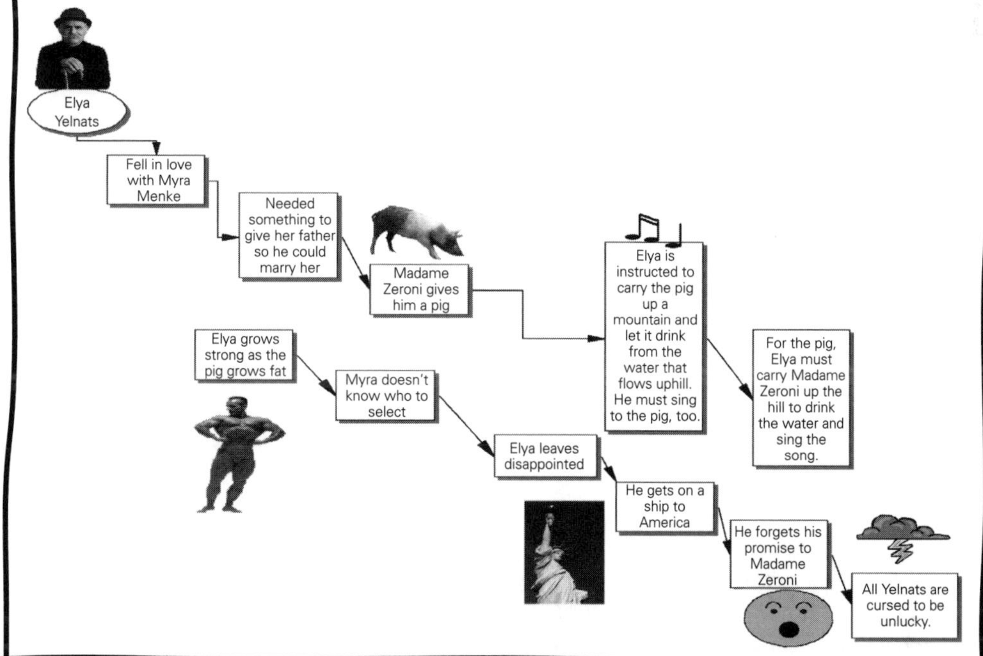

Linking Holes *to rap music and other text genres.* After students finished reading *Holes* and watched its movie version, I engaged the students in a culminating expressive project (see Figure 4.4). The project included comparing the book *Holes* to the movie *Holes*, completing a major themes worksheet, finding interesting words from the book, and completing an expressive project about

Figure 4.4   Culminating an Expressive Project: Filling in the Holes

To conclude our work with the book *Holes*, you must complete four items. All four of these items must be completed and turned in **by the end of the school day on Thursday, January 22, 2004**. I will be available after school to assist you, Tuesday through Friday, January 13–16, and January 20–22.

Complete a comparison of the book to the movie. (50 points)
Turn in a paper that lists at least 20 things that the movie added, left out, or changed from the book. You may work with a small group. All persons in the group must turn in their own paper.

Complete the major themes worksheet, using the examples from the story.
Please answer each question using full sentences. You will receive points for the effort and thoughtfulness you give in each answer. The questions under *Destiny* are each worth 5 points. The questions under *Change* are each worth 10 points.

Destiny
What is destiny?
How does someone find her or his destiny?
Which events lead up to Stanley's destiny?
What is your destiny?

Change
In what ways did Stanley change physically?
In what ways did Stanley change mentally?
In what ways did Stanley change emotionally?

Complete your blue book of interesting words. (50 points)
Your blue book needs to include at least 16 words you found new and/or interesting and their definitions.

Complete an expressive project. (50 points)
You will choose one of the following projects. Each project will be explained in depth and have a checklist to assist you. You must make a commitment to one of these projects by Monday, January 12, 2004.
    a. A rap about Stanley (we began this before the winter break). This can be written as a rap, song lyrics, or an epic poem.
    b. A persuasive essay (we will follow Ms. S's outline).
    c. An artistic collage that represents Stanley's journey toward his destiny.

Stanley's experience. Although most activities were familiar to my students, I anticipated that students needed some guidance on how to create a collage and on how to write a rap about Stanley.

To assist students in using a collage to express their understandings of Stanley's experiences and feelings, I provided them with a checklist for an artistic collage (see Figure 4.5; see also Reproducible A.3 in Appendix B). Figure 4.6 is a

Figure 4.5   Checklist for an Artistic Collage

A Checklist for an Artistic Collage
The purpose of a collage is to convey the story, meaning, and emotions through images. You may use magazines, drawings, words, painting, and fabric to create your collage. Each image should represent a particular incident, event, or feeling from the story.

When you present your collage, you will have the opportunity to enlighten the class as to why you selected your images and what they mean to you.

Remember, your collage must represent Stanley's journey to Camp Green Lake and back home again.

 ✓   My heading (name, date, and period) is on the BACK of the collage.
 ✓   I can explain what my images mean and why I chose them.
 ✓   This represents my best work.

Figure 4.6   A Student's Artistic Collage on Stanley's Experience

sample collage in which the student depicted, through the experiences of celebrities in the media, Stanley's journey to Camp Green Lake and back home again.

To assist students to write a rap about Stanley, I played a sample rap song, "All for a Purpose." As a class, we brainstormed ideas for a rap, song, or poem about Stanley's experience. Then students worked alone for the first day to think about their own ideas for a rap. During the second day, each student worked with a partner to create a rap about Stanley. I also provided students with a checklist to help them make certain that important events in Stanley's experience were included (see Figure 4.7; see also Reproducible A.4 in Appendix B). In Figure 4.8, one student detailed Stanley's experience in his rap.

Figure 4.7   Checklist for a Rap About Stanley

A Checklist for Stanley's Rap

Your assignment is to create lyrics for a song, a rap, or a poem that will describe Stanley's experience in the book *Holes*. The most powerful song lyrics help us to feel what the singer is feeling. Put yourself in Stanley's place. How do you feel about your life? How do you make sense out of what is happening to you now? How do you feel when you are successful?

Content

Include major experiences from the story.

✓	Why was Stanley sent to Camp Green Lake?
✓	Who does Stanley meet at the Camp?
✓	What is the curse on Stanley and his family?
✓	What does Stanley do for Zero?
✓	Why does Stanley run away?
✓	Where do Stanley and Zero go?
✓	Why do the boys come back to Camp Green Lake?
✓	What changes does Stanley go through?
✓	What happens in the end?

Writing Conventions	Yes	No
• My name, date, and period are on my paper.	✓	___
• I have indented my paragraphs.	✓	___
• I have put down one idea per sentence.	✓	___
• Each sentence begins with a capital letter.	✓	___
• Each sentence ends with a period.	✓	___
• I have used my best spelling.	✓	___
• I have reread my paper and corrected small mistakes.	✓	___

Figure 4.8   A Student's Rap About Stanley

I'm on the bus in my
seat, just waiting for some water
or something to eat. I'm here
'cause of my great grandfather
& his stinky curse that got
me bused, this verse.

I'm in this hole just digging
away, when I looked up it
took me all day, when all I wanted
to do was stay awake. I was walking under the bridge when I was
headed to my crib. Some shoes fell
on my head, and made me dizzy,
Hey look that policeman looks
frizzy.

He took me to court, I was
so scared I got some warts. I meet
some new friends name X-ray
Zig-Zag, David, Armpit, and Zero
who is my hero. I'm teaching
him how to read. Instead of
looking at this centipede.

I got to go dig my
holes while I'm making this money
for show.

Reflecting on the Use of Popular Culture in the Unit on *Holes*

California Content Standards and IRA and NCTE Standards

While using the media text set and engaging my students in various activities, I addressed many state-mandated reading and language arts standards (California Department of Education, 1999). The following are examples:

- Listening and Speaking Strategies 1.2 (sixth grade): Identify the tone, mood, and emotion conveyed in the oral communication.
- Literary Response and Analysis 3.6 (sixth grade): Identify and analyze features of themes conveyed through characters, actions, and images.

- Literary Response and Analysis 3.4 (seventh grade): Identify and analyze recurring themes across works (e.g., the value of bravery, loyalty, and friendship; the effects of loneliness).
- Writing Applications 2.4 (sixth grade): Write responses to literature:
  a. Develop an interpretation exhibiting careful reading, understanding, and insight.
  b. Organize the interpretation around several clear ideas, premises, or images.
  c. Develop and justify the interpretation through sustained use of examples and textual evidence.

Table 4.4 lists IRA and NCTE Standards for English Language Arts that I addressed during various literacy activities in this unit.

Table 4.4   IRA and NCTE Standards Addressed in Literacy Activities

Literacy Activities	IRA and NCTE Standards
1. Understanding Bullies Around Us	Standard 1 Standard 12
2. Small-Group Discussions About "Priscilla and the Wimps"	Standard 1 Standard 2 Standard 3 Standard 11 Standard 12
3. Understanding the Events in *Holes*	Standard 1 Standard 2 Standard 3 Standard 11 Standard 12
4. Linking *Holes* to Rap Music and Other Text Genres	Standard 2 Standard 3 Standard 5 Standard 6 Standard 11 Standard 12

The IRA and NCTE Standards are enumerated in this book's Introduction, pages 7–8.

The Power of Integrating Popular Culture Texts Into a Literacy Curriculum

Teaching struggling readers is taxing. It is difficult to motivate students who are mentally and emotionally *checking out* (choosing to remove themselves) from school, have poor skills, and serious self-esteem issues. These are the students who announce, "I hate this class!" as they enter the door. Introducing my students to various genres of texts—raps, websites, short stories, a film, and a novel—that are directly linked to students' interests has transformed my teaching experience.

Although the students regularly complained about each class assignment being *hard*, activities with this text set in no way stopped them from digging in and giving it their best effort. One of my students would regularly write two sentences of poor quality, claiming that he had finished his paragraph. As much as I prodded, assisted, and suggested, he rarely turned in work that would receive a passing grade in any class. But when I asked him to write a rap, I could not get him to stop writing. He bobbed his head to a beat that only he could hear and wrote with extreme concentration.

What has been most impressive is the volume and quality of student work from this unit. Students whom I have begged to write more than a three-sentence paragraph wrote full pages of their rap song. The initial explosion of excitement after receiving the assignment was something I had never experienced. Gone were the students' groans; they were replaced by students' bragging about who was going to have the best rap. The students were very appreciative of the opportunity to be creative while doing something they enjoyed. They rapped for each other and received praise from their classmates. Not once did I have to ask students to use good listening skills or manners.

Tensions in Integrating Popular Culture Texts

Depending upon your popular culture reference and your student population, you may have trouble finding content that is appropriate for school. To find a school-appropriate rap song to begin our theme, I went to a local Christian bookstore. I told them who I was and that I needed to find a rap song that would talk about justice without making overt references to Jesus. They walked me right over to the source. I found a reasonably good song. I felt it was important to strike a balance between respecting students' enjoyment of rap music and introducing them to other rap music that conveys different messages or exploring an issue from a different perspective. In so doing, I provided my students with an opportunity to learn other perspectives.

Not everyone will like the popular culture reference you select. All assignments had to be adapted to the extent that even those students who do not like rap could be included. For those students who are not musically interested, I adapted the assignment of an expressive project to include poetry writing. It is important that all students find a way to connect to the assignments.

Concluding Thoughts

Developing this unit did take more time than usual, partly because I needed to learn more about rappers and rap music. Even if the students' collective interest was a television show such as *One Tree Hill* (Davola, Hamilton, Robbins, Tollin, & Perry, 2005) or *Buffy the Vampire Slayer* (Greenwalt & Noxon, 1997), I would still have to immerse myself in that genre of popular culture text before I could effectively find themes and connect the interests to content standards.

Here is some advice I offer my colleagues: Most teenagers are passionate about music. It can be difficult to *control* a classroom when one student makes a connection to a rap song and seven people immediately pick up the rap. Suddenly, students are bobbing up and down at their desks and in the aisles. Keep a smile plastered on your face, thank them for the wonderful connection (even if you don't understand a word they are rapping), and immediately restore order. I have some chimes that are regularly used to signal silence and attention. They were used—a lot—during this unit of study.

I will be doing more units integrating popular culture text into the classroom. As much effort as this unit took, I must remember that I may not be able to repeat these activities. Next year, I may have students who do not value rap music. This process worked only because I was able to tap into *the students'* popular culture interest. Even so, I think the outcome in student work and pride was truly worth the effort.

PART 2

Integrating Popular Culture Texts in Your Classroom

Gaining Knowledge of Popular Culture Texts

This vignette portrays some realities that exist in today's classrooms. One is that students as young as 6 years old can be knowledgeable of and skillful at reading texts presented in a nontraditional format—a text with a combination of print, images, and sound and visual (e.g., color, font variations) effects. Another promising reality is that teachers are willing to become students of their students and to learn something from students—in particular, about the nontraditional texts that students are reading outside school settings. After witnessing what is described above, I have developed respect for Juan's teacher for taking up the status of an unknowledgeable novice of nontraditional texts, rather than trying to maintain the status of knowledgeable authority in the classroom, and for being willing to learn from her student.

In this chapter, I (Shelley) will describe some ways that help teachers learn about popular culture texts. I consider this step crucial because it is only when teachers become knowledgeable of these texts that they are able to identify their students' literacy knowledge and skills that would otherwise be invisible. It is only by learning about these texts that teachers can develop a better understanding of why students find popular culture texts engaging and appealing. Once teachers have become familiar with popular culture texts, they and their students can work together to make instructional decisions about incorporating popular culture texts into the literacy curriculum. Thus, teachers and students can make literacy learning more personally connected and interesting to students while addressing the mandated reading and language arts curriculum. (Note that pseudonyms are used for teachers and students throughout the chapter.)

Learning From Students About Popular Culture Texts

Teacher researchers, such as Mahar (2003), Morrell (2004), Norton (2003), and Vasquez (2003), have encouraged teachers to learn about students' popular culture texts. Some teachers have followed their recommendations and have become more knowledgeable of students' popular culture texts after discussion with students and self-exploration of such texts. In support of these teachers, some literacy researchers (e.g., Alvermann & Hagood, 2000; Mahiri, 2004) who have investigated students' outside of school literacy practices (in particular, those practices related to media texts, including popular culture texts) have pointed out the importance of developing "a better understanding of [students'] friendship networks and hierarchies, issues surrounding gender, interests, and skills beyond the classroom" (Mahiri, 2004, p. 470). In the following section, I describe three activities for you to gain some insights about your students' experiences, which are often quite different from yours, and for you to develop an understanding of why popular culture matters so much to your students.

Activity 1: Exploring Your Own and Your Students' Experiences

The types of popular culture texts with which teachers (or adults in general) interact and the ways that teachers engage with these texts in an outside of school setting can be very different from those of their students (Morrell, 2004; Xu, 2002b). To learn about similarities and differences in experiences with varied texts between themselves and their students, teachers can document different types of texts and the ways they engage with these texts during a period of several days, and also ask their students to do the same. The documented experiences will offer teachers an opportunity to reflect on their own and their students' engagement with popular culture texts. Specifically, it becomes possible for teachers to note that teachers do interact with popular culture texts in their daily life. More important, the differences in experiences with popular culture texts as shown in their documented experience will help teachers become more likely to accept the fact that the students and teachers do live in different worlds and belong to different Discourse communities (as discussed in chapter 1).

Table 5.1 shows, as the teacher, Sandi, documented, that what sixth grader Jane listened to, read, and watched was clearly different from what the teacher did. To Jane, the purpose of her interaction with different media texts seemed to be related largely to her age, with the possible exception of reading *Going Home* (Bunting, 1996), which could have been a school-assigned book. To Sandi, the purpose of engagement with popular media and other texts was to enjoy as a person, to become familiar with one particular genre of text (in this case children's literature) as a teacher, and to learn how to cook as a mother who cooks for the family. From the purpose of her *reading*, it is evident that Sandi had assumed multiple identities (i.e., a person, a teacher, and a mother), and that her experience with popular culture was closely related to who she is. Although Sandi and Jane were exposed to a set of texts with similar genres (e.g., movies, music), the content of each genre was very different. It is this kind of difference that made Sandi and Jane belong to different Discourse communities.

Table 5.1   Popular Culture Documentation of a Teacher and a Sixth-Grade Student

Date	Sandi (Teacher)	Jane (Sixth Grader)
May 22, 2001	• listening to KILL radio (a local radio station in west Texas; features country music, news, weather, and idle chatter) • reading morning newspaper • watching part of *Leave It to Beaver* (Cadiff, 1997; a movie) • scanning a few cookbooks • reading *Ladies Home Journal* (Meredith Corporation, 2005)	• reading *Going Home* (a book) • watching *JAG* (Bellisario, 2005; a television show) • watching *X-Files* (Carter, 1993–2002; a television show)
May 23, 2001	• listening to KILL radio • watching part of *McHale's Navy* (Spicer, 1997; a movie) • reading a few children's books	• watching *Ever After* (Sorla, Trench, & Tennant, 1998; a movie) • reading *Going Home* • watching *JAG*
May 24, 2001	• listening to KILL radio • listening to Christian music • doing crossword puzzle from the newspaper • reading children's books	• listening to Christina Aguilera's *My Kind of Christmas* (2000) album • listening to Celine Dion's *All the Way* (1999) album • listening to Martina McBride's *White Christmas* (1999) album

Activity 2: Exploring Your Own and Your Students' Literacy Knowledge and Skills

Another activity that teachers and their students might do together is to list genres of popular culture texts to which they have been exposed, and then to think about the literacy knowledge and skills that are required for them to enjoy each genre of text. This activity aids teachers in discovering "potentially interesting commonalities in the literacy skills needed to interpret" popular culture texts (Alvermann, Huddleston, Hagood, 2004, p. 538). As evident from Table 5.2, the

Table 5.2   Popular Culture Texts and Literacy Knowledge and Skills

Tina (Teacher)		Cindy (Second Grader)	
Text Genres	Literacy Knowledge/Skills	Text Genres	Literacy Knowledge/Skills
Television Shows • *Friends* (Bright, Goldberg-Meehan, Kaufman, Silveri, & Crane, 1994–2004) • *ER* (Chulack et al., 2005)	• predicting • making inferences based on music • making connections to personal experiences and other texts • using contextual clues (e.g., sound effects, action) to understand story line • differentiating reality and fantasy	Television Shows • *Rugrats* (Csupo & Klasky, 1991–2003) • shows on Cartoon Network (a U.S. television channel) • shows on Animal Channel (a U.S. television channel) • shows on Disney Channel (a U.S. television channel)	• predicting • making connections to personal experiences and other texts • differentiating reality and fantasy
Movies/Videos • *Dumb & Dumber* (Farrelly & Farrelly, 1994) • *Steel Magnolias* (Ross, 1989)	• differentiating reality and fantasy • making inferences • making connections to personal experiences and other texts • summarizing ideas based on story grammar	Movies/Videos • *Pokémon the Movie* (Yuyama, 2000) • *Wishbone II* (Guthrie & Duffield, 1995) • *Fantasia* (Algar et al., 1999) • *Allan Quatermain and the Last City of Gold* (Nelson, 1987) • *Shrek* (Jenson & Adamson, 2001) • *102 Dalmatians* (Biddle & Lima, 2000)	• differentiating reality and fantasy • making inferences • making connections to personal experiences and other texts

(continued)

Table 5.2 Popular Culture Texts and Literacy Knowledge and Skills
(continued)

Tina (Teacher)		Cindy (Second Grader)	
Text Genres	Literacy Knowledge/Skills	Text Genres	Literacy Knowledge/Skills
Music • George Strait • Lee Ann Womack • Shania Twain • Oldies • Soft Rock	• differentiating reality and fantasy • making inferences • making connections to personal experiences and other texts • figuring out unknown words based on contextual clues	Music • Britney Spears • Classic Disney songs • NSYNC • Backstreet Boys • Shania Twain	• making connections to personal experiences and other texts • using intonation clues to help understand the song lyrics
Websites • www.yahoo.com	• making inferences • making connections to other texts • using synonyms to find more information • trial and error	Websites • www.cartoon network.com • http://pokemon. com • http://disney.go. com • www.britney spears.com	• making connections to personal experiences and other texts • trial and error

literacy knowledge and skills that the student, Cindy, has used in her interaction with popular culture texts are actually the same ones or similar to those she is learning at school and using when interacting with readings from a basal reader series, all of which are part of the reading and language arts standards.

Activity 3: Exploring Your Own and Your Students' Views of Popular Culture Texts

In a third activity, a teacher chooses to explore a piece of unfamiliar popular culture text that is familiar to a student, and then to share with the student his or her views about the text. This activity not only helps a teacher learn about students' popular culture text, but, more important, it also allows the teacher to learn why this text is appealing to the student and why the teacher and the student hold different views of the text. The following dialogue is of second-grade teacher Dora's views of *SpongeBob SquarePants* (Hillenburg, 2005), a cartoon on Nickelodeon (a U.S. television channel), and her second-grade student's opinions about the show.

Dora: *SpongeBob SquarePants* is about a sponge named Bob who lives under the sea. Bob has a best friend, Patrick, who is a starfish, and they get into all types of mischief together. Bob has a neighbor, Squidward, who is a squid and can't stand Bob or his best friend because he thinks that they are goofballs. I am a cartoon fanatic, but this cartoon gets on my nerves a little bit because it is extremely silly. I really hate the theme song, too. Also, I find the neighbor to be obnoxious and rude most of the time. That is not [a] good role model for my students.

Fay: I love the theme song, "Oooooooh, who lives in a pineapple under the sea, SpongeBob SquarePants...." SpongeBob is very fun, because sometimes he is silly, and actually they [are] all funny.

While Fay just wanted to enjoy the humor and to have a good laugh, Dora was looking for educational materials from the show and was judging the quality of the show based solely on the show's educational value. In the following responses, fourth-grade teacher Maria explicitly expressed her negative opinion about Saliva's *Click, Click Boom* (2001) from the *Every Sixty Seconds* album (visit http://www.asklyrics.com/display/Saliva/Click_click_boom_lyrics/13536.htm for the lyrics), which contrasted with her second-grade student's opinion.

Maria: Personally, I didn't like this group. I felt their use of profanity isn't necessary to make good music. Being in a band kind of influences Juan's choice of music. The louder the better! The words are too negative and, of course, profanity is inappropriate. The beat is loud and the lyrics are not appropriate for elementary students. The music was so loud the words were hard to make out.

Juan: The beat of the music is most important than the lyrics. Profanity is part of their personality and culture. I don't take the lyrics seriously. [He is in a band and plays trombone.] I enjoy the *beat*. I sometimes don't take time to get the meaning of a song. Music is for *fun*.

Despite her disapproval of the song, Maria tried to understand why the song held some special meaning and appeal to Juan.

Learning About Popular Culture Texts

In the previous section, I discussed several activities in which you and your students can participate so that you can learn from them about what they are interested in *reading* and about what popular culture texts mean to them. Another effective (and interesting) way to familiarize yourself with students' popular culture texts is to explore different genres of popular culture texts. As listed previously in the Introduction, some common popular culture text genres are televisual and film texts, hypertexts and multimedia texts, musical texts, comic book texts, trading card texts, game texts, and zine or e-zine texts. In this chapter, I discuss each of these popular culture text genres separately and in detail.

Each of these text genres shares some similar textual structures with a print-based text (e.g., a picture book, an informational book) that students predominantly encounter at school, but each also has its own distinctive text features. In a similar way, while engaging with each text genre, students practice and reinforce many literacy skills that they use for reading and writing at school, and in the meantime, they acquire some new literacy skills or learn a new way to orchestrate different literacy skills for a context that exists only in an outside of school setting (e.g., playing a video game) (Alvermann & Heron, 2001; Gee, 2003). In the following section, I begin my discussion of the different genres with the most familiar text genre—televisual and film text—and move on to less familiar text genres (e.g., trading card text, game text).

Televisual and Film Text

Televisual and film texts seem familiar to most people because they have been around for a long time. Similar to print-based texts, both televisual and film texts are composed of linguistic units—words—that are spoken out rather than printed out as in a book. But there are some differences between a televisual and a film text:

- A television show may not have a complete story in one episode; some story problems are resolved after several episodes. A film usually tells a complete story.

- While watching a television show at home, viewers may not have a similar sensual experience that a movie theater can provide through cutting-edge multimedia technology.

- Viewers of a television show have more freedom to manipulate a televisual text than a film text. For example, a viewer can choose to turn on the closed-caption feature, increase or decrease the volume, and adjust the screen color background to achieve an optimal visual effect. Viewers of a film often cannot do any of these. Another interesting thing that viewers of a television show can do, but those of a film cannot, is to converse about the show before, during, and after the show. Viewers of a film, on the other hand, are required to remain quiet throughout the film but can discuss it before or after it.

Because a film text is very similar to a televisual text, except for the differences mentioned above, in the next section, I will focus on televisual text.

Similar to the structure of print text, a televisual text can be a narrative or an expository text. The narrative structure of a televisual text (e.g., one episode of *SpongeBob SquarePants* or *Friends* [a show about a group of adult friends]) is similar to that of a storybook. The presentation of and solution to a conflict are "a major storytelling mechanism" (Scharrer & Comstock, 2003, p. 183), and because of time constraints, a conflict often is resolved quickly in most televisual texts. A conflict in some television shows may be resolved after several episodes.

The expository structure of a televisual text (e.g., CBS *News* [CBS Broadcasting, Inc., 2005; a U.S. news television show], ABC's *20/20* [Arledge & Neufeld, 2005; a U.S. news show], PBS's *Nature* [Thirteen/WNET, 2005; a U.S. weekly feature television show]) shares a common feature—there are no headings and subheadings written out for viewers as in an informational book for readers. The structure of each text can vary from that of another similar text. For example, it is true that both CBS *News* and ABCs *20/20* do not list headings and subheadings for their viewers, but an overview of what is coming up after commercials serves the same function as headings and subheadings. Besides, a news program and a news magazine often have their own categories. In a news program, categories might be headlines, local news, world news, consumer report, weather, sports, and entertainment. In some programs without commercials (e.g., PBS's *Nature* and *Reading Rainbow* [Burton & Liggett, 2005]), before the show begins, the narrator does not always give information as to the content to be covered (although a title seems to tell clearly about the content) and the format of the information he or she is going to present.

For example, PBS's *Reading Rainbow* often begins with a theme song; the host, LeVar Burton, appears in a place related to the theme (e.g., in an aquarium or by a beach if the topic deals with ocean animals); he starts reading a book; he takes viewers to the place where experts or people working there provide information related to that place (e.g., different kinds of animals, their life cycles, and how to take care of animals); and finally, children who have read books on the topic of the show recommend the books. The show concludes with bibliographic information on the books. Although the show follows a consistent format across all episodes, the narrator does not provide viewers with headings and subheadings. Viewers of the show learn about its organization after multiple viewings and learn to summarize ideas based on their understanding of the relationship among ideas the narrator presents. The absence of headings and subheadings in an expository televisual text (and also in a documentary film) may present a challenge to viewers in terms of meaning making and organizing ideas while viewing it.

This challenge seems to be compensated by what makes televisual texts different from print-based texts, that is, the presence of nonlinguistic contextual clues—body language, gestures, animations, color and sound effects, and rapid action and pace (Goldman, 1996; Lee & Huston, 2003). These contextual clues provide viewers with additional support for meaning making. Coupled with "short sentences, lexical and syntactic simplification, and frequently exaggerated intonation" (Goldman, 1996, p. 15), nonlinguistic contextual clues offer comprehensible input for English-language learners and beginning readers.

With these unique nonlinguistic features, a televisual text may enhance the quality of the content that is originally presented in a book. According to Crane and

Chen (2003), in the television show *The Magic School Bus* (Loubert et al., 1994–1997), adapted from the book series by Joanna Cole, the teacher, Ms. Frizzle, engages her students in hands-on and inquiry-based learning of science, as opposed to teaching through lectures as portrayed in the book version. The students portrayed in the show are more active learners with unique personalities rather than the passive learners as described in the book. The unique features of a televisual text also tend to help engage students in mastering abstract literacy concepts and knowledge. Strickland and Rath (2000) report that kindergartners who watched 17 episodes (8.5 hours of viewing time) of *Between the Lions* (Cerf et al., 2005; a PBS show that teaches beginning readers phonemic awareness; phonics patterns; decoding; and enjoyment of reading through songs, stories, jokes, and performance) did better in the area of word knowledge, concepts about print, phonemic awareness, and letter–sound knowledge than their peers who did not watch the show.

Film and television producers can now present both televisual and film texts, classic (e.g., *Gone With the Wind* [Fleming, 1939]) or contemporary (e.g., *Friends*, in the format of a DVD (digital versatile disc), due to the advancement in technology. Although a movie or a television show on a DVD shares many similar features of televisual and film texts discussed above, it does have some unique features. For example, a DVD offers, in addition to an actual movie or television show, background information on the text. For a movie on a DVD, the audience may find several related features: (1) the trailers for the movie, (2) the process of making the movie (e.g., constructing a historical or futuristic setting, putting on makeup for a character with special appearance, adding special effects), (3) unedited or alternative scenes, (4) the soundtrack for the movie, (5) the historical background of the movie, and (6) an interview with the cast and crew (e.g., directors, actors, and actresses) or others (e.g., the real-life people that the movie portrays). These unique DVD features lend additional support to audiences for comprehending the text and often for deepening their understanding of the text. To some extent, this type of additional information, along with a movie or a television show on a DVD, may stimulate viewers' interests in exploring more about the movie or the show.

Hypermedia Text

A *hypertext* is a text on the Internet with links to other texts that may have additional links to other texts (Bruce, 2003). Hypertext is composed of linguistic units (words). For example, when you click on Meetings and Events on the International Reading Association's homepage (www.reading.org), you will get to a page with a list of conferences held in previous years and a conference to be held in the coming year. If you want to read about a conference to be held, you click the link of a conference to be held. Then you are led to another text page that lists all types of information related to the conference, each of which can be another hypertext.

A *hypermedia text* is a hypertext that is composed of linguistic units and multimedia, e.g., sound effects, animations, images, actions (as in a video clip), and pop-up windows (as in advertisements) (Myers & Beach, 2003). As discussed in chapter 1, a multimedia text has multimodes for meaning making. The images on the screen, for example, provide visual meanings that words may not be sufficient or effective to convey. An image of a paw print of the dog Blue (an icon for a link) on the website of *Blue's Clues* (Kessler, Twomey, Johnson, & Santomero, 1996–2004; www.nickjr.com/home/shows/blue/blue_live04/index. jhtml) is more easily recognized by a young child than the words *a paw print*. Many websites related to popular culture are hypermedia texts (e.g., http://pbskids.org and www.cartoonnetwork.com).

Although a hypermedia text provides additional (often nonlinguistic) contextual clues for readers to navigate the website and to comprehend the content presented in the website, the layout of any text on the Internet can pose some challenges to navigators. Specifically, they need either to transfer and adapt literacy skills acquired through reading print-based texts or to develop a new set of skills that can be applied successfully to reading a hypermedia text. A first challenge is that a hypermedia text has no point of entry as a traditional book does (Kress, 2003). The layout of information on the screen does not follow the concepts about print. There can be two-, three-, or even four-column text on a homepage. Navigators can first choose to read a right or middle column of text on the page. While reading a print text, readers always start reading from the left side of the page. With hypermedia text, navigators can click a link at the bottom of a page that is related to what they want to read without reading anything from the top of the page. Although when they get to the text they want, they do read, following the concepts about print.

Gaining adequate background knowledge of a topic presented on the Internet becomes another challenge. The layout on a homepage with headings and subheadings is very similar to a table of contents in an informational book. But unlike the table of contents where navigators locate a heading in a book and scan some subheadings under this heading to gain some background knowledge, a heading on the homepage does not always lead navigators to the next screen with subheadings. Often, a heading leads a navigator to another hypertext with more links. If a navigator is knowledgeable of a topic, he or she surely knows which heading to click on. For those who have limited knowledge about the topic, consecutively clicking each heading to see which one will lead to a hypertext with needed information is a common practice.

A last challenge is that a hypermedia text does not have any page numbers. While surfing the text, navigators have to quickly summarize information as they move from page to page. They may not remember which page to refer to, unless they want to start from the homepage. Navigators need to develop a graphic organizer of all the information they have read so far. Rereading a previously read portion of a text on the Internet is not so easy a task as reading a print text. Traditional print text is strictly linear; webpages branch out in many directions similar to a spider's web.

All the challenges confronting navigators make the literacy knowledge and skills they have acquired through interacting with print-based literacy more important, as they are a foundation for navigators' successful reading and comprehending experiences with hypertext and hypermedia texts. While students are navigating on the Internet, they are practicing and reinforcing their literacy skills and knowledge and also developing new ones. The materials (both print and nonprint) are often interesting to students, and the experience of reading these materials provides them with a sense of personal gratification and enjoyment. I invite you to visit a website related to your students' popular culture interests and to document what literacy skills and knowledge you are using while navigating the website (Table 5.3; see also Reproducible A.5 in Appendix B). In particular, note the same ones you have used for reading print-based texts and new ones you have developed or adapted for reading hypermedia texts. Put an *X* under either the *Same Ones* column or the *New or Adapted Ones* column.

Musical Text

A musical text consists of lyrics and music. If it is performed on stage or on a music television channel, the text also includes the images of an artist (e.g., clothing, dance) and the stage setting (e.g., lights, special effects). When a musical text is on a CD (compact disc) album, the image on the jacket also provides some clues as to the content of the musical text and the theme of all the songs on the album, which includes an album title and a list of songs and their performers, instruments, songwriters, length of song, and so forth. As discussed in chapter 1, both linguistic units (lyrics) and nonlinguistic context clues (e.g., images on a CD album) convey messages about the theme of the album and the meaning of each song. Visit a website featuring one of your students' popular artists and try to learn the theme of this artist's work and the message that an image on a CD cover tries to tell and sell you. You can write down your views of this artist and his or her work, share them with your students, and learn about your students' views (Table 5.4; see also Reproducible A.6 in Appendix B). The data you add to Table 5.5 can be tied into a minilesson on facts and opinions.

While many subgenres of musical texts have been around for a while (e.g., country, jazz, and rock), and they are relatively familiar to us, rap music, which is part of hip-pop culture, seems unfamiliar and often sounds strange to those of us who belong to a different generation and grew up in a different environment than that in which hip-hop culture developed. Hip-hop has gone mainstream and has become a dominant youth culture and popular culture in the United States and other parts of the world (Boyd, 2004; Piekarski, 2004). According to Piekarski (2004), hip-hop includes break dancing (a freestyle type of dance that is performed on cardboard laid on the street), graffiti, and rap music. He describes six different kinds of rap music:

1. Gangsta rap, which focuses on murder, money, and mayhem
2. Apolitical rap, which features a danceable beat and easy-going lyrics
3. Political rap, which is defined by socially analytical lyrics

Table 5.3   Literacy Knowledge and Skills Used With Hypermedia Text

Popular Culture Website and Address:

Yu-Gi-Oh! Cards   www.yugioh-card.com

Literacy Knowledge and Skills	Same Ones	New or Adapted Ones
Previewing headings on the homepage to gain background knowledge about Yu-Gi-Oh! cards	X	
Gathering additional information about the cards via reading the images (similar to illustrations in books)	X	
Referring to previous and next pages through links rather than page numbers		X
Downloading information to the desktop or a CD/disk rather than taking notes about the information		X
Locating certain portion of a text via the Find function on the menu		X

Table 5.4   Teacher's and Student's Views of a Popular Culture Artist and His or Her Work

Name of the Artist:	Title of a CD Album or Song:
Hilary Duff	*Song: What Dreams are Made off* *Album: The Lizzie McGuire Movie*
Teacher's View	**Student's View**
Most of her songs are okay. Some are sort of inspirational. She seems to be a better role model for female students than Britney Spears. She is a good pop star.	*I like Hilary Duff and her songs. But I also like Britney's and Christina's music. They have their unique styles. Hilary makes me feel confident about myself. It's okay that I am not as thin as Britney Spears and Christina Aguilera.*

4. Positive rap, which encourages listeners to become more aware of social and personal ills and to take steps to change them

5. Experimental rap, which continually modifies its style

6. Feminist rap, which challenges the implicit definition of rap as music created by and for males. (Piekarski, 2004, ¶ 2)

In a talk on *The Hip-Hop Phenomenon* of PBS's Online NewsHour (MacNeil/Lehrer Productions, 2005), Kaye describes hip-hop as "a culture and fashion beyond the music" (MacNeil/Lehrer Productions, 2005). Since its origination more than two decades ago in the south Bronx of New York City, New York, USA, rap music has continued to portray African Americans' urban life, and "the gritty, sometimes vulgar lyrics are often about life on the streets—poverty, drugs, sex, and violence" (Kaye, 1999, ¶15). I do not intend to ask teachers to promote rap music in an official school setting, nor do I intend to ask teachers to denounce rap music. Rather, I invite teachers to see, as Piekarski (2004) reminds us, beyond the negative surface elements in rap music:

Rap, of course, has a reputation for being violent, misogynistic, and hypermaterialistic. In many cases, these elements are indeed gratuitous; in others, they are an exaggeration for humor's sake, and sometimes they are a genuine reflection of a particular subculture and generation. A best selling rap CD may treat violence in all three ways. (¶ 8)

By becoming familiar with rap music, teachers are able to learn why it appeals to students and to think about the hope and positive experience that we teachers can provide students at school (which I will discuss in detail in chapter 6). Use a table as a guide to explore a rap artist, his or her music, and your view of the artist and music (Table 5.5; see also Reproducible A.7 in Appendix B).

Table 5.5   Explore Rap Music

Name of the Rap Artist	Title of the Rap Song
Bow Wow	I'm the Future in the Album of Beware of Dog (2000) Song.
Messages of the Song	Type of the Song (gangsta, apolitical, political, positive, experimental, and feminist)
• Telling his own success story of becoming a teen rap artist; • Showing self-confidence in his own future; • Implying the power of being a successful teen rap artist.	positive
Parts of the Song You Like	Parts of the Song You Dislike
• Bow Wow's success story • A preteen can be a rap artist if he or she works hard.	• glorifying too much about himself; and • Not telling other young people how to become successful.

In the article "Hip-Hop Till You Drop," Todd Boyd (2004), a professor of critical studies at the University of Southern California, helps educators who may hold a negative or resistant view toward rap music to see it in a historical context. He states, "Youth drives many forms of popular music, though. Rock 'n' Roll was once associated with youthful rebellion, but middle-aged figures like Bruce Springsteen and the Rolling Stones can continue to appeal to a core audience now despite their advancing age" (p. E44). Boyd continues to compare the influence of hip-hop with that of jazz:

> Believe it or not, anything young, vibrant and around long enough will grow old. Hip-hop is no different. There was a time when some people felt jazz was a corrupting influence, much the same way many people feel about hip-hop in the present. Today, jazz is regarded as high culture and celebrated in our most sacred cultural institutions. (p. E44)

In a similar manner, William Shakespeare wrote his plays for the general public, not for the nobles and the educated; now his plays are considered high culture and classical literature that are studied in high schools, colleges, and universities (Morrell, 2004). Interesting enough, rap music is not only used in advertisements (to which you may want to pay attention next time you watch television) but also in educational television shows. For example, high rapid movement, beats, and rhyming verse are actually used in part of *Between the Lions* (Cerf et al., 2005) for the purpose of engaging students.

Comic Book Text

In her study with 30 fifth, sixth, and seventh graders who are readers of *Archie* comic books, Norton (2003) discovered fantastic motivating power that comic books hold for the students and also confronted her "own fears and reservations about comic books in general and Archie comics more specifically" (p. 142). Again, before educators make any judgment on comic books in general, it is important for us to learn about them, which is a process that will help us see comic books from students' perspectives and then seek opportunities to capitalize on their interests in teaching.

In a short review of the evolution of comic books, Pellowski (1995) points out that the content of some comic books is derived from reality, such as politics, romance, crime, and war, "But most successful comic books use reality only as a springboard into a dimension beyond belief" (p. 7). The golden age of comics started in 1938, when superheroes appeared in comics. Although comics featuring superheroes predominate in the genre, other types of comic books are available. The following list comprises different types of comic books (Lavin, 1998; Pellowski, 1995):

Superheroes and superheroines: *Spiderman, X-Men, Wonder Woman, Catwoman*

Humor: *Blondie, Peanuts, Family Circus*

Crime and detective: *Pride and Joy*

Science fiction: *Star Wars, X-Files*

Horror: *Tales From the Crypt, Twilight Zone*

Mystery: *CSI: Thicker Than Blood* (Mariotte, 2003), *Sin City: The Hard Goodbye* (Miller, 2005)

Action, adventure, and fantasy: *Army Ants, Xena: Warrior Princess*

Television show: *The Simpsons*

Comic books have entertained and engaged readers and also stimulated them to think critically about current issues. *9-11: Artists Respond* (Vol. 1) (Dark Horse Comics, 2002) is a good example of a comic book being used as a powerful tool for documenting and portraying tragedies, triumphs, and human spirits. *Future 5: The Power of Your Mind!* (EDFUND & California Student Aid Commission, 2004; see Figure 5.1), a publication the Edfund and California Student Aid Commission produced in a comic book format, communicates with youth about the importance of going to college and about the information related to applying for community colleges, career schools, and colleges and universities.

Other two genres related to comic book text are mangas and graphic novels. *Mangas* are Japanese comic books that have characters from Japanese animations (animés) and have become increasingly popular in the United States and in other parts of the world (Weiner, 2002). One example of a manga is *Shonen Jump* (www.shonenjump.com), which features a comic book series and one-issue-length comics. A *graphic novel* is a novel written in a comic book format, whose theme is more than just superheroes or superheroines. Many graphic novels deal with conflicts similar to those portrayed in "accepted forms of literature" (Weiner, 2002, p. 55). For example, Art Spiegelman's *Maus: A Survivor's Tale* (1986), which won a Pulitzer Prize, is about the Jewish Holocaust survival. Comic authors and artists have rewritten some of Shakespeare's plays in a graphic-novel format to make the plays more accessible and comprehensible to young people. *Abraham Lincoln: The Civil War President* (Turner, 2004) is a biography written in a graphic-novel format. (Visit www.amazon.com for an inside look at this book.)

The text structure of a comic book is similar to that of a storybook in terms of story elements (e.g., characters, conflicts) and to that of a television show or a movie in terms of the visual images (e.g., pictures that tell a story). Yet, a unique structure of a comic book or a comic strip is that some characters do not age across time (e.g., characters in the comic strip *Peanuts*), while others grow older as their readers (e.g., characters in *Blondie*) do. Additionally, some story lines develop across time, which means readers will not find resolutions to conflicts in one issue of a comic book but will need to finish a whole series of the books. In other comic books, readers can find a complete story in one issue. The following summary illustrates the unique structural features of comic books (Pellowski, 1995; visit www.kiddonet.com).

Figure 5.1   *Future 5: The Power of Your Mind*

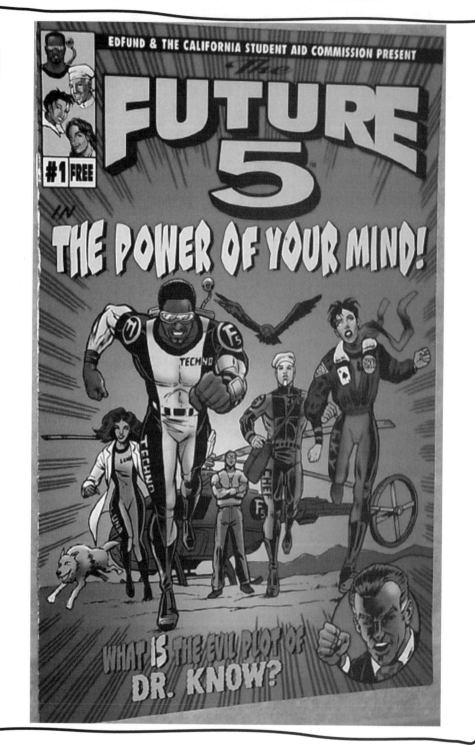

Directionality—In each picture (called a *panel* in comic books), a speech bubble on the left is read before the one on the right, and a bubble on the top is read before the one on the bottom. This process is similar to how print in a book is read. On each page of a comic book, there can be several pictures, or panels.

Speech, thought, and whispering bubbles—A speech bubble, which shows readers what a character is saying in a dialogue, is made up of solid lines with an arrow pointing to the character. A thought bubble, which allows readers to learn what a character is thinking, is made up of solid lines with a group of increasingly smaller bubbles pointing to the character. A whispering bubble, which shows a character is whispering to self or to another character, is made up of broken lines (or dotted lines) with an arrow pointing to the character.

Captions—Captions are used for time and location changes in setting, for setting a mood, or for content that cannot be conveyed in a dialogue. They often appear in a rectangular box.

Language—Everything said in speech, whispering, and thought bubbles or in captions needs to be as concise and to the point as possible. What is said often resembles oral language, that is, short sentences. At times, keywords are bolded or italicized to draw readers' attention. All words are capitalized.

Special effects—Special effects are used to achieve exaggeration and humor.

Sound—Sound effects are achieved through onomatopoeia (the pronunciation of a word that imitates a sound, e.g., *boom, bang*) and also through an image (e.g., the word *crash* may be framed in a jagged box to indicate broken fragments).

Visual—Visual effects can be achieved through exaggerated depiction of a character, such as disproportionally large or small body parts, out-of-ordinary facial expressions, and movements.

Color—Hot colors (e.g., red, orange) make a character more visible against its background.

Although a comic book contains a limited number of words with short sentences and simple sentence patterns, reading it may require some skills because readers need to follow pictures for a story line (Weiner, 2002) and make inferences based on pictures and a limited number of linguistic units. There is a wide range of comic books for young and older readers and for males and females (see Appendix A for the resources on comic books). Two major publishers of comic books are Marvel Comics (www.marvelcomics.com) and DC Comics (www.dccomics.com), whose websites provide helpful information on comic books.

Trading Card Text

The types of trading cards range from sports (e.g., baseball, football) to movies (e.g., *Spiderman* [Raimi, 2002]) to comic books (e.g., *Catwoman*) to cartoons (e.g.,

SpongeBob SquarePants) to collectible toys (e.g., Beanie Babies). What are new about trading cards that our students are collecting are those related to animé (Japanese animation) where the characters battle or fight against evil (e.g., *Yu-Gi-Oh!* [Kenney, 2005], *DragonBall Z* [Fukunga, Fukunga, Watson, & Fukengama, 1996–2003]). Unlike other trading cards, a trading card related to Japanese animés, in addition to providing information on the character (e.g., special power), tells how to use this card while playing. At the website of the *Yu-Gi-Oh!* Trading Card Game (www.upperdeckentertainment.com/yugioh/en/deck.aspx), detailed information is available about different types of trading cards needed to play a Duel Monsters game just like the characters in the cartoon. Other trading cards related to animés include *Pokémon* (Grossfeld, Kahn, & Kenney, 2005), *Digimon* (Rollman & Tufoya-Booton, 1999–2003; a Japanese animé similar to Pokémon in characters and in story lines), and *DragonBall Z*. Visit Splash Page Comics' index of animé trading cards at www.splashpagecomics.com/animcard.htm to learn about the trading cards and their animés.

A trading card has its own structure. Because of its limited space on a card, the words on the card must be concise and to the point. The language on the card may be beyond a student's grade level, which is particularly true for those students in the primary grades. For example, one of the *Yu-Gi-Oh!* trading cards, Red-Moon Baby, reads, "A monster destroyed by this card can be Special Summoned in face-up Attack or Defense Position at the end of the Battle Phase to your side of the field" (Takahashi, 1996, n.p.). The instruction contains words that are less familiar to students, such as *summon* and *phase*, and the structure of the sentence contains a past participle (*destroyed*) that serves as a modifier for the state of the subject (*monster*). In addition, readers cannot understand the true meaning of all the words on the card unless they belong to a Discourse community of *Yu-Gi-Oh!* players and have played the Duel Masters game. For example, What is a *face-up attack*? What is the *field*? Students who rely on players to explain the instruction rather than reading it by themselves would lose the game. Thus, in order to win the Duel Masters game with the *Yu-Gi-Oh!* trading cards, students have to be able to read the instruction on each card and be very familiar with the rules of the game.

Game Text

Game playing on a variety of platforms (e.g., PC, PlayStation 2, X Box, GameCube, N-Gage, and handhelds such as Palm Pilots, Game Boy, or Pocket PCs) has become part of childhood in today's multimedia-saturated society (Facer, Furlong, Furlong, & Sutherland, 2003; Gee, 2003). Teachers and parents often wonder what is so special about game playing that hooks young people, children, and adolescents for hours, days, months, and years, regardless of how hard a game is. In an interesting, provocative, and thought-provoking book, *What Video Games Have to Teach Us About Learning and Literacy*, Gee (2003) provides, based on his experience of playing various types of games, some insights about the unique and appealing features of games and 36 learning principles that game players apply to playing a well-designed game. Some of the 36 learning principles (e.g., active principle, critical learning principle, and design principle) have been evident in Vasquez's nephew's experience with playing *Pokémon* games, as documented by Vasquez (2003).

The game genres include action–adventure, simulation, fantasy, role-playing, and educational (Gee, 2003). Each game has the following four features:

1. an introduction to the game that presents a conflict or a task for the game player to resolve or to accomplish;
2. written texts that appear throughout each level of the game, as feedback on how a game player is doing so far, as helpful hints or strategies, as menus for the game player to make a choice for his or her next move, or as presentations of new problems;
3. the sound and visual (three-dimensional) effects that make the context of the game more realistic; and
4. instant rewards that allow a game player to move on to the next higher and more challenging level.

Each game has its own manual, which offers background information about the game and strategies. Another resource existing outside a game itself, but inside a particular game player's Discourse community, may be a network of game players who play the same game(s) on a similar theme, or games designed by the same company. These game players frequently exchange ideas, hints, strategies, and cheats online (Gee, 2003). A *cheat* is a way for a game player to edit a file in the program so that it will do something to allow him or her to successfully complete the level. For example, a cheat for *Spider-man* to gain extra health is to do this (please note that the words and symbols make little or no sense to those who do not belong to a Discourse community of game players):

> Use a text editor to edit the Gamestat.ini file in the \Spider-man2\system folder. Inside the game file, locate the file
>
> MaxHealth = 100//200 is upgraded value and change it to
>
> MaxHealth = 1000//2000 is upgraded value.... (Abby-cheat, 2004, n.p.)

Magazines for game players (e.g., *PC Gamers* [Future Network USA, 2005], *GamePro* [IDG Communications, 2005; www.gamepro.com.au]) also provide cheats and strategies related to particular games.

Games are "a new form of media, enabling true 'interactivity' for the first time, as the user is said to control and determine narrative in a way impossible in traditional linear media such as television, books or film" (Facer et al., 2003, p. 71). Besides, games offer players exciting, challenging, and rewarding experiences. However, if a game player depends on written feedback, he or she is most likely to lose the game soon after the game is started. As Facer and colleagues (2003) put it, "the experience of handling large and indeterminate amounts of information presented graphically, numerically and in text was a central feature of many games" (p. 75).

In Gee's (2003) book, he captures well the "reflective practice" in which successful game players are engaged while playing a game. He calls this "reflective practice" the "probe, hypothesize, reprobe, and rethink cycle," in which expert practitioners in professions such as teaching, medicine, and law are often involved (p. 90). In the beginning, game players probe the game by clicking on different icons to see where each icon will take them and trying out some moves to see if they can complete the current level. After the initial probes, game players ponder over their successful or unsuccessful trials and then formulate a hypothesis about how to effectively play the game. For example, a game player may make the hypothesis that using a certain button or key will make a character run faster so that an enemy will not catch the character. Once the game player formulates the hypothesis, he or she wants to reprobe the game to see if it is possible to make the character run faster. While reprobing, the game player reflects on how the hypothesis has worked and then decides either to accept the previously formulated and newly tested hypothesis as a useful strategy or to formulate another hypothesis if the previous hypothesis has not worked. This "probe, hypothesize, reprobe, and rethink cycle" (p. 90) continues as the game player moves from one level to another, but certain parts of the cycle can be shortened or skipped. For example, expert game players may not do much probing while playing a new game because they may bring some intertextual knowledge gained through a rich experience of game playing to help formulate hypotheses that they are ready to test.

Now, I invite you to play a free game from one of the websites listed in Appendix A, or you may play any game to which you have access. Try to see how the probe, hypothesize, reprobe, and rethink cycle works in your case and document your experience (Table 5.6; see also Reproducible A.8 in Appendix B). Through this experience, you will discover that playing a game is not a waste of time, which many people, including educators in particular, have perceived; rather, playing a game requires a game player to develop and practice, in an engaging context, literacy and critical thinking skills. The cycle may also show that initial learning of something new may not be positive and rewarding, much like the experience some children have at the beginning stage of literacy learning in school. But reflecting on and rethinking about the not-so-successful experience, as you may discover later, is an important step to a successful experience in the long term. This practicing and reflecting process, a metacognitive one, is similar to that of the literacy learning process, which is, unfortunately, missing in those who are not successful readers (but who may be skillful game players). Teachers who have experienced this metacognitive process through exploring game playing possibly have a better chance to communicate with their students about the process and

Table 5.6   Probe, Hypothesize, Reprobe, and Rethink Cycle

Title of the Game:	Tonka Space Station: Adventure Game

Stage of the Cycle	What Did You Do?
Probe	To drive the Terra Racer, a space-racing machine in the sporting arena, I used, as the user's manual instructs, the Ctrl key for forward movement and Left/Right arrow keys for steering the vehicle.
Hypothesize	To avoid crashing the racer into an open pit, a gate, or a wall, I needed to constantly use Left/Right arrow keys to keep the racer on its course.
Reprobe	The constant use of the Left/Right arrow keys kept the racer avoiding open pits, gates, and walls. But when the racer has hit a wall I didn't know how to get the racer back to the course again.
Rethink	To get the racer back to its course, as I have figured out, I needed to use Left/Right arrow keys just enough (not too much, not too few) to back the racer (just as we back our car).

Overall Reflections:

Following the user's manual does not always help me successfully play the game. I felt that I was constantly testing my hypotheses and strategies and that the experience of testing hypotheses gave me ideas for revising them. This cycle continued during my playing this game.

help them note the similar metacognitive process across academic literacy learning at school and leisure game playing outside of school.

Zine and E-Zine Text

Guzzetti, Campbell, Duke, and Irving (2003) define *zines* (pronounced /zeens/) as "self-published alternatives to commercial magazines. They are a form of 'indie media,' or independent media, that represent and reflect the ideas, ideologies, and ideals of their creators, who are known as 'zinesters'" (¶ 1). Zines are print-based publications, and most zines are written by and for women and teens. With the advancement of technology and easy access to computers and the Internet, e-zines have become popular (Warnick, 2002). Although e-zines may be no different from any other hypertexts or multimedia texts, they are unique in the sense of their content focuses. Like zines, e-zines continue to focus on current and pressing issues that matter to women and teens, ranging from homework to peer relationships to college and career to dating to fashion to sex. These issues are often presented in a form of forum, poll, or chat. For example, at the website of gURL (iVillage, 1995–2005, www.gurl.com), users can respond to whether an anti-anorexia ad with a straightforward tone would work. In the ad, the parents pick up some food from a table with many different kinds of food while their pale-and ghost-looking and skinny-to-the bone daughter is standing by. The caption for the picture reads, "You'll be dead [*dead* was highlighted by a flashy brown color] before you are thin enough [*thin* was highlighted by a flashy brown color]." In a piece cowritten by Guzzetti and three zinesters (Guzzetti et al., 2003), the authors describe the zines produced by the three zinesters as "a balanced mix of social justice issues, liberal politics, humor, entertainment, reviews, and personal reflections" (¶ 1).

Besides a discussion of issues, many e-zines for teens post the latest news related to them or to women in general and peer reviews of books, poems, and popular culture media, and they offer resources via links to other websites (see Appendix A for a list of e-zines). Other characteristics of e-zines, as Warnick (2002) describes, include targeted audience, purpose, and safe and supportive environment. A focus of an e-zine defines its own targeted audience, or each e-zine targets one particular Discourse group or community based on ethnicities, political affiliations, age, interests, sexual orientations, and so on. Despite the differences in content focuses, all e-zines have one primary purpose, that is, to provide their audience with resources and emotional support. In a similar way, a safe and supportive environment in each e-zine is created largely by the way that authors and users freely voice their opinions and, to some degree, by the rules set up for the authors who contribute to the website. One interesting characteristic of e-zines is their interactive and dynamic nature. A person can be a passive user of an e-zine in one minute while reading information on the website and instantly become an author in the next minute when the user decides to participate in a discussion. The dynamic nature of e-zines is further evident in updated information on users' opinions and the issues pressing to users.

Concluding Thoughts

At the conclusion of this chapter, you may have come to an understanding that many structural features of the popular culture text genres resemble those of traditional literary genres (e.g., a story, a poem) that students are learning at school. You may also have noted that users of different types of popular culture texts often apply similar literacy knowledge and skills as they do with print-based texts (Alvermann, Huddleston, & Hagood, 2004). In some cases, however, users have to modify these skills and develop new ones in order for them to comprehend these popular culture texts. With that said, students' engagement with popular culture texts does not seem to be a waste of time or meaningless as many have perceived. I hope that your own exploration of various popular culture text genres listed in this chapter will help you view these texts from a different perspective. Similarly, your study of students' engagement with media texts may offer you some insights into how you may capitalize on their acquired literacy skills by teaching in a way that makes connections between students' personal literacy practices with popular culture texts and their learning of traditional school texts.

Using Popular Culture Texts to Enhance Literacy Learning

6

VIGNETTE 6.1

In an informal talk with the preservice teachers from a nearby university, Mary, who has taught primary grades for 20 years, stresses, "You've got to keep up with the kids, know what they like and don't like, and what they do outside school. The times have changed. You have to consider their interests in teaching. For example, I need to make a connection between the characters of *SpongeBob SquarePants* and those in a storybook so that the students would be interested in learning about the characters. Otherwise, my teaching will never be more interesting to them than their Game Boys and television shows."

---

n this vignette, a veteran teacher, Mary, portrays a realistic picture of what students are interested in and why teachers should change or adapt the way they teach in response to students' experiences brought to school. What Mary does with students' popular culture interests is similar to the third approach (*celebrating popular culture*) discussed in chapter 1 (see pp. 22–23), in contrast to the first approach (*banning popular culture*), the second approach (*critically analyzing popular culture*), and the fourth approach (*celebrating and critically analyzing popular culture*). In this chapter, I (Shelley) provide some examples of using both the third and the fourth approaches in literacy teaching. Please keep in mind that these examples are not perfect, as they reflect a process of teachers' exploring the use of the third and fourth approaches, nor are they models for teachers to follow step by step. Rather, these examples illustrate what the third and fourth approaches might look like in your teaching. As you read this chapter, I invite you to reflect on how you might do things differently if you were the teacher in each example.

While reading and reflecting on the examples presented in this chapter, I would like you to keep in mind three other issues. The first issue is the ephemeral nature of popular culture. What is popular as illustrated in this chapter (and in this book) may have become outdated when you are reading this book. Therefore, becoming an expert on one particular piece of popular culture text is not as important as developing ways to learn about students' popular culture interests and to capitalize on these interests to make school relevant to them. An appropriate analogy for this would be the strategy of the literature circle (the teacher and students share their responses to literature they have read and discuss questions about the book). If you know how to effectively use the strategy of the literature circle, you can apply it with chapter books, picture books, and other literary genres. You do not need to learn again how to use the literature circle every time you use this strategy with a new book or a new literary genre. The relationship between a piece of literature and the use of the literature circle strategy with the literature is very similar to the relationship between a particular piece of popular culture text and the ways to use the text.

The second issue, how to identify a commonality among a wide range of students' popular culture interests in teaching, is a concern that teachers often have. In a classroom with 20 first graders, for example, you may have 5 students who are fans of *SpongeBob SquarePants* (Hillenburg, 2005), another 10 students who are interested in *Yu-Gi-Oh!* (Kenney, 2005; from the television show and trading cards), and the remaining 5 students may be not interested in either of these two popular culture texts at all. While respecting the interests of a majority of the students but not overlooking others' interests, you may want to find a commonality among varied interests, and at times, students may help you to do so. In this example, the commonality of the television shows and books can be character development and character traits. You may ask students to explore how characters are portrayed in a television show, a book, or other media forms (e.g., comic books or trading card related to a television show). In so doing, you have incorporated all students' interests and do not devalue any particular student's interests.

The third issue is a sensitive and subtle one. The findings from studies with adolescents (e.g., Alvermann & Heron, 2001; O'Brien, 1997) have informed us that "when teachers attempt to situate popular media texts alongside the more traditional texts of classroom, they run the risk of burying youth's pleasure by exposing them to adult critique" (Alvermann & Heron, 2001, p. 121). This could happen when students voice opinions that they think their teachers want to hear about their favorite popular culture, but are reticent about openly expressing their pleasure in their favorites. Alvermann and Heron further remind us that "it is unlikely that teachers can ever recreate the contexts that facilitate students' discussions and other transactions with popular culture media texts that occur outside or despite the 'regular' curriculum" (p. 121). Indeed, it is not an easy task to balance respecting students' pleasure and engaging them in critically analyzing popular culture texts. Teachers' experiences described in this book may somehow reflect their struggle with this issue. I invite all teachers to explore this issue in their own teaching.

In the following section, I share some promising possibilities of using popular culture texts. You may try in your teaching one idea or a combination of several ideas. Your experience of exploring may inspire you to come up with your own ways of infusing popular culture texts into teaching. Always share your new ideas with school administrators and parents to gain their support (which I discuss in chapter 7) and with your colleagues to help them see other ways to address required standards in teaching.

Sharing the Pleasure of *Reading* Popular Culture Texts

In kindergarten and sometimes in first or second grade, where show-and-tell (or sharing) is one of the daily literacy activities for children, teachers may use that time to allow students to show and tell their interests in popular culture. (Be aware of the extreme excitement this will generate!) Students can bring in items related to their interests (e.g., a book, a trading card, a T-shirt, a video game manual) and tell the class what an item is and why the item is important to them. This kind of show-and-tell provides teachers with an abundance of information about who our students are and what literacy knowledge they have, which, in turn, assists teachers in making teaching personally relevant to their students. During this process, teachers also gain knowledge about students' popular culture and may become interested in exploring these texts. It might be helpful for teachers to jot down their students' popular culture interests and then identify commonality across different interests, which would allow teachers to recognize a shared interest's relevancy to curriculum content and standards.

In a log of show-and-tell across a two-month period (Table 6.1), a kindergarten teacher discovered not only her students' individual and common interests but also some possible focuses for her teaching. In this example, the teacher identified a shared interest in popular culture texts by genres; specifically, all the television shows are narratives (i.e., the commonality) that are composed of story elements (i.e., curriculum content). Most of the narratives listed are fantasy in nature (e.g., *Digimon* [Rollman & Tufoya-Booton, 1999–2003], *Power Rangers* [Aronowitz, Kalish, & Sakamoto, 2005]), though some tell stories that could happen in people's lives (e.g., *Arthur* [Charest, Taylor, & Greenwald, 2005], *Dora the Explorer* [Walsh, Gifford, & Johnson, 2005]). Thus, fantasy-versus-reality is the commonality across these television shows, and it is also part of the curriculum content. In addition to identifying a commonality across various interests through genres, teachers can recognize a similarity among popular culture texts through themes. For example, the television shows listed in Table 6.1 have two themes—one is good versus evil (e.g., *Spider-man* [Gendel, Ungar, Arad, Caracciolo, & Lee, 2004], *PowerPuff Girls* [McCracken, Miller, & Potamkin, 2005]) and the other is friendship and getting along (e.g., *Arthur*, *SpongeBob SquarePants*).

Table 6.1 Learning From Students' Show-and-Tell

Student Name	Popular Culture Interest	Reasons Students Like It
Abby	*SpongeBob SquarePants*	funny, silly
Ameha	*Blue's Clues* (Kessler, Twomey, Johnson, & Santomero, 1996–2004)	I am happy when I can solve the mystery (interactive).
Anna	*Dora the Explorer*	I help Dora to solve the problem (interactive).
Cathy	*Dora the Explorer*	fun
Chad	*Power Rangers*	Good guys always win.
Demitri	*SpongeBob SquarePants*	silly, all about ocean animals
George	*Blue's Clues*	cute
James	*SpongeBob SquarePants*	funny
Jose	*Arthur*	don't know
Juan	*SpongeBob SquarePants*	fun to watch
June	*PowerPuff Girls*	They are strong, have super power.
Kevin	*Yu-Gi-Oh!*	exciting
LaTesha	*Spider-man*	All in my family watched the movie.
Maria	*Spider-man*	He climbs.
Mary	*Rugrats* (Csupo & Klasky, 1991–2003)	funny
May	*Pokémon*	They always fight.
Mei	*Dora the Explorer*	I walk along with Dora and Boots (interactive).
Peter	*Yu-Gi-Oh!*	play Duel Monsters game
Shawn	*Yu-Gi-Oh!*	They fight.
Tony	*Digimon*	special power

Tallies of the Interests From the Class

1 *Arthur*
1 *Digimon*
1 *Pokémon*
1 *Power Rangers*
1 *PowerPuff Girls*
1 *Rugrats*
2 *Blue's Clues*
2 *Spider-man*
3 *Dora the Explorer*
3 *Yu-Gi-Oh!*
4 *SpongeBob SquarePants*

(continued)

Table 6.1   Learning From Students' Show-and-Tell *(continued)*

Possible Connection to Curriculum Standards
- story elements
- fantasy and reality
- retelling a familiar story
- lessons learned from a story
- need to locate books with an exciting plot or with silly and funny characters or characters who are physically strong
- need to help students understand that physical power is not always the only trait for a character; need to find books with characters who use wisdom to solve problems

Teachers in other grade levels where show-and-tell is not part of daily literacy activities need to find time and space for students to talk about their outside of school literacy experiences with popular culture. The teachers that I have worked with in the past several years were often astonished to note an extremely high level of excitement when students were asked to share their interests. The time spent on this type of activity will pay off in the near future. The following examples are some possible ideas for teachers to try:

- In a literature discussion, students share their thinking on the similarities and differences between the characters in a picture book or a chapter book and those in popular culture media (e.g., comparing Brian in *Hatchet* [Paulsen, 1999] and *Brian's Winter* [Paulsen, 1996] or Julie in *Julie of Wolves* [George, 1972] with contestants in the CBS reality show *Survivor* [Burnett, 2005] or Chuck Noland in the movie *Cast Away* [Zemeckis, 2000]).

- In a discussion of character traits, students discuss the traits of their favorite characters in popular media (e.g., SpongeBob from *SpongeBob SquarePants*, Timmy from Nickelodeon's *Fairly Odd Parents* [Hartman & Seibert, 2005; a 10-year-old boy with parents who work full time and have a babysitter and other relatives to take care of him]).

- In a discussion of character traits, students describe how a character in a book is differently portrayed in a media text (e.g., Ms. Frizzle from the *Magic School Bus* series).

- In sharing favorite parts of a book, students make an intertextual connection through talking about a favorite part of a popular culture text that is similar to a favorite part of the book (e.g., PowerPuff Girls in the television animation *PowerPuff Girls* defeated the villain, Mojo, in a similar way that the sisters killed the bad wolf who tried to eat them in Young's book, *Lon Po Po: A Red-Riding Hood Story From China*, 1989).

Using the Media Format

When your students have expressed diverse interests in popular culture media, one of the commonalities might be the media formats that popular culture producers use to convey ideas. For example, visual representation (drawings) is a primary medium to tell a story in comic books, comic strips, and cartoons. Rachael vividly described in chapter 3 how she took advantage of her students' interests in comic books and cartoons and built on them to enhance her students' learning. You may allow your students to use the medium of drawing, in addition to printed words, to demonstrate their understanding. Please be aware that printed words are often a medium of communication that is used along with other media formats. Teachers should encourage students to use multiple media formats to convey ideas.

At the KiddoNet website (www.kiddonet.com), there is an Interactive Comics, My Comic Strip section where students can create their own illustrations and text for the strip. In the three panels, or pictures, are speech bubbles and two characters without any facial expressions. Students can add dialogue and then select facial expressions for the characters that are consistent with the mood reflected from the dialogue. Because of the limited space for words, students have to think about using only keywords in each speech bubble. (This activity can be helpful to beginning readers and writers, those who are struggling with reading and writing, and those who are developing English proficiency.) The limited number of words required to fill in a bubble does not seem too intimidating or challenging to these students.

Another way to use a media format is to apply a trading card format in designing cards about concepts related to content area. The Solar System Trading Cards website (http://amazing-space.stsci.edu/resources/explorations/trading/game.htm?sssssscsss) is an example of effective use of the design of trading cards in summarizing information related to each planet in the solar system. Figure 6.1 is a generic format similar to a trading card that you may use for your students to summarize information related to particular content (see also Reproducible A.9 in Appendix B).

A first-grade student, Charlie, designed a new *Pokémon* card for his newly invented *Pokémon* character, Octawave (Figure 6.2), and a card of a corresponding animal in nature, an octopus (Figure 6.3). In designing a card of a new *Pokémon* character, Charlie had to use his knowledge of *Pokémon*—the characters' resemblance to animals in nature, strengths (the environment in which they can survive and the way they attack their enemies), and weaknesses (the environment in which they cannot survive and the way they would be defeated if their enemies use this device). And he had the freedom to make Octawave as imaginary as possible. On the other hand, when he designed the card of an octopus, Charlie had to write facts about it, based on his knowledge about it. As seen from both cards, Charlie applied his literacy knowledge (reading and writing) gained from reading *Pokémon* books, comic books, trading cards; watching *Pokémon* shows; and interacting with his classmates and friends who share a same interest in *Pokémon*. In addition, he demonstrated his scientific knowledge about the real

Figure 6.1   Generic Format of a Trading Card

A picture that illustrates or describes a content, which can be an animal (wolf), a natural disaster (a hurricane), or an event (Martin Luther King, Jr., gave a speech). Students may color the picture.

Information Related to the Content in the Picture:

Figure 6.2   Trading Card of Octawave

Figure 6.3   Trading Card of Octopus

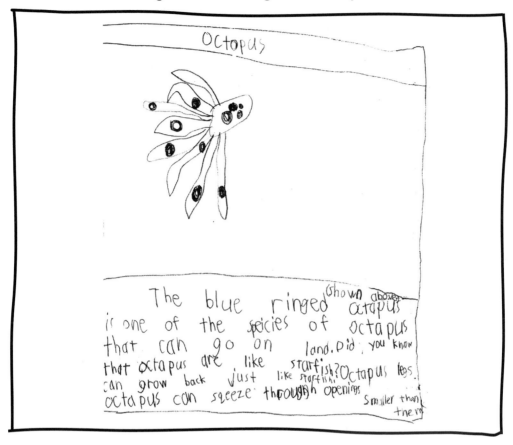

octopus. In a classroom, teachers may not have time for students to design trading cards, but teachers can provide students with a choice of either writing facts about a subject (e.g., an animal, the solar system) using a traditional format of writing (e.g., in paragraphs) or in a trading card format. This choice may offer those who are reluctant writers and readers a motivation to do the assignment and another possible chance to succeed.

Exploring the Social and Historical Context of a Popular Culture Text

The entertainment industry has developed popular media based on other literary genres. For example, Disney has adapted a majority of movies from classical fairy tales. The evolution of other media has a history associated with the changing cultural and political climate in a society. Rap music, for example, which was born in the ghettos of the south Bronx in New York, was mainly music by and for African Americans, and it now enjoys a trend of going mainstream in United States and abroad. Teachers can engage students in investigating the social (including cultural and political) and historical context of popular culture media. This type of investigation can also be tied to critical literacy practices in which students examine any biases and stereotypes in gender, age, race, physical appearance, and cultural and family values.

Hanzl (2001) provides an example of examining social and history backgrounds of a popular culture text. Primary-grade teachers, she suggests, may use the Disney film *Aladdin* (Clements & Musker, 1992) as a springboard to study its sources in a unit on *The Arabian Nights*. In studying its sources (e.g., *The Tales From the Arabian Nights* [Riordan, 1985] and *The One Thousand and One Arabian Nights* [McCaughrenn, 1996]), teachers and students explore the time the books were written, the setting in which each story took place, and the culture and people each story reflected. Students may also make a compare and contrast of stories for each story's popularity. Another activity is to ask students to view each story from a perspective of compilers or publishers of *The Arabian Nights*. Hanzl (2001) provides a good example, which has been adapted here:

> What criteria do you think modern compilers or publishers of *The Arabian Nights* tales might use when choosing which stories to include in a collection?
>
> Popularity and accessibility of each story
>
> Age of intended audience—these stories were originally intended for adult audiences, and more complete collections include many stories that are very down to earth and bawdy
>
> Content and language of story
>
> Balance of stories with strong male or female characters
>
> Budgetary considerations (p. 87)

In addition to a closer look at the social and historical background information related to the stories and the movie, the unit includes a study of setting, characters and characterization, plot, theme, and culture-specific concepts (e.g., palace, curse, and feast) of *Aladdin*. For the details of this unit, please read Anne Hanzl's chapter in *Critical Literacy and Children's Literature: Exploring the Story of Aladdin* (2001) .

Another way to explore the social and cultural context of a popular culture text is to help students note the connection between the text and the content curriculum they are studying. In Vignette 6.1, sixth-grade teacher Cristina capitalized on her students' interests in *Yu-Gi-Oh!* in developing a unit on ancient Egypt. In the unit, Cristina's students participated in the following literacy activities:

Table 6.2   A Text Set on *Yu-Gi-Oh!* and Ancient Egypt

Boehm, R.G., Hoone, C., McGowan, T.M., McKinney-Browning, M.C., Miramontes, O.B., & Porter, P.H. (2000). *Ancient civilizations.* Orlando, FL: Harcourt Brace.

Crosher, J. (1992). *Ancient Egypt.* United Kingdom: Hamlyn Children's Books.

Millmore, M. (1997). *Egyptian games.* Retrieved October 10, 2003, from www.eyelid.co.uk/games.htm

Quie, S. (1998). *Myths and civilizations of the ancient Egyptians.* New York: Peter Bedrick.

Shuter, J. (1998). *Egypt.* Austin, TX: Raintree Steck-Vaughn.

Shuter, J. (1999). *Pharaohs & priests.* Des Plaines, IL: Heinemann.

Takahashi, K. (2003). *Yu-Gi-Oh!* Retrieved October 10, 2003, from www.yugiohkingofgames.com

- Cristina and her students explored websites about *Yu-Gi-Oh!* and Egyptian games (see Table 6.2 for the text set).
- Students played Yu-Gi-Oh!'s Duel Monsters game in an after-school class.
- Cristina and her students read about ancient Egyptian rituals, games, gods, and goddesses.
- Cristina and her students each watched an episode of *Yu-Gi-Oh!* at home. (The students informed her when the show was on television.)
- Students transcribed hieroglyphic messages.
- Students played *senet* (a popular board game in ancient Egypt) after school. (For more information, visit www.humanities-interactive.org/ancient/tut/senet and www.fortunecity.com/victorian/lion/193/Senet.html).
- Cristina and her students identified main ideas relating to *Yu-Gi-Oh!* and the people, culture, and language of ancient Egypt.
- Cristina and the students outlined the relationship between *Yu-Gi-Oh!* and ancient Egypt (see Figure 6.4).
- Students wrote an essay comparing *Yu-Gi-Oh!* to ancient Egypt (see Figure 6.5).

During this unit, Cristina was both a student of her students and their teacher. Specifically, as a student, she observed her students playing the Duel Monsters game and took notes while watching one episode of *Yu-Gi-Oh!* As a teacher, she facilitated the discussions about *Yu-Gi-Oh!* and ancient Egypt, and provided feedback to her students on their outlines and essays. At the conclusion of the unit, Cristina not only witnessed a change in her students' motivations and interests in social studies, but also addressed specific curriculum standards in the areas of reading and language arts, technology, and social studies. She addressed the following standards:

- Reading and Language Arts: organizing thoughts in an outline, including key ideas with supporting details in an essay; understanding specific terms related to a game (e.g., *defensive* and *attack mode*, *supreme dragon*, *scapegoat*, *field* and *land card*); using complex and critical thinking skills in game playing.
- Technology: using the features of a website to find information; learning to cut, paste, and edit in word processing.
- Social Studies: reading books and websites about ancient Egypt.

Figure 6.4   Outline of an Essay Comparing *Yu-Gi-Oh!* to Ancient Egypt

I. Yu-Gi-Oh
   A. Game
      1. Struggle between good and evil
      2. Popular game played by kids, mainly boys
   B. Monsters
      1. Winged Dragon of Ra
      2. Milus Radius – resembles the Sphinx
      3. Flame Cerebrus – of the afterlife
      4. Obelisk
      5. Three Egyptian God Cards – powerful
         a. Exodia
         b. Dark Exodia – defeat Exodia
   C. Television Episode
      1. Tomb keeper – waiting for the pharaoh
      2. Hieroglyphs, pyramids
      3. Ouija board – hands move the piece to spell "Final"

II. Ancient Egypt
   A. Games
      1. Senet
         a. Game symbolizing struggle of good against evil
         b. Popular ancient Egyptian board game played by all, but mainly by wealthy adults
      2. Ouija boards
         a. luck boards used to tell the future
   B. Gods & Goddesses
      1. Amun-Ra – two gods combined to form Creator God
      2. Anubis – prepare for afterlife

   C. Embalming
      1. took out brain and other body parts
      2. preserve the body for the afterlife

Reprinted with permission by Cristina Barber.

Figure 6.5   Essay Comparing *Yu-Gi-Oh!* to Ancient Egypt

Yu-Gi-Oh is about a boy who loses his grandfather. His grandfather is kidnapped and he must fight the monsters, like the winged dragon of Ra and Dark Exodia to get him back. Dark Exodia is one of the three most powerful god cards of the Egyptian god cards.

The ancient Egypt Pharaohs did not have monsters. They had gods and goddesses and there names were like the Yu-Gi-Oh names. There was Amun-Ra and Obelisk. I think that is cool how the creator of Yu-Gi-Oh used real life names to teach us about what Egypt was like.

Developing a Text Set

In the previous section, you have already seen an example of text set on *Yu-Gi-Oh!* and ancient Egypt that blends different text genres in covering both topics. In this section, I will discuss several other ways to develop a text set.

Different Text Genres on a Popular Culture Interest

Audiences often interact with their popular culture texts in more than one genre. For example, the original genre of Spider-man is a comic book, and its other text genres include two movies (*Spider-man* [Raimi, 2002], *Spider-man 2* [Raimi, 2004]), trading cards, websites, and soundtracks. As discussed in chapter 5, each text genre has its own unique ways to convey messages through linguistic (i.e., words) and nonlinguistic (e.g., sound, visual effects) units. When students are exposed to only one text genre, their process of meaning making is based on the linguistic and nonlinguistic units that this particular text genre has. Exposure to and engagement with different text genres provide students with an opportunity to make an intertextual connection and to become increasingly familiar with the content. This opportunity has a potential to make meaning making less of a challenge for those who are struggling and who are English-language learners (ELLs). If children have watched a television show (e.g., *PowerPuff Girls*), they are familiar with the story elements (e.g., characters, plot). When these children are reading a book based on the show, they would focus more on making sense of the words rather than trying to develop some background knowledge about the story while reading. Table 6.3 lists some examples of students' popular culture texts in different genres. When incorporating students' popular culture interests in teaching, teachers need to make available to students different genres of texts of interest rather than just one genre.

Different Perspectives on a Popular Culture Text

Cinderella has been a classic fairy tale in American culture. The recently released movie (at the time this book was being written), *A Cinderella Story* (Rosman, 2004), starring Hilary Duff, a singer-turned-actress who is very popular among

Table 6.3   Popular Culture Texts in Multiple Genres

Popular Culture Interest	Text Genres							
	Book	Comic Book or Manga	Game	Movie	Sound-track or CD Album	Trading Cards	Television Show	Website
50 Cent					X			X
Blue's Clues	X		X				X	X
DragonBall Z	X	X	X			X	X	X
Garfield (Hewitt, 2004)	X	X		X	X			X
Pokémon	X	X	X	X	X	X	X	X
Rugrats	X		X	X	X	X	X	X
Scooby-Doo	X		X	X	X	X	X	X
Spider-man	X	X	X	X	X	X	X	X
Superman	X	X	X	X	X	X	X	X
Yu-Gi-Oh!	X	X	X	X	X	X	X	X

students of all ages, would probably bring back students' interest in the story and theme in both Disney's *Cinderella* (Luske & Johnson, 1950) and Warner Bros. modern-day *A Cinderella Story* (Rosman, 2004). A text set on Cinderella may include Cinderella-like tales from around the world that are set in different cultures, told from different perspectives, and written by authors of different nationalities. Table 6.4 is a list of books related to Cinderella. After reading some or all of the books, students can complete a chart such as the one in Table 6.5 (see also Reproducible A.10 in Appendix B) to guide them in discussing multiple perspectives. Other movies that may help you develop a text set that examines different perspectives are *Shrek* (Jenson & Adamson, 2001), *Shrek 2* (Vernon & Adamson, 2004), *Spider-man*, and *Spider-man 2*.

A Text Set Beyond a Popular Culture Interest

One way for teachers to encourage students to read texts beyond their immediate popular culture interests is to develop a text set that is related to the theme, story line, or characters of a popular culture text. For example, the television show or movie *Scooby-Doo* (Hanna & Barbera, 1978) provides a springboard for teachers to develop a text set with a focus on mystery (Table 6.6). The genres can be fiction and nonfiction (e.g., how detectives solve mysteries).

Table 6.4   Text Set on Cinderella

Africa
Climo, S. (1989). *The Egyptian Cinderella*. New York: Crowell.

Antarctica
Marceau-Chenkie, B. (1999). *Naya, the Inuit Cinderella*. Union Bay, British Columbia, Canada: Raven Rock.

Asia
Climo, S. (1993). *The Korean Cinderella*. New York: HarperCollins.
Climo, S. (1999). *The Persian Cinderella*. New York: HarperCollins.
Coburn, J.R., & Lee, T.C. (1996). *Jouanah: A Hmong Cinderella*. Arcadia, CA: Shen's Books.
Coburn, J.R. (1998). *Angkat: The Cambodian Cinderella*. Fremont, CA: Shen's Books.
de la Paz, M.J. (2001). *Abadeha: The Philippine Cinderella*. Auburn, CA: Shen's Books.
Hickox, R. (1998). *The golden sandal: A Middle Eastern Cinderella*. New York: Holiday House.
Jaffe, N. (1998). *The way meat loves salt: A Cinderella tale from the Jewish tradition*. New York: Holt.
Louie, A. (1982). *Yeh-Shen: A Cinderella Story from China*. New York: Philomel.
Pollock, P. (1996). *The turkey girl: A Zuni Cinderella story*. New York: Little, Brown.
Sierra, J. (2000). *The gift of the crocodile: A Cinderella story*. New York: Simon & Schuster Books for Young Readers.

Europe
Climo, S. (1996). *The Irish Cinderlad*. New York: HarperCollins.
Daly, J. (2000). *Fair, brown and trembling: An Irish Cinderella story*. New York: Farrar Straus Giroux.

North America
Coburn, J.R. (2000). *Domitila: A Cinderella tale from the Mexican tradition*. Auburn, CA: Shen's Books.
Craft, K.Y. (2000). *Cinderella*. New York: SeaStar.
San Souci, R.D. (1994). *Sootface: An Ojibwa Cinderella Story*. New York: Delacorte.
San Souci, R.D. (1998). *Cendrillon : A Caribbean Cinderella*. New York: Simon & Schuster Books for Young Readers.
San Souci, R.D. (2000). *Little Gold Star: A Spanish American Cinderella Tale*. New York: Morrow Junior Books.
Schroeder, A. (1997). *Smoky Mountain Rose: An Appalachian Cinderella*. New York: Dial Books for Young Readers.

South America
Boada, F. (2001). *Cinderella/Cenicienta* (M. Fransoy, Trans.). San Francisco: Chronicle.

Adapted from Table 7.1 of Barone, D.M., Mallette, M.H., & Xu, S.H. (2005). *Teaching early literacy: Development, assessment, and instruction* (p. 146). New York: Guilford.

Table 6.5   Exploring Cinderella Around the World

Book Title	Setting	Story Plot	Comparing to Disney's Cinderella A Cinderella Story		Comparing to Warner Bros.	
			Similar	Different	Similar	Different
Fair, Brown, and Trembling: An Irish Cinderella Story	Ireland	Trembling, mistreated by her sisters, won the heart of a prince.	• mistreated • hard-working • magic • happy ending	• mistreated by her own father and two old sisters • the henwife had magic	• mistreated • hard-working • magic • happy ending	• a modern day version of the Cinderella story
Little Gold Star: A Spanish American Cinderella	New Mexico	Teresa, mistreated by her stepmother and sisters, was blessed by Virgin Mary with a gold star.	• mistreated • hard-working • magic • happy ending	• the woman who had magic turned out to be the Virgin Mary	• mistreated • hard-working • magic • happy ending	• a modern day version of the Cinderella story
The Korean Cinderella	Korea	Peach Blossom, mistreated by her stepmother, was rescued from her misery by a nobleman.	• mistreated • hard-working • magic • happy ending	• the animals had magic	• mistreated • hard-working • magic • happy ending	• a modern day version of the Cinderella story
Yeh-Shen: A Cinderella Story from China	China	Yeh-Shen, mistreated by her stepmother and stepsister, married the king who appreciated her kindness and beauty.	• mistreated • hard-working • magic • happy ending	• the animals had magic	• mistreated • hard-working • magic • happy ending	• a modern day version of the Cinderella story

Table 6.6   Texts With a Focus on Mystery

Series Books
A to Z Mysteries by Ron Roy, published by Random House Books for Young Readers
Boxcar Children Mysteries by Gertrude Chandler Warner, published by Albert Whitman
Cam Jansen Adventure by David A. Adler, published by Puffin
Encyclopedia Brown by Donald J. Sobol, published by Yearling
Lizzie McGuire Mysteries by Lisa Banim, published by Disney Press
Nancy Drew by Carolyn Keene, published by Grosset & Dunlap
Nate the Great by Marjorie Sharmat, published by Yearling Books
The Adventures of the Bailey School Kids by Debbie Dadey, published by Scholastic
The Hardy Boys by Franklin W. Dixon, published by Grosset & Dunlap

Other Books
Shannon, G. (1985). *Stories to solve: Folktales from around the world*. New York: Green
   Willow Books.
Shannon, G. (1994). *More stories to solve: Fifteen folktales from around the world*.
   New York: Beech Tree Books.
Sobol, D. (2004). *Two minute mysteries*. New York: Scholastic.
Steig, W. (1973). *The real thief*. New York: Farrar Straus Giroux.
Yolen, J. (1992). *Piggins*. New York: Voyager.

Engaging Students in Critical Literacy Practices

While celebrating and respecting students' enjoyment of popular culture texts, teachers also have a responsibility to help students become critical consumers and reproducers of texts related to popular media (Morrell, 2004). Developing students' critical awareness requires teachers to guide students to see beyond what is familiar (e.g., their favorite female or male character, a typical way people from certain backgrounds are portrayed) and to explore what is unfamiliar and at times strange, which can be others' views, experiences, and perspectives (Luke & Freebody, 1997; Marsh, 2000; Vasquez, 2000). There are many ways that teachers can use popular culture texts to enhance students' critical awareness. I discuss three ideas in this section. Please feel free to think along and come up with your own.

Problematizing a Popular Culture Text

One way to engage students in critically reading a popular culture text (often a familiar one) is to ask them to *problematize* (i.e., to make an accepted text less acceptable or to make it controversial from a different perspective) the text, which involves reading the text from another perspective. Consider the images of artists on music CD jackets: Commonly, male artists and male bands are fully clothed, while female artists and female bands are revealing some parts of their body. When people view the text of the female images from a feminist perspective, the images convey the message of women being sex objects, which is demeaning to women and which reflects the poor choice and taste of the recording company. To help students problematize a familiar popular culture text, teachers may use three guiding principles identified by Comber (2001):

1. Reposition students as researchers of language.
2. Respect student resistance and explore minority culture constructions of literacy and language use.
3. Problematize classroom and public texts. (p. 92)

To translate these three principles into action, teachers guide students to become "researchers of language" (Comber, 2001, p. 92) by asking them to look at how certain characters are portrayed and what kind of language is used (e.g., positive adjectives versus negative adjectives). During this scaffolding process, teachers try not to impose their own opinions about a text on their students, but rather invite students to learn about teachers' comments on the text. Teachers, however, do need to guide students to problematize (often familiar) texts by asking students to view the texts from other perspectives.

For example, *Spider-man*, either in a movie genre or a comic book genre, deals with a classic literary theme—good versus evil. And it enjoys popularity among children and adolescents. When a teacher asks students to conduct a multiple reading of the text, that is, to watch the movie or read the book again from another perspective, students may not be willing to do so. The teacher may respect students' resistance to reading it from another perspective. But the teacher can offer students a chance to explore this familiar text from other perspectives by posing these five questions to students:

1. Is Spider-man always powerful?
2. Does Mary Jane (Spider-man's neighbor) have to be saved by Spider-man?
3. What if she were not saved by Spider-man—does that mean she can't save herself?
4. Why can't Mary Jane save the children?
5. In comparison to Spider-man, what type of person is Mary Jane portrayed as in the movie?

By discussing these questions, the teacher helps students see the different ways that a male and a female character are portrayed. Spider-man, for example, does not seem to fit, to some extent, into a traditional image of a superhero who is powerful and is able to defeat villains and save the innocent. Spider-man, as a superhero, does not have bulky muscles and has average weight and height. He seems to be an average guy. But the portrait of the female character, Mary Jane, continues to reflect a long-standing, stereotypical tradition—women are weak and need to be saved.

Using Critical Media Literacy Frameworks to Explore a Popular Culture Text

Another way to engage students in critical literacy practices is to use one or more of the critical media literacy frameworks as a guide to analyze a popular media text (see Table 6.7).

Table 6.7   Critical Media Literacy Frameworks, Codes, and Guiding Questions

Lloyd-Kolkin & Tyner (1991)

Media agencies	Who is communicating and why?
Media categories	What type of text is it?
Media technologies	How is it produced?
Media audiences	Who receives it and what sense do they make of it?
Media representations	How does it present its subject?

Lusted (1991)

Language	What language (visual/print/oral) is used? How do we understand this language?
Narrative	What stories/themes/beliefs/characters are being told and evoked?
Institution	In what social contexts does this text occur?
Audience	For whom is this text intended? What is its purpose? How does the audience understand this text?
Representation	Who is speaking? To whom? Who/what is represented and how?
Production processes	How was this text produced?

Messaris (1994)

Concrete representations	These are similar to notions of signs and symbols. What elements are in the text?
Abstract representations	What do they mean?
Empirical evidence	These are descriptions of data and response to support interpretations.

Lester (1995)

Personal perspectives	What do I think or feel about this? What meanings do I create from it?
Historical perspectives	When was this text produced? How does it reflect values, technologies, events, and understandings from its time?
Technological perspectives	What artistic and technical devices are used?
Ethical perspectives	What values does this text convey and reflect? Who constructed it and why? What moral impacts does it have on viewers?

(continued)

Table 6.7   Critical Media Literacy Frameworks, Codes, and Guiding Questions *(continued)*

Cultural perspectives	Whose point of view is represented by the text? Who is left out? How does it reflect information, knowledge, events, and values? What are these?
Critical perspectives	What ideologies are conveyed through this text? How does it establish and/or maintain power relations and social institutions?

Pailliotet (1995, 1998)

Action/Sequence	What happens? In what order? When and how long?
Semes/Forms	What objects are observed? What are their traits?
Discourse/Actors	What words are used? Who "speaks"? How do we understand them?
Proximity/Movement	What sorts of movements and space use occur? What is implied? What is missing? Where are authors and actors in this text situated historically and culturally?
Effects/Processes	What technologies, artistic devices, and production processes were used to construct this text?

Luke (1999, p. 623)

Coding practice	What analytic skills can I apply to crack the codes of this text? How does this text work?
Text meaning practice	What different cultural readings and meanings does this text enable? How does this combination of language, ideas, and images hold together to produce ideas?
Pragmatic practice	How does this text work in different contexts? How does context shape its uses? What does this text mean to me and what might it mean for others in different situations and cultural contexts?
Critical practice	How does this text attempt to position me? Who is the ideal person this text addresses? Whose interests are served in this text? Who is present and absent in this text?

Considine & Haley (1999, p. 28)

Who?	(Source, structure/organization/ownership of the media)
Says what?	(Statement, content, values, ideology)
To whom?	(Audiences)
In what way?	(Form, style, codes, conventions, technologies)
With what effect?	(Influence and consequences)
Why?	(Purpose, profit, motivation)

From Pailliotet, A.W., Semali, L., Rodenberg, R.K., Giles, J.K., & Macaul, S.L. (2000). Intermediality: Bridging to critical media literacy. *The Reading Teacher, 54,* 208–219.

Teachers can choose questions from one or more of the frameworks and engage students in discussing their favorite texts. Through students' responses to the selected questions, teachers can note if students have gone beyond the familiar to explore other aspects. For example, Figure 6.7 lists seventh grader Jose's responses to the questions from Lusted's (1991) framework. This "deep viewing activity" (Pailliotet, 1998, p. 127) was on a Japanese animé, *DragonBall Z* (Fukunga, Fukunga, Watson, & Fukengama, 1996–2003), during which the student viewed one episode of the show multiple times and then wrote down his thoughts

Figure 6.7   Deep Viewing Activity With *DragonBall Z*

Deep Viewing Activity – Lusted (1991)

What language (visual/print/oral) is used? How do we understand this language?
It's visual, action involved, it was made in Japan in the late 80's.

What stories/themes/beliefs/characters are being told and evoked?
Good vs. Evil search for Dragonball to make wishes, and train to get strong enough to to beat what ever comes up.

In what social contexts does this text occur?
Fiction.

For whom is this text intended? What is its purpose? How does the audience understand this text? Mainly for males (8-25) mostly for entertainment. The text become intended as viewers keep up with the show on a daily bases, and get to know the characters good vs. Evil.

Who is speaking? To whom? Who/what is represented and how?
Every character has their own involvement in the story, each character ties into the story.

How was this text produced?
First made as a comic, and then into animation.

related to the questions posed. The student's response to Lusted's (1991) third question (In what social contexts does this text occur?) seemed to be superficial, overlooking a context beyond the text genre. There can actually be several social contexts related to *DragonBall Z* (this animé has over 300 characters). First, *DragonBall Z* was introduced to the United States after the popularity of a series of Japanese products (e.g., *Pokémon*, Game Boy games, manga). The fighting scenes and adult humor made it appealing to people of all ages, thus making the company that produces the animé a great profit. Second, this success motivated the company to carry on a massive advertising campaign and to produce multiple text genres based on the animé, including a television show, a movie, a website, books, trading cards, and games. Third, the United States has a long tradition of enjoying cartoon style of story telling, which contributes to *DragonBall Z's* success. After taking a closer look at students' responses to the questions, the teacher can sense what is missing in the students' critical viewing of the text, and accordingly guide students to explore the text in depth.

Figure 6.8 lists the responses of sixth-grade ELL Jesus to questions based also on Lusted's (1991) framework. Read the responses carefully and think about what aspect(s) the student considered and did not consider, and about what you might do if you were his teacher to help the student see beyond the familiar. Use a table to

Figure 6.8   Deep Viewing Activity With *Pokémon*

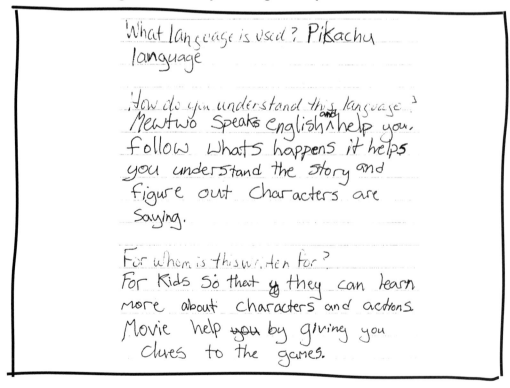

What language is used? Pikachu language

How do you understand this language? Mewtwo speaks English and help you. follow whats happens it helps you understand the story and figure out characters are saying.

For whom is this written for? For kids so that they can learn more about characters and actions. Movie help you by giving you clues to the games.

Table 6.8   Considering Other Perspectives

Student's Response	What Aspect(s) Is (Are) Considered?	What Aspect(s) Is (Are) Not Considered?	What Might You Do to Help Students See Other Perspectives?
What language is used? Pikachu language	the language used by the Pokémon character, Pikachu	the actual language used in the show to tell the story	Have students watch the show with first-time viewers and learn about their opinion of the language
How do you understand this language? Mewtwo speaks English, and it helps you follow what's happening. It helps you understand the story and figure out what characters are saying.	Use the knowledge of the storyline and familiarity with the language used by the Pokémon characters	Use the skills needed for understanding a TV show and use contextual clues (e.g., actions of the characters, facial expressions) to understand the language of the show and of the Pokémon characters	Have students watch the show with first-time viewers and learn about how the viewers would use strategies (e.g., using images and sound effects) to help understand the storyline.
For whom is this written? For kids so that they can learn more about characters and actions. The movie helps by giving you clues to the games.	those who are fans of Pokémon and those who understand the language the Pokémon characters speak	those who are not interested in the show and those who don't understand the language the Pokémon characters speak	Have students watch the show with first-time viewers and learn about how the viewers feel about the show (e.g., interesting, violent, easy to understand.)

record your thinking and ideas, such as the characters, language they used, and the targeted audience of the text (Table 6.8; see also Reproducible A.11 in Appendix B).

Reality Checking a Popular Media Text

Involving students in exploring the reality depicted in a popular culture text can be another way to foster students' critical awareness of popular culture media. Many popular culture texts tend to give their readers or audience a false reality. For example, female characters in a movie are often very young, slender, beautiful, and relatively free from wrinkles. In reality, however, not all females are young and slender, and even beautiful females in reality do not fit into the images created by many media texts. In the Entertainment section on PBS's website Don't Buy It: Get Media Smart! (2002–2004) (http://pbskids.org/dontbuyit/entertainment), viewers are asked to explore behind-the-scenes secrets in the entertainment world. On the Cover Model Secrets page, viewers will learn about how many makeup artists work hard and creatively to make models look beautiful and flawless. The Take the Television vs. Life Quiz invites viewers to select a choice out of several choices that best describes a reality. For example, for the first quiz item, viewers are asked about how often a police officer fires a gun per year in reality: once a year, once a month, once a week, or none of the above. Once viewers have selected an answer, the next screen shows the reality of how often a police officer in reality fires a gun.

> The answer is none of the above. A television cop is likely to draw his or her weapon at least once per episode, and shoot it more than once per season. Most real police officers will never use a gun in the line of duty. (Don't Buy It: Get Media Smart! 2002–2004)

On the website's Money and Mu$ic page, viewers learn about how music ends up in a commercial or why we can hear music from radio.

The Don't Buy It: Get Media Smart! (2002–2004) website provides teachers with some ideas about guiding students to do some reality checking about what is portrayed in popular culture texts. Reality checking is also a way to help students read a media text beyond the familiar and surface level. For example, teachers may engage their students in learning more about their idols in popular culture texts. This deep learning would involve students reading varied text genres (e.g., biography, Internet text, movie or other televisual texts, lyrics), and will help students understand that it is not just their idols' fame and wealth but also their inspiration and diligence that earn students' worship. Students can record on a table what they have discovered from an exploration of their idols (Table 6.8; see also Reproducible A.12 in Appendix B). Some students, for example, tend to be blinded by many rap artists' stylish clothing, flashy jewelry, and multimillion-dollar sale profits, forgetting the fact that many of them have painful memories of growing up in ghettos and that their hard work and music talent played an important role in their success. The activity of reality checking helps these students read a popular culture text (which includes images, such as how a pop culture idol is photographed in a magazine) beyond a surface level.

Concluding Thoughts

At this point, you have probably developed a sense of how popular culture texts might be incorporated into teaching to support students' learning. Many of you may have come up with ideas better than those presented in this chapter. I hope that

Table 6.8   Learning More About My Idol

My Idol	What I Know About Him or Her From the Media	What I Now Know About Him or Her After the Exploration	Sources of Exploration
Francisco Muniz from Fox-TV's Malcolm in the Middle	• He is funny, smart, and lucky. • He is a great actor. • He may not spend a lot of time studying due to his schedule of shooting the show.	• He is not a genius, but he got all As when he was in school. • He is from a happy family, not a dysfunctional one as in the show. • Like Malcolm, he was bullied at school.	Morreale, M. T. (2000). Class acts: Celebrity confession sessions. New York: Scholastic.

now you may feel more comfortable with and confident in trying some ideas with your students. Please keep in mind that the ideas presented here may not work perfectly with your students. Always remember to consider your students as one of the major resources for your learning about their interests and to involve them in planning any learning experience related to media texts—their everyday texts.

CHAPTER 7

Managing an Integration of Popular Culture Texts

VIGNETTE 7.1

Maria is a sixth-grade teacher of Latino and African American students in a Title I school where *Pokémon* (Grossfeld, Kahn, & Kenney, 2005) is a forbidden subject. During Maria's implementation of her unit on *Pokémon*, several of her colleagues report to Maria's principal what she is doing with the unit on *Pokémon* in her classroom. Maria's principal responds, "I know, she has told me about that. Maria is using *Pokémon* to get her students interested in reading, language arts, and math. It's OK. I'm fine with that."

This vignette illustrates that school administrators can be supportive of teachers' innovative approaches to teaching as long as teachers present a convincing case for an innovative approach, that is, why it may be a better approach for the students. As Rachael has written in chapter 3, her principal was proud of what her students had accomplished in the unit on Dream to Jobs, and she even invited the regional director of the school district to visit her classroom to learn about her innovative approach. Based on the experiences of many teachers with whom I have worked in the past several years, many school administrators do have a sincere interest in teachers' innovative ways of teaching, and they are interested in learning about how these ways may possibly improve students' learning outcomes. In this chapter, I (Shelley) address dealing with censorship issues in relation to gaining support from school administrators, parents, and the community during the process of educators' integration of popular culture texts. Another important issue I discuss is time management—how teachers can incorporate popular culture texts as additional instructional materials into a prescribed program or into a large amount of required curriculum content.

Censorship becomes an issue when a text contains some messages that are not acceptable to people whose values, beliefs, and experiences do not support these messages. In traditional print-based texts, the following elements can cause censorship via either language or content (e.g., Agee, 1999; Simmons & Dresang, 2001): profanity; stereotypes; racism; antiminority, antifemale, antichildren, or antireligious sentiments; violence; sexual activities; homosexuality; witchcraft; and the supernatural. When communicating with and gaining support from school administrators and parents, always remember to share your ways of dealing with these issues. It would be more effective if addressing a controversial issue is tied into teaching students critical literacy practices.

Gaining Support From School Administrators

Popular culture texts, unlike canonical literature, are subject to close scrutiny by school administrators if brought into classrooms from unofficial sources outside the school world. When teachers make a decision to incorporate popular culture texts into teaching, they should follow the principle of open communication with their school administrators. Open communication is an effective strategy that teachers need to employ whenever a text used for teaching may be challenged (Agee, 1999). Teachers should also remember to check the school and school district policies concerning the use of materials that are not traditionally used at school (Simmons & Dresang, 2001). The following are some steps that teachers need to take in order to keep their school administrators informed during the whole process of implementing popular culture texts.

Before an Integration: Explicitly Explaining Rationales

In an NCTE starter sheet, *Rationales for Teaching Challenged Books* (www.ncte.org/library/files/About_NCTE/Issues/rationalesforbooks.pdf), Jean Brown and Elaine Stephens (1994) offer detailed steps on writing a rationale for each book before using it for teaching. Although the steps on writing rationales are mainly related to books, Brown and Stephens's advice also applies to the use of popular culture texts, most of which are multimedia. They offer the following guidelines for writing a rationale:

1. The bibliographic citation
2. The intended audience
3. A brief summary of the work
4. The relation of the book to the program
5. The impact of the book
6. Potential problems with the work
7. Collection of information about the book
8. Collection of supplementary information (p. 2)

Table 7.1 provides a detailed explanation of each step and a written rationale for the use of the movie *Spider-man* (Raimi, 2002). (Reproducible A.13 in Appendix B offers guidelines for writing a rationale for using a popular culture text.)

Table 7.1   Writing a Rationale for a Popular Culture Text

Guidelines	Explanation*	An Example of Popular Culture Text
1. The Bibliographic Citation	• author, title, publication date and place, and publisher	Rami, S. (Director). (2002). Spiderman. United States: Columbia Pictures.
2. The Intended Audience	• appropriate grade levels • instructional settings (independent reading, or during small-group or large-class instruction or discussion)	• second grade and up • as a whole class for viewing and for discussion; as a small group for discussion; as an independent viewing at home
3. A Brief Summary of the Work	• main ideas of the text	A teen bitten by a laboratory spider suddenly became capable of many acts beyond what a regular teen can do. He was able to climb walls and jump from one skyscraper to another. Most impressive of his act is his ability to defeat villains to make his neighborhood safe.
4. The Relation of the Book to the Program	• relationship of the text to the standards • relationship of the text to other canonical texts • a list of standards to be addressed with the use of the text • the ways the teacher and students use the text • the ways the teacher assess students' learning outcome with the use of this text	• The movie serves as an electronic text to address the standards related to characterization and theme • The movie presents a literary genre on one particular theme: good vs evil. Standard 2 (IRA/NCTE): • Students read a wide range of literature from many periods in many genres to build an understanding of the many dimensions (e.g., philosophical, ethical, aesthetic) of human experience. (continued)

Table 7.1   Writing a Rationale for a Popular Culture Text (continued)

Guidelines	Explanation*	An Example of Popular Culture Text
		• The teacher and students may use the text in the following ways: 1) The teacher reviews the movie if the students have seen it, and highlights key events in the movie. 2) The teacher guides the students in describing the main characters and discussing how an author portray the characters in the movie (e.g., via action, facial expressions). 3) The students can do a compare and contrast, via a Venn Diagram (2 overlapping circles), between the main character with other characters from their familiar books, movies, or television shows. 4) The teacher and students discuss how the character is similar to or different from other superheroes portrayed in other literary genres (e.g., comic books) • The teacher assesses students' learning through their participation in the discussion and their completed Venn Diagram.
5. The Impact of the Book	• impact that this text has on learning that other texts may not have	• Since this text is popular among students, learning involving this text brings familiarity to students and generates interests in learning.

(continued)

Table 7.1 Writing a Rationale for a Popular Culture Text *(continued)*

Guidelines	Explanation*	An Example of Popular Culture Text
		• The text relies on visual images to tell a story would help students to better understand the key components related to characterization Multiple sources of contextual clues (e.j., words, visual images) make it easier for ELLs and struggling readers to understand.
6. Potential Problems With the Work	• potential issues that might cause school administrators and parents or guardians to be concerned • possible ways to address the issues	• Some fighting scenes, violence, gender stereotype. • The teacher engages students in a discussion if fighting is the only solution to a problem; what might be some alternative solutions to the problem; if females are always weak and need to be saved by males; and who are some female superheroines students know.
7. Collection of Information About the Book	• reviews of the text	Reviews of Spiderman movie and other media texts can be found at these sites. • Los Angeles Times www.calendarlive.com/movies • The New York Times www.nytimes.com/pages/movies • Newsweek www.msnbc.msn.com/id/3032542/site/newsweek • Roger Ebert & Richard Report http.//tvplex.go.com/buena vista/ebertandroeper/today.html

(continued)

Table 7.1   Writing a Rationale for a Popular Culture Text *(continued)*

Guidelines	Explanation*	An Example of Popular Culture Text
		• Rolling Stone Magazine www.rollingstone.com/?rnd=10959731699398 has-player=trued Version=6.b.11.847 • San Francisco Chronicle www.sfgate.com/eguide/movies • USA Today www.usatoday.com/life/movies/fall-movie-preview.htm • Washington Post www.washingtonpost.com/ac2/wp-dyn?node=entertainment/search&type=movie event &sort =recommended-desc
8. Collection of Supplementary Information	• any information related to the text	Texts related to the movie • Rami, S. (Director).(2002) Spiderman [DVD] New York: Sony Pictures. • Richards. k.(2002). Your friendly neighborhood Spiderman. New York: Avon. • Coll. S. (2002). Spiderman: The movie storybook. New York: HarperFestival. • Straczynski, J. M. (2004). Amazing Spiderman Vol. 7. New York: Marvel.
9. Alternative Works an Individual Student Might Read	• other texts related to the text (either based on the theme, on a similar topic, or on a similar character) that bring in different perspectives	Texts related to the theme of Superheroes or good vs. evil • Fisch, S. (2000). Batman beyond: No place like home. New York: Random House. *(continued)*

145

Table 7.1   Writing a Rationale for a Popular Culture Text (continued)

Guidelines	Explanation*	An Example of Popular Culture Text
		• Hoffman, E. (1999). Heroines and heroes/Heroínas y héroes (E. de la Vega, Trans.) St. Paul, MN: Redleaf. • Isaacs, A. (1994). Swamp angel. New York: Dutton. • Kellogg, S. (1995). Sally Ann Thunder Ann Whirlwind Crockett. New York: Morrow. • Mooney E-S. (2000) The PowerPuff Girls: Snow-off. New York: Scholastic. • Peterson. S. (2000) Batman beyond: New hero in town. New York: Random House. • Whatley, B. (1999). Captain Pajamas. New York: HarperCollins. • Wisniewski, D. (2002). Sumo mouse. San Francisco: CA: Chronicle Books.

* In the explanation I have used *text* instead of *book* (as used in Brown and Stephens's guideline) to reflect a broad and multimedia nature of what is read in today's society. The guidelines and part of the explanation are taken from Brown, J.E., & Stephens, E.C. (1994). *Rationales for teaching challenged books*. Urbana, IL: National Council of Teachers of English. Copyright © 1994 by the National Council of Teachers of English. Reprinted with permission.

During and After an Integration: Sharing Changes in Students' Affective Domain and Learning Outcomes

Throughout the process of integrating popular culture texts, teachers need to keep school administrators informed about any learning outcomes that they have noted. For example, many teachers with whom I have worked, such as Rachael and Lark, often notice a high level of student engagement in learning and a positive change in student attitude and motivation toward learning that was not present when teachers used other types of texts. Although the change is mainly in students' affective domain, it is an important step that leads to changes in learning outcomes. Without engagement, interest, and motivation, active student learning would not be possible. So when teachers have witnessed a change in students' affective domain, they should share this information with their school administrators and invite them to observe literacy activities with popular culture texts.

Documenting any changes in students' affective domain and learning outcomes is another good way to prove to school administrators that using popular culture texts as alternative texts has made some differences. The teachers I know have taken photographs or anecdotal notes when their students were participating in literacy activities with popular culture texts. Some teachers have shared students' improved writing samples with their school administrators. Billy's engagement in his writing, as Lark described in chapter 4, illustrated that the choices (e.g., a song, a rap, or an essay) that she offered her students for expressing an understanding of the main character, Stanley, in *Holes* (Sachar, 1998) provided Billy with an opportunity to have meaningful interaction with writing that would not have been possible for him if the traditional way of expressing ideas in a paragraph format was the only choice. In Table 7.2, Lark documented Billy's changes in attitude, interest, motivation, and learning outcomes. I strongly encourage teachers to use this form to document students' changes in affective domain and in learning outcomes (see Reproducible A.14 in Appendix B), which serve as powerful evidence for what positive impact popular culture texts can have on students' learning.

Sharing Positive Changes With Colleagues

Sharing positive changes in students' interests, attitudes, and learning outcomes should not be limited to school administrators, but needs to include colleagues. Colleagues can offer feedback to your innovative ways of teaching and suggestions for improving your use of popular culture texts, and in the meantime, they learn something from you that they may apply later in their own teaching. In the future, you will benefit from gaining your colleagues' support. When other colleagues start incorporating popular culture texts and collecting evidence of students' enhanced learning, it will make your argument for the use of popular culture texts even more convincing.

Gaining Support From Parents or Guardians and the Community

The principle of open communication certainly applies when teachers want to gain support from parents (or guardians for some students—I will use *parents* as a general term) and the community. Teachers also need to inform parents of the rationales for using a particular popular culture text and of any positive changes in

Table 7.2   Changes in Affective Domain and Learning Outcomes

Student Name:	Popular Culture Texts Used:	Date:
Billy	• Davis, A. (2003). Holes. [DVD]. Burbanks, CA: Disney. • Maj, DJ. (2003). All for a purpose. • Rap Artists and Lyrics www. ohhla.com	
Areas of Change	Before an Integration	During and After an Integration
Attitude	low	high
Interest	low	high
Motivation	low	high
Learning Outcomes	• He usually wrote two sentences of poor quality. • He would not receive a passing grade for a development reading class.	• He could not stop writing a rap about Stanley the main character in Holes (Sacher, 1998) • His writing reflected his good understanding of the character.

student attitudes, interests, motivation, and learning outcomes. In open communication with parents and community, teachers need to consider two crucial factors.

One factor is related to the culture of a community and a family. It would be more likely for a teacher to gain support from a community where rap music is a mainstream form of music than from a community where other forms of music (e.g., classics, country, or jazz) are dominant. In a similar way, parents who have never heard of rap music or who may possess a negative view of the music would be less ready to offer their support for the use of rap music in your teaching. In this case, teachers need to provide parents and community with information that they have shared with school administrators, and in particular the rationales for using rap music to address curriculum standards.

Informing parents of their children's popular culture interests and literacy experiences associated with these interests can be a crucial step in gaining their support. Not all parents are aware of their children's interests. Based on my numerous informal and formal conversations with preservice and inservice teachers who have children, I have noted that teachers as parents do not often know about their own children's interests. Even if they know about the interests, parents (who are teachers) often lack a deeper knowledge of one particular popular culture text. Often a negative impression of the text results not from their own exploration of the text, but from other parents' comments. For example, when the Harry Potter series became popular, many parents, including those who were teachers, expressed to me their objections to its use in school. But when people who had read the series asked about how they developed their negative impression about the series, their responses were often similar to this: "I heard it is about witchcraft. It is not good. I do not want to read it and do not want my kids to read it." So educating parents about their children's popular culture interests and inviting them to explore the texts can be a helpful way to gain their support.

Another important factor to consider is that parents may not see a direct connection between a popular culture text (which is often considered as a means of entertainment) and literacy learning (which has been traditionally involved with print-based text). It thus becomes crucial for teachers to communicate with parents about literacy knowledge and skills that students demonstrate in their engagement with popular culture texts. Such a presentation of linkage between students' engagement and literacy learning lends support for a rationale of using a popular culture text. Table 7.3 demonstrates a second grader's interest in the television show *SpongeBob SquarePants* (Hillenburg, 2005) and literacy knowledge and skills (related to IRA and NCTE standards) demonstrated in her interaction with the text. (See Reproducible A.15 in Appendix B for a blank chart you can use.) In addition, I suggest that teachers inform parents in a letter of their rationales for using popular culture texts and the relevance to student learning outcomes. It is better to explain such a letter at an open house at the beginning of a school year rather

**Table 7.3   Literacy Knowledge and Skills Demonstrated in an Engagement
With the Television Show *SpongeBob SquarePants***

IRA and NCTE Standards	Literacy Knowledge or Skills Related to Watching *SpongeBob SquarePants*
1. Students read a wide range of print and nonprint texts to build an understanding of texts, of themselves, and of the cultures of the United States and the world; to acquire new information; to respond to the needs and demands of society and the workplace; and for personal fulfillment. Among these texts are fiction and nonfiction, classic and contemporary works.	• Enjoying a story presented in a genre of televisual text • Understanding story elements: setting, characters, plot, problems, problem solution(s), and theme
2. Students read a wide range of literature from many periods in many genres to build an understanding of the many dimensions (e.g., philosophical, ethical, aesthetic) of human experience.	• Enjoying a story presented in a genre of a televisual text
3. Students apply a wide range of strategies to comprehend, interpret, evaluate, and appreciate texts. They draw on their prior experience, their interactions with other readers and writers, their knowledge of word meaning and of other texts, their word identification strategies, and their understanding of textual features (e.g., sound-letter correspondence, sentence structure, context, graphics).	• Using comprehension strategies (e.g., activating prior knowledge, making connections, making inferences) to help understand a story • Developing an understanding of a televisual text (how a story is told in a television show)
4. Students adjust their use of spoken, written, and visual language (e.g., conventions, style, vocabulary) to communicate effectively with a variety of audiences and for different purposes.	None

(continued)

Table 7.3   Literacy Knowledge and Skills Demonstrated in an Engagement With the Television Show *SpongeBob SquarePants (continued)*

IRA and NCTE Standards	Literacy Knowledge/Skills Related to Watching *SpongeBob SquarePants*
5. Students employ a wide range of strategies as they write and use different writing process elements appropriately to communicate with different audiences for a variety of purposes.	None
6. Students apply knowledge of language structure, language conventions (e.g., spelling and punctuation), media techniques, figurative language, and genre to create, critique, and discuss print and nonprint texts.	• Sharing responses to the show (e.g., what I liked about the show and what I don't like about the show) • Evaluating the show (e.g., what is real? What is not real? What is funny? What should have been done to make it funnier?)
7. Students conduct research on issues and interests by generating ideas and questions and by posing problems. They gather, evaluate, and synthesize data from a variety of sources (e.g., print and nonprint texts, artifacts, people) to communicate their discoveries in ways that suit their purpose and audience.	None
8. Students use a variety of technological and information resources (e.g., libraries, databases, computer networks, video) to gather and synthesize information and to create and communicate knowledge.	• Reading books, watching television shows or movies, or visited websites related to the ocean animals
9. Students develop an understanding of and respect for diversity in language use, patterns, and dialects across cultures, ethnic groups, geographic regions, and social roles.	• Gaining an understanding of getting along with people different from self (one of the themes of the show)

(continued)

**Table 7.3   Literacy Knowledge and Skills Demonstrated in an Engagement
With the Television Show *SpongeBob SquarePants (continued)***

IRA and NCTE Standards	Literacy Knowledge/Skills Related to Watching *SpongeBob SquarePants*
10. Students whose first language is not English make use of their first language to develop competency in the English language arts and to develop understanding of content across the curriculum.	• Enabling English language learners to have some exposure to English oral language • Developing some interests in science
11. Students participate as knowledgeable, reflective, creative, and critical members of a variety of literacy communities.	• Using literacy as a medium of entertainment • Applying literacy knowledge and skills learned at school in an outside-school setting
12. Students use spoken, written, and visual language to accomplish their own purposes (e.g., learning, enjoyment, persuasion, the exchange of information).	• Enjoying a television show and laughing

The IRA and NCTE Standards are enumerated in this book's Introduction, pages 7–8.

than simply sending the letter home just before your use of popular culture texts. (Figure 7.1 [see pp. 153–156] is a sample letter including many key points that teachers need to communicate to parents. Feel free to modify the letter to fit your situation, or use Reproducible A.16 in Appendix B.)

**Figure 7.1   Sample Letter to Parents or Guardians Concerning
the Use of a Popular Culture Text**

Dear Parents/Guardians of ___*Many Du*___ (Student):

This year, I will try to incorporate students' interests in popular culture into teaching. Popular culture texts are often multimedia and include television shows, movies, music, video games, Internet, and magazines. Popular culture texts hold familiarity and interests for students, and thus have potential to motivate and engage students. In this letter, I will share with you my reasons for using students' popular culture texts as listed below and my ways of using them. I also invite you to explore these texts along with your child and to share with me your opinions about the texts.

I have conducted an informal survey of the class during the first couple weeks of this school year. Here are the students' popular culture interests:
(List These Interests)

- Spiderman (movie, comic book)

- Yu-Gi-Oh! (movie, manga, trading cards, TV show)

- PowerPuff Girls (movie, books, TV show)

- Bionicles (toy, books), Captain Underpants series

- The Incredibles (movie, books)

After a close examination of all the interests, I have noted this common interest across the whole class. (State this Common Interest) ___Good vs Evil,___
___Superheroes___

I am going to build on this common interest in my teaching of (State Content)
___Characterization___

I will use these following popular culture texts in my teaching of (State Content)
___Characterization___

(continued)

(List the Bibliographic Information for Each Text)

- Bird, B. (Director). (2004). The Incredibles [DVD]. Emeryville, CA: Pixar.

- Coll, S. (2002). Spiderman: The movie storybook. New York: HarperFestival.

- Farshtey, G. (2003). The official guide to Bionicle. New York: Scholastic.

- Mooney, E. S. (2000). The PowerPuff girls: Snow-off. New York: Scholastic.

- Yu-Gi-Oh! Website: www.yugioh.com

   The purpose of using these texts is to address curriculum standards in an innovative way that may better engage and motivate students. Here are the standards that the use of these popular culture texts will address:

(List the Curriculum Standards)

- NCTE/IRA Standard 2: Students read a wide range of literature from many periods in many genres to build an understanding of the many dimensions of human experience.
- NCTE/IRA Standard 3: Students apply a wide range of strategies to comprehend, interpret, evaluate, and appreciate texts.
- NCTE/IRA Standard 6: Students apply knowledge of language structure, language conventions (e.g. spelling and punctuation), media techniques, figurative language, and genre to create, critique, and discuss print and non-print texts.
- NCTE/IRA Standard 11: Students participate as knowledgeable, reflective, creative, and critical members of a variety of literacy communities.
- NCTE/IRA Standard 12: Students use spoken, written, and visual language to accomplish their own purposes (e.g. for learning, enjoyment, persuasion, and the exchange of information).

   I have personally read all of the texts listed above, and noted some controversial issues that may arise in my teaching. I am sharing possible ways to address these issues and inviting you to share your suggestions.

(continued)

Issues	Ways to Deal With the Issues
• Violence	Engaging students in discussing alternative solutions to a problem
• gender stereotype	Engaging students in discussing if superheroines can have similar power superheroes have, and vice versa
• inappropriate language	Engaging students in discussing other expressions that can replace the inappropriate language

Here is a list of some professional literature that supports the use of popular culture texts to enhance literacy learning. You may be interested in reading some from the list. Please feel free to ask me for a copy of the listed literature and share with me your opinions about the literature.

(List the Literature)

- Alverman, D. Z., & Xu, S. H. (2003). Children's Everyday literacies: Intersections of popular culture and language arts instruction. Language Arts, 81, 145-154.
- Marsh, J. (2000). Teletubby tales. Popular culture in the early years language and literacy curriculum. Contemporary Issues in Early Childhood, 1, 119-123.
- Nonton, B. (2003). The motivating power of comic books. The Reading Teacher, 57, 140-147.
- Vasquez, V. (2003). What Pokémon can teach us about learning and literacy. Language Arts, 81, 118-125.
- Whipple, P. (1998). Let's go to the Movies: Rethinking the role of film in the elementary classroom. Language Arts, 76, 144-150.

Please send the following consent slip back to me, indicating your consent for your child to participate in literacy activities involving all or some of the popular culture texts listed. If you object to the use of the texts, I'd appreciate that you share your reasons so that I can plan a set of alternative texts for your child during the activities.

Thank you for your support of my exploration of innovative ways of teaching.

Sincerely,

Mrs. Xu

(continued)

Consent Slip

Child's Name: _____

_____ I give my consent for my child to participate in literacy activities with popular culture texts.

_____ I DO NOT give my consent for my child to participate in literacy activities with popular culture texts. Here are the reasons:

(List the Reasons)

_____

_____

_____

_____

Dealing With Time Issues

The time issues involved with planning and implementing a unit in which some popular culture texts are included, as Rachael and Lark have confessed in their respective chapters, can be a big barrier to an integration, even if teachers are supported by school administrators and parents. These issues become more pressing given the political and social context in which school districts pressure teachers to use a prescribed program or give little freedom to add other texts to the approved literacy curriculum. In addition to seeking support from school administrators and parents, teachers need additional time or freedom to use their instructional time in a way that would benefit their students most. The following are some ideas that may be helpful in planning and implementing literacy activities when teachers infuse popular culture texts into the regular curriculum.

- Plan to use popular culture texts not only for their intrinsic value but also as a springboard to motivate your students to participate in the regular curriculum or as additional or alternative texts for some students who find traditional texts uninteresting or too difficult. The multimedia nature of popular culture texts offers multiple contextual clues that lend support for comprehension. (See chapter 5 for details about the multimedia nature of popular culture texts.)

- Pair with a colleague in your grade level who is interested in a similar unit based on popular culture texts. Divide the tasks of planning between you and share resources (rather than shopping around to buy individual copies of the texts) throughout the implementation.

- Seek resources on the Internet that offer current information on popular culture texts. You can print or download information for class use in a matter of minutes.
- Involve students in the planning. Ask students to suggest possible titles of popular culture texts related to the unit and the sources for you to learn about the texts. In so doing, you show students about your interests in learning about their interaction with popular culture and about your willingness to consider them as your teachers. Additionally, students' suggested texts may allow you to understand their perspective, which will assist you in bringing to the unit texts written from other perspectives.
- Use center time (time for small-group activities) in primary grades to allow students to engage in literacy activities involved with popular culture texts and other regular activities. In intermediate and upper grades, assign activities related to popular culture texts as homework, and then ask students to share in class their experiences or work.
- To share students' accomplishments during the unit with school administrators, colleagues, and parents, assign different groups of students the responsibility of guiding visitors to the classroom as Rachael did with her students. In so doing, you give your students a sense of pride and ownership for what they have achieved.
- Always save everything you have created and used, as you may use some of the resources again in the following years.

Concluding Thoughts

Teachers, as Simmons and Dresang (2001) point out, often can locate, from various sources, professional literature that supports the use of one particular piece of classical or canonical literature (e.g., Shakespeare's plays), but not much literature is available that supports the use of particular young adult literature (e.g., Lemony Snicket's *A Series of Unfortunate Events: The Bad Beginning*, 1999). Professional literature on multimedia texts and, in particular, popular culture texts also is sparse. The rapid advancement in technology and students' increasing engagement with multimedia texts have outpaced the development in research studies related to the positive effects of integrating media texts into teaching. Research on the positive results that multimedia texts and, in particular, popular culture texts have on students' school literacy learning is still a relatively new area in the literacy field. Thus, it becomes crucial for teachers to read professional journals and books to keep abreast of new developments in this area. (Be sure to read the articles and books in this area that are listed in the References section at the end of this book.) The newly gained information that is supported by scholarship will later become useful to teachers who are making a convincing case to school administrators and parents for using popular culture texts.

Resources for Teachers

Television Shows and Movies

Online Resources

American Film Institute: www.afi.com
This official website of the American Film Institute offers AFI award-related news, nominees, and past winners. The AFI 100 Year List downloads include songs, heroes and villains, passions, laughs, thrills, stars, and movies.

Animé Web Turnpike: www.anipike.com
This extremely comprehensive website offers readers almost everything about Japanese animation (animés). This website features animé fan club listings, manga industry, manga series, fandom pages, fan fiction, and games. It offers links to websites about Japanese culture and to websites of other animés and mangas.

Cartoon Network: www.cartoonnetwork.com
This official website for the Cartoon Network channel features cartoons for various age groups. For each show, there is a synopsis, news, schedule, and even a clip of the show. This website also has information for parents regarding television shows.

Disney Online: www.disney.go.com/disneychannel/index.html
This official website for Disney Online has links to the Disney Channel, which has information about the shows, and to Disney theme parks in the United States and around the world. It also has information on classic and contemporary movies produced by Disney.

DragonBall Z: www.dragonballz.com
This official website has featured characters from *DragonBall Z*, which has more than 300 characters so far, and news of video and movie release.

Fox Kids Channel: www.foxkids.com
This official website for Fox Kids Channel features information related to cartoons (most of which are superhero shows), ranging from a poll on a favorite character in a cartoon to an advertisement for show-related merchandise.

The Internet Movie Database: www.imdb.com
This website provides information related to a movie from its cast to director(s), producer(s), and movie synopses. It also has information related to other media genres (e.g., music) and short biographies of entertainers.

Nickelodeon Channel: www.nick.com
This official website for the Nickelodeon channel features cartoons for various age groups. In addition to a synopsis of each show and an online shop for show-related merchandise, this website also has games, e-cards, and links to Teenick (for teenagers) and Nick, Jr. (for young children).

Nielsen Media Research: www.nielsenmedia.com

This website, which offers a listing that ranks top television programs on a weekly basis, illustrates the popularity of television shows and programs.

Oscar: www.oscar.com

This official website of the Academy of Motion Pictures Arts and Sciences lists current Oscar nominees and past winners, the academy history, ceremony history, and Oscar questions and answers (Q & A).

Pokémon: www.pokemon.com

This website has information on *Pokémon*, ranging from synopses of the shows to trading cards, comic books, movies, and news.

TV Tome: www.tvtome.com

This comprehensive website offers information on past and current television shows and series. The information ranges from a summary of a show or series, to cast and crew information, schedules, and interesting facts about the show or series.

WB Television Network: www.thewb.com

This official website of the WB Television Network features cartoons and television shows for various age groups. The website lists the shows (including schedule, synopsis, news, and advertisement for merchandise), the actors and actresses in the shows, music heard on the shows, and chats about the show.

Yu-Gi-Oh!: www.yugioh.com

This comprehensive website offers all one needs to know about *Yu-Gi-Oh!* It includes the show schedule on the Cartoon Network channel, show synopsis, steps of playing a Duel Monsters card game, movie soundtrack, free wallpapers and e-cards, and an official Yu-Gi-Oh! store.

Books About Movies

Minow, N. (2004). *The movie mom's guide to family movies* (2nd ed.). Lincoln, NE: iUniverse.

This 590-page book has synopses of many family movies and answers to questions asked by parents about their children's engagement with different types of movies.

Music

Online Resources

Hip-Hop Website: www.hiphopsite.com

This website provides background information about the bands, artists, and songs in an album. People can share their review of an album through an online forum.

Lyrics.com: www.lyrics.com

This comprehensive website allows people to search the lyrics from an artist's album. The artists are listed in an alphabetical order, and the music they perform ranges from soft rock to rap, pop songs, and country music.

MTV Network: www.mtv.com

This official MTV Network website provides up-to-date information on television shows on the channel and movies. It also features artists in the movie and music industry, and reviews of albums and movies.

**New Haven Teacher's Institute:
www.yale.edu/ynhti/curriculum/units/1993/4/93.04.04.x.html**

This website features an article, *The Evolution of Rap Music in the United States*, written by Henry A. Rhodes, who also shares his lesson plans on integrating hip-hop culture into a literacy curriculum. Films, rap records, and a teacher–student bibliography are provided.

The Original Hip-Hop Lyrics Archive: www.ohhla.com

This hip-hop lyrics archive has a comprehensive list of information on lyrics, hip-hop artists, new lyrics, frequently asked questions (FAQs), press releases, reviews, top 30 songs, and links to other hip-hop lyrics websites. This is a place to add lyrics to the archive and a place to correct any mistakes in the lyrics added to the archive by other fans.

Rap Search: www.rapsearch.com

This largest and comprehensive online hip-hop portal features news headlines, hip-hop discussion, and a RapSearch link directory. The directory has links to hip-hop artists and bands, breakdance, record labels around the world, graffiti, boards and forum, magazines, and news.

Rap Songs and Artists: www.rapmusic.com

This comprehensive website features live hip-hop events, reviews of CDs, and highlights of artists, producers, games, and shopping for CDs.

***Rolling Stone* Magazine: www.rollingstone.com**

This website has entertainment-related news and features reviews of music CDs and movies.

**Worldwide Internet Music Resources:
www.music.indiana.edu/music_resources**

This comprehensive website provides links to websites of artists and musicians of all genres, plus types of music, research and study, journals and magazines, and composers and compositions.

**Yahoo's List of Websites With Music Reviews:
http://dir.yahoo.com/Entertainment/Music/Reviews**

This website lists music reviews of different genres. People can search a review via genre, popularity, or an alphabetic list.

Comic Books and Graphic Novels

Online Resources

Comic Books for Young Adults:
http://ublib.buffalo.edu/libraries/units/lml/comics/pages/index.html
This comprehensive website, which is intended for librarians, is certainly useful for classroom teachers. It features comic formats and genres, guidelines for selecting comic books, recommended comics, rationales for an inclusion of comic books and graphic novels in libraries, and other relevant Internet resources.

Dav Pilkey: www.pilkey.com
This official website of children's book author Dav Pilkey, whose Captain Underpants series enjoys popularity among children in primary and upper grades, features the published books and those in progress, jokes related to the books, games, ideas for using the books in teaching, and a brief biography of the author (including his unpleasant school experience).

DC Comics www.dccomics.com
This official DC Comics website features comic books, graphic novels, and mangas. The website provides news related to the comics world, sneak previews of soon-to-be-released comics, and features of some popular comics.

Garfield: www.garfield.com
This official website for the *Garfield* comic strip features Garfield collectibles, news, games, and comics and cartoons. The website also has a link to www.garfieldgame.com and www.garfieldstuff.com.

King Features Syndicate:
www.kingfeatures.com/features/comics/comics.htm
This official website of King Features Syndicate offers a comprehensive list of popular comic strips. The website provides a brief history for each comic strip series and a search function that allows readers to find any strip published during the previous month.

Marvel Comics: www.marvelcomics.com
This official Marvel Comics website provides comprehensive information about the comic books and graphic novels published by the company. The website provides a sneak preview of soon-to-be-released comics and a relatively complete list of comics ever published on one particular series (e.g., *Spider-man* series).

Peanuts: www.unitedmedia.com/comics/peanuts
This website provides comprehensive information about one of the most popular comic strips, which ranges from the history of the comics to news of Peanuts; its creator, Charles Schulz; and its characters. A search function on the website allows readers to find any comic strip published in the past month and to send it via e-mail to a friend. Wallpapers and e-cards are other features of this website.

ShonenJump Manga: www.shonenjump.com
This official website of the world's most popular manga has news about Japanese animés, a preview of an upcoming issue, manga titles, downloads (e.g., online manga, wallpapers, and e-cards), and features (e.g., contests and reader surveys).

Books and Articles About Comic Books and Graphic Novels

Barrier, M., & Williams, M. (Eds.). (1981). *Smithsonian book of comic-book comics*. Washington, DC: Smithsonian Institution Press; New York: H.N. Abrams.
This is a series of reprints of comics of different genres that were originally produced by different companies.

Benton, M. (1989). *The comic book in America: An illustrated history*. Dallas, TX: Taylor.
This book chronicles the history of comic books in the United States.

Benton, M. (1994). *Masters of imagination: The comic book artists Hall of Fame*. Dallas, TX: Taylor.
This book features 13 comics artists who have made an impact on comic book history.

Callahan, B. (2004). *The new Smithsonian book of comic book stories: From crumb to clowes*. Washington, DC: Smithsonian Books.
This anthology includes classic and contemporary comics and graphic novels from the 1960s to the present.

Glubok, S. (1979). *The art of the comic strip*. New York: Macmillan.
This book presents a history of comic strips, which includes a detailed description of some classic comic strips.

Gorman, M. (2003). *Getting graphic! Using graphic novels to promote literacy with preteens and teens*. Worthington, OH: Linworth.
This book is an excellent resource for classroom teachers and school librarians who want to introduce graphic novels to students ages 10 and up. The book provides background information on fiction and nonfiction graphic novels, a summary list of graphic novels appropriate for students ages 10–18, and practical ideas of integrating graphic novels into teaching.

Gorman, M. (2004). Graphic novels for younger readers. *Book Links, 13*(5), 51–54.
This article discusses several nonfiction graphic novels (e.g., *Amelia Earhart Free in the Skies*) appropriate for primary-grade students.

McCloud, S. (1993). *Understanding comics*. Northhampton, MA: Tundra Publications.
McCloud writes this book in a comic format and explains the history of comics, the meaning of comic art, and the ways people read and understand comics.

Pellowski, M.M. (1995). *The art of making comic books.* **Minneapolis, MN: Lerner.**
This book presents a brief history of comic books and offers detailed steps for making your own comic books.

Scott, E. (1993). *Funny papers: Behind the scenes of the comics.* **New York: Morrow Junior Books.**
This book chronicles the history of cartoons, comic strips, and comic books. Comments by cartoonists of famous comic strips or books are included.

Tatchell, J. (1987). *How to draw cartoons and caricatures.* **London: Usborne.**
This book offers details and tips for children who are interested in drawing cartoons and comic strips.

Trading Cards

Online Resources

Animé Trading Cards Index: www.splashpagecomics.com/animcard.htm
This index provides information on animé cards for sale.

Parents' (and Grandparents') Guide to *Pokémon*:
www.geocities.com/ResearchTriangle/Campus/3229/pokemon.html
This comprehensive and excellent website offers parents and grandparents a wide range of information related to Pokémon, including video games, television shows, and merchandise. The website also has a section with responses to FAQs from parents (e.g., What is Pokémon? What is a GameCube?). Many links to other websites are provided.

Solar System Trading Cards: http://amazing-space.stsci.edu/resources/explorations/trading/game.htm?sssssssscsssss
This website is an example of using the trading card format to convey information about the solar system. A player is asked to choose one card with a planet and to answer questions related to the chosen planet. Feedback on the responses is provided. This website also has links to other websites on the solar system.

Yu-Gi-Oh! Trading Card Game:
www.upperdeckentertainment.com/yugioh/en/train.aspx
This helpful website explains the Duel Monsters trading game, including the cards in a deck, the ways to use the cards, the rules of the game, and FAQs.

Games

Online Resources

Abby-cheat: www.abby-cheat.com
This website lists cheats, cheat codes, trainers, and walkthroughs.

Game Daily Downloads: www.pcgamer.com/gigex50.html

This website lists free game demos that are downloadable for gamers to play on a specific platform (e.g., PC, PlayStation 2).

Game Downloads: www.FilePlanet.com

This comprehensive website provides a description for each game and lists the top 50 newest and the top 50 most popular games. Each game can be searched by genre or by file type. The website lists gamers' comments on a game and has free downloads for some games.

GameTalk: www.gametalk.com

The website features forums for gamers to share ideas and tips for games as well as reviews of games of all genres.

Game Zone Online: www.gamezone.com

This website features reviews of newly released games, strategies shared by gamers, and the top 50 demos.

Gamecritics.com: www.gamecritics.com

This website includes reviews of games, a forum, news, and features of gamers and game designers.

GamePro.com: www.gamepro.com

This comprehensive website features demos and newly released or popular games on various platforms. Games can be searched by genre or by platform. The website also list cheats, strategies, reviews, and news.

GameSpy: www.gamespy.com

This comprehensive website provides news, previews, and reviews of games, cheats, and downloads. It also lists links to other websites. Subscription to the website, which allows a subscriber to play Internet games, is required.

KiddONet: www.kiddonet.com

This website features a wide range of free games just for children.

Miniclip: www.miniclip.com

This website features a wide range of free online games for children and adults.

***PC Gamer* Magazine: www.pcgamer.com**

This comprehensive website provides the magazine's online version and highlights features from its print version. The website has descriptions for games, forums for gamers to share reviews, and the top 50 downloadable demos.

Womengamers.com: www.womengamers.com

This website is geared for women gamers. It lists previews and reviews of games, discusses women portrayed in games, has a hardware Q & A section, provides downloads, and features game-related news.

E-Zines

Online Resources

gURL.com: www.gurl.com

This popular website for teenage girls covers a wide range of topics, including music, movies and media, friends and family, school and careers, body image, and fashion and styles. For each topic, one can take a poll, join in an ongoing conversation, and read responses to posted questions or answer the questions.

John Labovitz's E-Zine-List: www.e-zine-list.com

This is a relatively comprehensive list of all e-zines on almost every subject.

Teen Ink: http://teenink.com

This website features reviews of movies, music, and books. It also publishes essays in various genres, which are all written by and for teens. *Teen Ink* is also published as a printed magazine.

Teen Space: www.ipl.org/div/teen/browse/ae9000

This website lists links to e-zines for teens.

Reproducibles

A.1 Literacy as Social Practice

Key Concepts of Literacy as Social Practice	Your Understanding
Meaningfulness in Social Contexts	
Domains and Discourse	
Social Institutions and Power Relationship	
Critical Literacy Practices	
Multiliteracies	
Changing Literacy	

A.2 Four Approaches to Using Popular Culture Text

1. Popular Culture Text:	
2. How You Might View and Use It:	**2. How Your Partner Might View and Use It:**
3. Your Approach(es):	**3. Your Partner's Approach(es):**

Similarities in Approach(es) Between You and Your Partner:

Differences in Approach(es) Between You and Your Partner:

A.3 Checklist for an Artistic Collage

Checklist for an Artistic Collage

The purpose of a collage is to convey the story, meaning, and emotions through images. You may use magazines, drawings, words, painting, and fabric to create your collage. Each image should represent a particular incident, event, or feeling from the story.

When you present your collage, you will have the opportunity to enlighten the class as to why you selected your images and what they mean to you.

Remember, your collage must represent Stanley's journey to Camp Green Lake and back home again.

_____ My heading (name, date, and period) is on the BACK of the collage.

_____ I can explain what my images mean and why I chose them.

_____ This represents my best work.

A.4 Checklist for a Rap About Stanley

A Checklist for _____

Your assignment is to create lyrics for a song, a rap, or a poem that will describe Stanley's experience in the book *Holes*. The most powerful song lyrics help us to feel what the singer is feeling. Put yourself in Stanley's place. How do you feel about your life? How do you make sense out of what is happening to you now? How do you feel when you are successful?

Content

Include major experiences from the story.

_____ Why was Stanley sent to Camp Green Lake?

_____ Who does Stanley meet at the Camp?

_____ What is the curse on Stanley and his family?

_____ What does Stanley do for Zero?

_____ Why does Stanley run away?

_____ Where do Stanley and Zero go?

_____ Why do the boys come back to Camp Green Lake?

_____ What changes does Stanley go through?

_____ What happens in the end?

Writing Conventions	Yes	No
• My name, date, and period are on my paper.	_____	_____
• I have indented my paragraphs.	_____	_____
• I have put down one idea per sentence.	_____	_____
• Each sentence begins with a capital letter.	_____	_____
• Each sentence ends with a period.	_____	_____
• I have used my best spelling.	_____	_____
• I have reread my paper and corrected small mistakes.	_____	_____

A.5 Literacy Knowledge and Skills Used With Hypermedia Text

Popular Culture Website and Address:		
Literacy Knowledge and Skills	Same Ones	New or Adapted Ones

Name of the Artist:	Title of a CD Album or Song:
Teacher's View	Student's View

A.7 Explore Rap Music

Name of the Rap Artist	Title of the Rap Song
Messages of the Song	Type of the Song (gangsta, apolitical, political, positive, experimental, and feminist)
• • • • • • •	• • • • • • •
Parts of the Song You Like	Parts of the Song You Dislike
• • • • • • •	• • • • • • •

A.8 Probe, Hypothesize, Reprobe, and Rethink Cycle

Title of the Game:

Stage of the Cycle	What Did You Do?
Probe	
Hypothesize	
Reprobe	

(continued)

A.8 Probe, Hypothesize, Reprobe, and Rethink Cycle (*continued*)

Title of the Game:

Stage of the Cycle	What Did You Do?
Rethink	

Overall Reflections:

Picture:

Information Related to the Content in the Picture:

A.10 Exploring Cinderella Around the World

Book Title	Setting	Story Plot	Comparing to Disney's *Cinderella*		Comparing to Warner Bros. *A Cinderella Story*	
			Similar	Different	Similar	Different

A.11 Considering Other Perspectives

Student's Response	What Aspect(s) Is (Are) Considered?	What Aspect(s) Is (Are) Not Considered?	What Might You Do to Help Students See Other Perspectives?
What language is used?			
How do you understand this language?			
For whom is this written?			

A.12 Learning More About My Idol

My Idol	What I Know About Him or Her From the Media	What I Now Know About Him or Her After the Exploration	Sources of Exploration

Guidelines	Explanation	An Example of Popular Culture Text
1. The Bibliographic Citation		
2. The Intended Audience		
3. A Brief Summary of the Work		
4. The Relation of the Book to the Program		
5. The Impact of the Book		

(continued)

Guidelines	Explanation	An Example of Popular Culture Text
6. Potential Problems With the Work		
7. Collection of Information About the Book		
8. Collection of Supplementary Information		
9. Alternative Works an Individual Student Might Read		

A.14 Changes in Affective Domain and Learning Outcomes

Student Name:	Popular Culture Texts Used:	Date:
Areas of Change	Before an Integration	During and After an Integration
Attitude		
Interest		
Motivation		
Learning Outcomes		

A.15 Literacy Knowledge and Skills Demonstrated in an Engagement With a Television Show

IRA and NCTE Standards	Literacy Knowledge or Skills Related to Watching _____
1. Students read a wide range of print and nonprint texts to build an understanding of texts, of themselves, and of the cultures of the United States and the world; to acquire new information; to respond to the needs and demands of society and the workplace; and for personal fulfillment. Among these texts are fiction and nonfiction, classic and contemporary works.	
2. Students read a wide range of literature from many periods in many genres to build an understanding of the many dimensions (e.g., philosophical, ethical, aesthetic) of human experience.	
3. Students apply a wide range of strategies to comprehend, interpret, evaluate, and appreciate texts. They draw on their prior experience, their interactions with other readers and writers, their knowledge of word meaning and of other texts, their word identification strategies, and their understanding of textual features (e.g., sound-letter correspondence, sentence structure, context, graphics).	
4. Students adjust their use of spoken, written, and visual language (e.g., conventions, style, vocabulary) to communicate effectively with a variety of audiences and for different purposes.	
5. Students employ a wide range of strategies as they write and use different writing process elements appropriately to communicate with different audiences for a variety of purposes.	
6. Students apply knowledge of language structure, language conventions (e.g., spelling and punctuation), media techniques, figurative language, and genre to create, critique, and discuss print and nonprint texts.	

(continued)

IRA and NCTE Standards	Literacy Knowledge/Skills Related to to Watching _____
7. Students conduct research on issues and interests by generating ideas and questions, and by posing problems. They gather, evaluate, and synthesize data from a variety of sources (e.g., print and nonprint texts, artifacts, people) to communicate their discoveries in ways that suit their purpose and audience.	
8. Students use a variety of technological and information resources (e.g., libraries, databases, computer networks, video) to gather and synthesize information and to create and communicate knowledge.	
9. Students develop an understanding of and respect for diversity in language use, patterns, and dialects across cultures, ethnic groups, geographic regions, and social roles.	
10. Students whose first language is not English make use of their first language to develop competency in the English language arts and to develop understanding of content across the curriculum.	
11. Students participate as knowledgeable, reflective, creative, and critical members of a variety of literacy communities.	
12. Students use spoken, written, and visual language to accomplish their own purposes (e.g., for learning, enjoyment, persuasion, and the exchange of information).	

A.16 Sample Letter to Parents or Guardians Concerning the Use of a Popular Culture Text

Dear Parents/Guardians of _____(Student):

This year, I will try to incorporate students' interests in popular culture into teaching. Popular culture texts are often multimedia and include television shows, movies, music, video games, Internet, and magazines. Popular culture texts hold familiarity and interests for students, and thus have potential to motivate and engage students. In this letter, I will share with you my reasons for using students' popular culture texts as listed below and my ways of using them. I also invite you to explore these texts along with your child and to share with me your opinions about the texts.

I have conducted an informal survey of the class during the first couple weeks of this school year. Here are the students' popular culture interests:

-
-
-
-
-

After a close examination of all the interests, I have noted this common interest across the whole class. _____

_____

I am going to build on this common interest in my teaching of _____

_____. I will use these following popular

culture texts in my teaching of _____
(Bibliographic Information)

-
-
-
-
-

The purpose of using these texts is to address curriculum standards in an innovative way that may better engage and motivate students. Here are the standards that the use of these popular culture texts will address:
(Curriculum Standards)

-
-
-
-
-

(continued)

•••

I have personally read all of the texts listed above, and noted some controversial issues that may arise in my teaching. I am sharing possible ways to address these issues and inviting you to share your suggestions.

Issues	Ways to Deal With the Issues

-
-
-
-

Here is a list of some professional literature that supports the use of popular culture texts to enhance literacy learning. You may be interested in reading some from the list. Please feel free to ask me for a copy of the listed literature and share with me your opinions about the literature.
(Literature)

-
-
-
-

Please send the following consent slip back to me, indicating your consent for your child to participate in literacy activities involving all or some of the popular culture texts listed. If you object to the use of the texts, I'd appreciate that you share your reasons so that I can plan a set of alternative texts for your child during the activities.

Thank you for your support of my exploration of innovative ways of teaching.
Sincerely,

- -

Consent Slip

Child's Name:_____

_____ I give my consent for my child to participate in literacy activities with popular culture texts.

_____ I DO NOT give my consent for my child to participate in literacy activities with popular culture texts. Here are the reasons:

_____

_____

_____

REFERENCES

Abby-cheat.com. (1995–2005). *Abby-cheat.com*. Retrieved April 6, 2005, from http://www.abby-cheat.com

Agee, J. (1999). There it was, that one sex scene: English teachers on censorship. *English Journal*, *89*(2), 61–70.

Alexander, P.A. (2003). Profiling the developing reader: The interplay of knowledge, interest, and strategic processing. In C.M. Fairbanks, J. Worthy, B. Maloch, J.V. Hoffman, & D.L. Schallert (Eds.), *52nd yearbook of the National Reading Conference* (pp. 47–65). Oak Creek, WI: National Reading Conference.

Allington, R.L., & Johnston, P.H. (2002). *Reading to learn: Lessons from exemplary fourth-grade classrooms*. New York: Guilford.

Alvermann, D.E. (2001). Reading adolescents' reading identities: Looking back to see ahead. *Journal of Adolescent & Adult Literacy*, *44*, 676–690.

Alvermann, D.E., & Hagood, M.C. (2000). Fandom and critical media literacy. *Journal of Adolescent & Adult Literacy*, *43*, 436–446.

Alvermann, D.E., Hagood, M.C., & Williams, K.B. (2001, June). Image, language, and sound: Making meaning with popular culture texts. *Reading Online*, *4*(11). Retrieved August 10, 2004, from http://www.readingonline.org/newliteracies/lit_index.asp?HREF=/newliteracies/action/alvermann/index.html

Alvermann, D.E., & Heron, A.H. (2001). Literacy identity work: Playing to learn with popular media. *Journal of Adolescent & Adult Literacy*, *44*, 118–122.

Alvermann, D.E., Huddleston, A., & Hagood, M.C. (2004). What could professional wrestling and school literacy practices possibly have in common? *Journal of Adolescent & Adult Literacy*, *47*, 532–540.

Alvermann, D.E., Moon, J.S., & Hagood, M.C. (1999). *Popular culture in the classroom: Teaching and researching critical media literacy*. Newark, DE: International Reading Association.

Alvermann, D.E., & Xu, S.H. (2003). Children's everyday literacies: Intersections of popular culture and language arts instruction. *Language Arts*, *81*(2), 145–154.

Anderson, S. (1999). *So, you wanna be a rock star? How to create music, get gigs, and maybe even make it big!* Hillsboro, OR: Beyond Words.

Barone, D.M., Mallette, M.H., & Xu, S.H. (2005). *Teaching early literacy: Development, assessment, and instruction*. New York: Guilford.

Barrier, M., & Williams, M. (Eds.). (1981). *Smithsonian book of comic-book comics*. Washington, DC: Smithsonian Institution Press; New York: H.N. Abrams.

Barton, D., & Hamilton, M. (1998). *Local literacies: Reading and writing in one community*. London: Routledge.

Bear, D.R., Invernizzi, M., Templeton, S., & Johnston, F. (2000). *Words their way: Word study for phonics, vocabulary, and spelling instruction* (2nd ed.). Englewood Cliffs, NJ: Prentice Hall.

Benton, M. (1989). *The comic book in America: An illustrated history*. Dallas, TX: Taylor.

Benton, M. (1994). *Masters of imagination: The comic book artists Hall of Fame*. Dallas, TX: Taylor.

Berghoff, B., & Harste, J.C. (2002). Semiotics. In B.J. Guzzetti (Ed.), *Literacy in America: An encyclopedia of history, theory, and practice* (pp. 580–581). Santa Barbara, CA: ABC-CLIO.

Block, C.C., Gambrell, L.B., & Pressley, M. (Eds.). (2002). *Improving comprehension instruction: Rethinking research, theory, and classroom practice*. San Francisco: Jossey-Bass.

Block, C.C., & Pressley, M. (Eds.). (2002). *Comprehension instruction: Research-based best practices*. New York: Guilford.

Boyd, T. (2004, March 14). Hip-hop till you drop. *Los Angeles Times*, p. E44.

Brown, J.E., & Stephens, E.C. (1994). *Rationales for teaching challenged books*. Urbana, IL: National Council of Teachers of English. Retrieved April 5, 2004, from http://www.ncte.org/library/files/About_NCTE/Issues/rationalesforbooks.pdf

Brozo, W.G. (2002). *To be a boy, to be a reader: Engaging teen and preteen boys in active literacy*. Newark, DE: International Reading Association.

Bruce, B.C. (Ed.). (2003). *Literacy in the information age: Inquiries into meaning making with new technologies*. Newark, DE: International Reading Association.

Buckingham, D. (Ed.). (1993). *Reading audience: Young people and the media*. New York: Manchester University Press.

Buckingham, D. (1998). Introduction: Fantasies of empowerment? Radical pedagogy and popular culture. In D. Buckingham (Ed.), *Teaching popular culture: Beyond radical pedagogy* (pp. 1–17). London: UCL Press.

California Department of Education. (1999). *Reading/language arts framework for California public schools: Kindergarten through grade twelve*. Sacramento, CA: Author.

Comber, B. (2001). Classroom explorations in critical literacy. In H. Fehring & P. Green (Eds.), *Critical literacy: A collection of articles from the Australian Literacy Educators' Association* (pp. 90–102). Newark, DE: International Reading Association.

Considine, D.M., & Haley, G.E. (1999). *Visual messages: Integrating imagery into instruction* (2nd ed.). Englewood, CO: Teacher Ideas Press.

Crane, V., & Chen, M. (2003). Content development of children's media. In E.L. Palmer & B.M. Young (Eds.), *The faces of televisual media: Teaching, violence, selling to children* (2nd ed., pp. 60–82). Mahwah, NJ: Erlbaum.

Duffy, G.G. (2003). *Explaining reading: A resource for teaching concepts, skills, and strategies*. New York: Guilford.

Dyson, A.H. (1997). *Writing superheroes: Contemporary childhood, popular culture, and classroom literacy*. New York: Teachers College Press.

Echevarria, J., Vogt, M., & Short, D.J. (2000). *Making content comprehensible for English language learners: The SIOP model*. Boston: Allyn & Bacon.

Evans, J. (2005). Beanie Babies: An opportunity to promote literacy development, or a money-spinner for the business tycoons? In J. Evans (Ed.), *Literacy moves on: Popular culture, new technologies, and critical literacy in the elementary classroom* (pp. 106–126). Portsmouth, NH: Heinemann.

Facer, K., Furlong, J., Furlong, R., & Sutherland, R. (2003). *Screenplay: Children and computing in the home*. New York: Routledge/Falmer.

Fairclough, N. (1989). *Language and power*. New York: Longman.

Field, A. (2004). Beyond superman: Superheroes in picture books. *Book Links, 13*(5), 25–27.

Freire, P. (1970). *Pedagogy of the oppressed* (M. Bergman Ramos, Trans.). New York: Herder & Herder.

Future Network USA. (2005). *PC gamers* [Magazine]. Brisbane, CA: Author.

Gee, J.P. (1996). *Social linguistics and literacies: Ideology in discourses* (2nd ed.). London: Falmer.

Gee, J.P. (2003). *What video games have to teach us about learning and literacy*. New York: Palgrave Macmillan.

Gee, J.P., Hull, G., & Lankshear, C. (1996). *The new work order: Behind the language of the new capitalism*. Boulder, CO: Westview Press.

Glubok, S. (1979). *The art of the comic strip*. New York: Macmillan.

Goldman, M. (1996). If you can read this, thank TV. *TESOL Journal, 6*(2), 15–18.

Gorman, M. (2003). *Getting graphic! Using graphic novels to promote literacy with preteens and teens*. Worthington, OH: Linworth.

Gorman, M. (2004). Graphic novels for younger readers. *Book Links, 13*(5), 51–54.

Guthrie, J.T. (2004). Teaching for literacy engagement. *Journal of Literacy Research, 36*(1), 1–30.

Guthrie, J.T., Van Meter, P., Hancock, G.R., Alao, S., Anderson, E., & McCann, A. (1998). Does concept-oriented reading instruction increase strategy use and conceptual learning from text? *Journal of Educational Psychology, 90*(2), 261–278.

Guzzetti, B.J. (2002). Zines. In B. Guzzetti (Ed.), *Literacy in America: An encyclopedia of history, theory, and practice* (p. 699). Santa Barbara, CA: ABC-CLIO.

Guzzetti, B.J., Campbell, S., Duke, C., & Irving, J. (2003, July/August). Understanding adolescent literacies: A conversation with three zinesters. *Reading Online, 7*(1). Retrieved January 10, 2004, from http://www.readingonline.org/newliteracies/lit_index.asp?HREF= guzzetti3

Hagood, M.C. (2001). Media literacies: Varied but distinguishable. In J.V. Hoffman, D.L. Schallert, C.M. Fairbanks, J. Worthy, & B. Maloch (Eds.), *50th yearbook of the National Reading Conference* (pp. 248–261). Chicago: National Reading Conference.

Hagood, M.C. (2002). Popular culture. In B.J. Guzzetti (Ed.), *Literacy in America: An encyclopedia of history, theory, and practice* (pp. 440–443). Santa Barbara, CA: ABC-CLIO.

Hanzl, A. (2001). Critical literacy and children's literature: Exploring the story of Aladdin. In H. Fehring & P. Green (Eds.), *Critical literacy: A collection of articles from the Australian Literacy Educators' Association* (pp. 84–89). Newark, DE: International Reading Association.

Harste, J.C., Ariogul, S., Sanner, D., East, D., Enyeart, J.A., Lehman, B.M., et al. (2003). New times: First-person shooter games go to college. In C.M. Fairbanks, J. Worthy, B. Maloch, J.V. Hoffman, & D.L. Schallert (Eds.), *52nd yearbook of the National Reading Conference* (pp. 218–229). Oak Creek, WI: National Reading Conference.

Heath, S.B. (1983). *Ways with words*. New York: Cambridge University Press.

Hill, B.C., Noe, K.L.S., & King, J.A. (2003). *Literature circles in middle school: One teacher's journey*. Norwood, MA: Christopher-Gordon.

IDG Communications. (2005). *Game pro* [Magazine]. St. Leonards, Australia: Author.

International Reading Association & National Council of Teachers of English. (1996). *Standards for the English language arts*. Newark, DE, Urbana, IL: Authors.

iVillage (1995–2005). *gURL*. Retrieved February 16, 2005, from http://www.gurl.com

Jenkins, H. (1992). "Strangers no more, we sing": Filking and the social construction of the science fiction fan community. In L.A. Lewis (Ed.), *The adoring audience: Fan culture and popular media* (pp. 208–236). New York: Routledge.

Johns, J. (2001). *Basic reading inventory: Preprimer through grade twelve and early literacy assessments* (8th ed.). Dubuque, IA: Kendall/Hunt.

KCTS Television. (2002–2004). *Don't buy it: Get media smart!* Retrieved August 15, 2004, from http://pbskids.org/dontbuyit/entertainment/tvvslife_1_result.html?quizquestion= 1&quiz=b&x=25&y=10)

Keene, E.O., & Zimmerman, S. (1997). *Mosaic of thought*. Portsmouth, NH: Heinemann.

Klingner, J.K., & Vaughn, S. (1999). Promoting reading comprehension, content learning, and English acquisition through collaborative strategic reading (CSR). *The Reading Teacher, 52,* 738–747.

Kress, G. (2003). *Literacy in the new media age*. New York: Routledge.

Lankshear, C., & Knobel, M. (2003). *New literacies: Changing knowledge and classroom teaching*. Philadelphia: Open University Press.

Lavin, M.R. (1998). Comic books and graphic novels for libraries: What to buy. *Serials Review, 24*(2), 31–46.

Lee, J.H., & Huston, A.C. (2003). Educational televisual media effects. In E.L. Palmer & B.M. Young (Eds.), *The faces of televisual media: Teaching, violence, selling to children* (2nd ed., pp. 83–106). Mahwah, NJ: Erlbaum.

Lester, P.M. (1995). *Visual communication: Images with messages*. Belmont, CA: Wadsworth.

Lloyd-Kolkin, D., & Tyner, K.R. (1991). *Media and you: An elementary media literacy curriculum*. Englewood Cliffs, NJ: Educational Technology.

Long Beach Unified School District. (n.d.). *Long Beach unified school district: Office of research, planning, and evaluation*. Retrieved April 5, 2005, from http://www.lbusd.k12.ca.us/research/demographics/index.asp

Luke, A., & Freebody, P. (1997). Shaping the social practices of reading. In S. Muspratt, A. Luke, & P. Freebody (Eds.), *Constructing critical literacies: Teaching and learning textual practice* (pp. 185–225). Cresskill, NJ: Hampton.

Luke, C. (1999). Media and cultural studies in Australia. *Journal of Adolescent & Adult Literacy, 42*, 622–626.

Lusted, D. (Ed.). (1991). *The media studies book: A guide for teachers*. New York: Routledge.

Mahar, D. (2003). Bringing the outside in: One teacher's ride on the animé highway. *Language Arts, 81*(2), 110–117.

Mahiri, J. (1998). *Shooting for excellence: African American and youth culture in new century schools*. New York: Teachers College Press.

Mahiri, J. (2004). Researching teacher practices: "Talking the talk" versus "walking the walk." *Research in the Teaching of English, 38*, 467–471.

Marsh, J. (2000). Teletubby tales: Popular culture in the early years language and literacy curriculum. *Contemporary Issues in Early Childhood, 1*(2), 119–123.

Marsh, J. (2003, April). *Taboos, tightropes and trivial pursuits: Pre-service and newly-qualified teachers' beliefs and practices in relation to popular culture and literacy*. Paper presented at the 2003 Annual Meeting of American Educational Research Association, Chicago.

McCloud, S. (1993). *Understanding comics*. Northhampton, MA: Tundra Publications.

Messaris, P. (1994). *Visual literacy: Image, mind and reality*. Boulder, CO: Westview.

Minow, N. (2004). *The movie mom's guide to family movies* (2nd ed.). Lincoln, NE: iUniverse.

Moll, L.C., Amanti, C., Neff, D., & Gonzalez, N. (1992). Funds of knowledge for teaching: Using a qualitative approach to connect homes and classrooms. *Theory Into Practice, 31*(1), 132–141.

Moll, L.C., & Gonzales, N. (1994). Lessons from research with language-minority children. *Journal of Reading Behavior, 26*(4), 439–456.

Morrell, E. (2004). *Linking literacy and popular culture: Finding connections for lifelong learning*. Norwood, MA: Christopher-Gordon.

Myers, J., & Beach, R. (2003). Hypermedia authoring as critical literacy. In B.C. Bruce (Ed.), *Literacy in the information age: Inquiries into meaning making with new technologies* (pp. 233–246). Newark, DE: International Reading Association.

New London Group. (1996). A pedagogy of multiliteracies: Designing social futures. *Harvard Educational Review, 66*(1), 60–92.

Nieto, S. (2004). Series foreword. In V.M. Vasquez (Ed.), *Negotiating critical literacies with young children* (pp. ix–xii). Mahwah, NJ: Erlbaum.

Norton, B. (2003). The motivating power of comic books: Insights from Archie comic readers. *The Reading Teacher, 57*, 140–147.

O'Brien, D.G. (1997). Multiple literacies in a high-school program for "at risk" adolescents. In D.E. Alvermann, K.A. Hinchman, D.W. Moore, S.F. Phelps, & D.R. Waff (Eds.), *Reconceptualizing the literacies in adolescents' lives* (pp. 3–26). Mahwah, NJ: Erlbaum.

Ogle, D.M. (1986). KWL: A teaching model that develops active reading of expository text. *The Reading Teacher, 39*, 564–570.

Online NewsHour. (1999, February 24). *The hip-hop phenomenon*. Retrieved April 20, 2004, from http://www.pbs.org/newshour/bb/entertainment/jan-june99/hiphop_2-24.html

The original hip-hop lyrics archive. (2002). Retrieved October 20, 2003, from http://www.ohhla.com

Pailliotet, A.W. (1995). "I never saw that before." A deeper view of video analysis in teacher education. *The Teacher Educator, 31*(2), 138–156.

Pailliotet, A.W. (1998). Deep viewing: A critical look at texts. In S. Steinberg & J.L. Kincheloe (Eds.), *Unauthorized methods: Strategies for critical teaching* (pp. 123–136). New York: Routledge.

Pailliotet, A.W., Semali, L., Rodenberg, R.K., Giles, J.K., & Macaul, S.L. (2000). Intermediality: Bridging to critical media literacy. *The Reading Teacher, 54*, 208–219.

Pellowski, M.M. (1995). *The art of making comic books* (H. Bender, Ill.). Minneapolis, MN: Lerner.

Piekarski, B. (2004, July 15). The rap on hip-hop. *Library Journal.* Retrieved August 10, 2004, from http://www.libraryjournal.com/article/CA434408?display=searchResults&stt=001 &text=piekarski

Rasinski, T.V., Linek, W., Sturtevant, E., & Padak, N. (1994). Effects of fluency development on urban second-grade readers. *Journal of Educational Research, 87*(3), 158–165.

Rhodes, H.A. (2004). *The evolution of rap music in the United States.* Retrieved April 19, 2004, from http://www.yale.edu/ynhti/curriculum/units/1993/4/93.04.04.x.html

Scharrer, E., & Comstock, G. (2003). Entertainment televisual media: Content patterns and themes. In E.L. Palmer & B.M. Young (Eds.), *The faces of televisual media: Teaching, violence, selling to children* (2nd ed., pp. 161–193). Mahwah, NJ: Erlbaum.

Science Research Associates/McGraw-Hill. (2000). *Open court reading (Grade 4, Level 1, Book 1).* Columbus, OH: Author.

Scott, E. (1993). *Funny papers: Behind the scenes of the comics.* New York: Morrow Junior Books.

Shaw, D. (2003, November 30). Media matters: Information inundation imperils our children. *Los Angeles Times*, p. E20.

Simmons, J.S., & Dresang, E.T. (2001). *School censorship in the 21st century: A guide for teachers and school library media specialists.* Newark, DE: International Reading Association.

Smolin, L.I., & Lawless, K.A. (2003). Becoming literate in the technological age: New responsibilities and tools for teachers. *The Reading Teacher, 56*, 570–577.

Storey, J. (1996). *Cultural studies and the study of popular culture: Theories and methods.* Athens: University of Georgia Press.

Street, B.V. (1984). *Literacy in theory and practice.* New York: Cambridge University Press.

Street, B.V. (1995). *Social literacies: Critical approaches to literacy in development, ethnography and education.* London: Longman.

Strickland, D.S., & Rath, L.K. (2000, August). Between the Lions: Public television promotes early literacy. *Reading Online, 4*(2). Retrieved February 15, 2005, from http://www.reading online.org/articles/strickland

Tatchell, J. (1987). *How to draw cartoons and caricatures.* London: Usborne.

TV Turnoff Network. (2004). *TV facts and figures.* Retrieved January 10, 2004, from http://www.tvturnoff.org/images/facts&figs/factsheets/Facts%20and%20Figures.pdf

U.S. Department of Commerce, Bureau of the Census. (2003). [Current population survey, October 1997 and September 2001]. Unpublished data, U.S. Department of Commerce.

Vasquez, V. (2000). Our way: Using the everyday to create a critical literacy curriculum. *Primary Voices, K–6, 9*(2), 8–13.

Vasquez, V. (2003). What Pokémon can teach us about learning and literacy. *Language Arts, 81*(2), 118–125.

Vasquez, V. (2004). *Negotiating critical literacies with young children.* Mahwah, NJ: Lawrence Erlbaum.

Warnick, B. (2002). *Critical literacy in a digital era: Technology, rhetoric, and the public interest.* Mahwah, NJ: Erlbaum.

Weiner, S. (2002). Beyond superheroes: Comics get serious. *Library Journal, 127*(2), 55–59.

Xu, S.H. (2001). Exploring diversity issues in teacher education. *Reading Online, 5*, 1–17. Retrieved February 15, 2005, from http://www.readingonline.org/newliteracies/action/xu

Xu, S.H. (2002a). Teachers' full knowledge of students' popular culture and the integration of aspects of that culture in the literacy instruction. *Education, 122*(Summer), 721–730.

Xu, S.H. (2002b). Teachers integrate diverse students' "funds of knowledge" with popular culture in literacy instruction. In D.L. Schallert, C.M. Fairbanks, J. Worthy, B. Maloch, & J.V. Hoffman (Eds.), *51st yearbook of the National Reading Conference* (pp. 407–419). Oak Creek, WI: National Reading Conference.

Xu, S.H. (2003). [Popular culture texts and literacy curriculum]. Unpublished raw data.

Xu, S.H. (2004). Teachers' reading of students' popular culture texts: The interplay of students' interests, teacher knowledge, and literacy curriculum. In J. Worthy, M. Maloch, J.V. Hoffman, D.L. Schallert, & C.M. Fairbanks (Eds.), *53rd yearbook of the National Reading Conference* (pp. 417–431). Oak Creek, WI: National Reading Conference.

Literature Cited

Alexander, S. (1985). *World famous Muriel and the scary dragon*. Boston: Little, Brown.

Bennett, W.J. (1997). *The children's book of heroes*. New York: Simon & Schuster.

Boada, F. (2001). Cinderella/Cenicienta (M. Fransoy, Trans.). San Francisco: Chronicle.

Boehm, R.G., Hoone, C., McGowan, T.M., McKinney-Browning, M.C., Miramontes, O.B., & Porter, P.H. (2000). *Ancient civilizations*. Orlando, FL: Harcourt Brace.

Bunting, E. (1996). *Going home*. New York: HarperCollins.

Callahan, B. (2004). *The new Smithsonian book of comic book stories: From crumb to clowes*. Washington, DC: Smithsonian Books.

Climo, S. (1989). *The Egyptian Cinderella*. New York: Crowell.

Climo, S. (1993). *The Korean Cinderella*. New York: HarperCollins.

Climo, S. (1996). *The Irish Cinderlad*. New York: HarperCollins.

Climo, S. (1999). *The Persian Cinderella*. New York: HarperCollins.

Coburn, J.R., & Lee, T.C. (1996). *Jouanah: A Hmong Cinderella*. Arcadia, CA: Shen's Books.

Coburn, J.R. (1998). *Angkat: The Cambodian Cinderella*. Fremont, CA: Shen's Books.

Coburn, J.R. (2000). *Domitila: A Cinderella tale from the Mexican tradition*. Auburn, CA: Shen's Books.

Craft, K.Y. (2000). *Cinderella*. New York: SeaStar.

Creech, S. (2001). *A fine, fine school*. New York: HarperCollins.

Crosher, J. (1992). *Ancient Egypt*. New York: Penguin.

de la Paz, M.J. (2001). *Abadeha: The Philippine Cinderella*. Auburn, CA: Shen's Books.

Daly, J. (2000). *Fair, brown and trembling: An Irish Cinderella story*. New York: Farrar Straus Giroux.

Dark Horse Comics. (2002). *9-11: Artists respond* (Vol. 1). Milwaukie, OR: Author.

Derrien, P. (2002). *Super H*. New York: Rouergue.

Farshtey, G. (2003). *The official guide to Bionicle*. New York: Scholastic.

Fisch, S. (2000). *Batman beyond: No place like home*. New York: Random House.

George, J.C. (1972). *Julie of the wolves* (J. Schoenherr, Ill.). New York: Harper & Row.

Graham, B. (2000). *Max*. Cambridge, MA: Candlewick.

Hess, K. (1999). *Just juice*. New York: Scholastic.

Hickox, R. (1998). *The golden sandal: A Middle Eastern Cinderella*. New York: Holiday House.

Hoffman, E. (1999). *Heroines and heroes/Heroínas y héroes* (Eida de la Vega, Trans.). St. Paul, MN: Redleaf Press.

Isaacs, A. (1994). *Swamp angel*. New York: Dutton Children's Books.

Jaffe, N. (1998). *The way meat loves salt: A Cinderella tale from the Jewish tradition*. New York: Holt.

Kellogg, S. (1995). *Sally Ann Thunder Ann Whirlwind Crockett: A tall tale*. New York: Morrow Junior Books.

Lester, J. (1994). *John Henry*. New York: Dial Books for Young Readers.

Louie, A. (1982). *Yeh-Shen: A Cinderella story from China*. New York: Philomel.

Marceau-Chenkie, B. (1999). *Naya, the Inuit Cinderella*. Yellowknife, NT, Canada: Raven Rock.

McCann, J.L. (2000). *Scooby-Doo and the weird water park*. New York: Scholastic.

McCaughrean, G. (1996). *One thousand and one Arabian nights*. New York: Oxford University Press.

McPhail, D. (1995). *Little Red Riding Hood*. New York: Scholastic.

Meredith Corporation. (2005). *Ladies home journal* [Magazine]. San Francisco: Author.

Millmore, M. (1997). *Egyptian games*. Retrieved October 10, 2003, from http://www.eyelid.co.uk/games.htm

Mooney, E.S. (2000). *The PowerPuff girls: Snow-off*. New York: Scholastic.

Paulsen, G. (1996). *Brian's winter*. New York: Delacorte.

Paulsen, G. (1999). *Hatchet*. New York: Aladdin.

Peck, R. (2004). Priscilla and the Wimps. In *Past, perfect, present tense: New and collected stories*. New York: Dial Books.

Peterson, S. (2000). *Batman beyond: New hero in town*. New York: Random House Books for Young Readers.

Pilkey, D. (1997). *The adventures of Captain Underpants*. New York: Blue Sky Press.

Pilkey, D. (2000a). *Captain Underpants and the perilous plot of Professor Poopypants*. New York: Blue Sky Press.

Pilkey, D. (2000b). *Ricky Ricotta's giant robot: An adventure novel*. New York: Blue Sky Press.

Pilkey, D. (2000c). *Ricky Ricotta's giant robot vs. the mutant mosquitoes from Mercury*. New York: Blue Sky Press.

Pilkey, D. (2001a). *Captain Underpants and the wrath of the wicked Wedgie Woman*. New York: Blue Sky Press.

Pilkey, D. (2001b). *Ricky Ricotta's giant robot vs. the voodoo vultures from Venus*. New York: Blue Sky Press.

Pilkey, D. (2002a). *Ricky Ricotta's mighty robot vs. the Jurassic jackrabbits from Jupiter*. New York: Blue Sky Press.

Pilkey, D. (2002b). *Ricky Ricotta's mighty robot vs. the mecha-monkeys from Mars*. New York: Blue Sky Press.

Pilkey, D. (2003a). *Captain Underpants and the big, bad, battle of the Bionic Booger Boy, part 1: The night of the nasty nostril nuggets*. New York: Blue Sky Press.

Pilkey, D. (2003b). *Captain Underpants and the big, bad, battle of the Bionic Booger Boy, part 2: The revenge of the ridiculous Robo-Boogers*. New York: Blue Sky Press.

Pinkney, B. (1997). *The adventures of Sparrowboy*. New York: Simon & Schuster Books for Young Readers.

Pollock, P. (1996). *The turkey girl: A Zuni Cinderella story*. New York: Little, Brown.

Quie, S. (1998). *Myths and civilizations of the ancient Egyptians*. New York: Peter Bedrick.

Riordan, J. (1985). *The tales from the Arabian nights*. Richmond, KY: Rand McNally & Company.

Sachar, L. (1998). *Holes*. New York: Farrar Straus Giroux.

San Souci, R.D. (1994). *Sootface: An Ojibwa Cinderella Story*. New York: Delacorte.

San Souci, R.D. (1998). *Cendrillon: A Caribbean Cinderella*. New York: Simon & Schuster Books for Young Readers.

San Souci, R.D. (2000). *Little Gold Star: A Spanish American Cinderella tale*. New York: Morrow Junior Books.

Schanzer, R. (2001). *Davy Crockett saves the world*. New York: HarperCollins.

Schroeder, A. (1997). *Smoky Mountain Rose: An Appalachian Cinderella*. New York: Dial Books for Young Readers.

Shakespeare, W. (1938). Sonnet 29: When in disgrace with fortune and men's eyes. In T. Thorpe (Ed.), *Shakespeare's sonnets*. London: P. Lund, Humphries & Co. (Original work published 1609)

Shannon, G. (1994). *More stories to solve: Fifteen folktales from around the world*. New York: Beech Tree Press.

Shannon, G. (2000). *Stories to solve: Folktales from around the world*. New York: Greenwillow Books.

Shuter, J. (1998). *Egypt*. Austin, TX: Raintree Steck-Vaughn.

Shuter, J. (1999). *Pharaohs & priests*. Des Plaines, IL: Heinemann.

Sierra, J. (2000). *The gift of the crocodile: A Cinderella story*. New York: Simon & Schuster Books for Young Readers.

Snicket, L. (1999). *A series of unfortunate events: The bad beginning*. New York: HarperCollins.

Sobol, D. (2004). *Two minute mysteries*. New York: Scholastic.

Spiegelman, A. (1986). *Maus: A survivor's tale*. New York: Pantheon.

Steig, W. (1973). *The real thief*. New York: Farrar Straus Giroux.

Takahashi, K. (2003). *Yu-Gi-Oh!* Retrieved October 10, 2003, from http://www.yugiohkingof games.com

Turner, G. (2004). *Abraham Lincoln: The Civil War president* (S. Tiwari, Ill.). Belmont, CA: Gossamer.

Whatley, B. (1999). *Captain Pajamas*. New York: HarperCollins.

Whitman, W. (1937). *Leaves of grass*. New York: Doubleday, Doran, and Company. (Original work published 1855)

Wisniewski, D. (2002). *Sumo mouse*. San Francisco: Chronicle.

Yolen, J. (1992). *Piggins*. New York: Voyager.

Young, E. (1989). *Lon Po Po: A red-riding hood story from China*. New York: Philomel.

Music Cited

Aguilera, C. (2000). *My kind of Christmas* [CD]. Tukwila, WA: RCA Records.

Dion, C. (1999). *All the way* [CD]. New York: Sony Music Entertainment.

Maj. (2003). All for a purpose. On *The ringleader: Mixtape volume 3* [CD]. Brentwood, TN: Gotee Records.

McBride, M. (1999). *White Christmas* [CD]. Tukwila, WA: RCA Records.

Prosper, M. (2000). Who let the dogs out? [Recorded by Baha Men] on *Baha Men* [CD]. New York: Antemis Records.

Quintanilla, A., & Los Kumbia Kings. (1999). Azucar. On *Amor, familia y respeto* [CD]. Miami Beach, FL: Emi Music Publishing.

Saliva. (2001). Click, click boom. On *Every six seconds* [CD]. New York: Island Records.

Comic Books, Graphic Novels, and Mangas Cited

Diehl, D. (1996). *Tales from the crypt: The official archives* (1st ed.). New York: St. Martin's Press.

EDFUND & California Student Aid Commission (2004). *Future 5: The power of your mind!* Rancho Cordova, CA: Author.

Edginton, J. (2000). *Xena: Warrior princess #10* [Comic book]. Milwaukie, OR: Dark Horse Comics.

Groening, M. (2005). *The Simpsons comics barn burner* [Comic book]. New York: HarperCollins.

K.K. Publications. (1962–1982). *Twilight zone* [Comic book]. Poughkeepsie, NY: Author.

Mariotte, J. (2003). *CSI: Thicker than blood*. San Diego, CA: IDW Publishing.

Miller, F. (2005). *Sin City: The hard goodbye* (2nd ed.). Milwaukie, OR: Dark Horse Comics.

Scarpelli, H., & Boldman, C. (2004). *Archie* [Comic book]. Mamaroneck, NY: Archie Comic Publications.

Takahashi, K. (1996). *Yu-Gi-Oh!* [Manga]. San Francisco: Viz Comics.

Topps Comics. (1995–1998). *X-files* [Comic book]. New York: Author.

Vertigo Comics. (1997). *Pride and joy* [Comic book]. El Paso, TX: Author.

Viz Comics. (2005). *Shonen jump* [Manga]. San Francisco: Author.

Television Productions, Motion Pictures, Animations, Videos, and Games Cited

Algar, J., Brizzi, G., Brizzi, P., Butoy, H., Glebas, F., Goldberg, E., et al. (Directors). (1999). *Fantasia* [Motion picture]. Burbank, CA: Disney.

Arad, A., Donner, R., & Lee, S. (Producers), & Singer, B. (Director). (2000). *X-Men* [Motion picture]. Los Angeles: Twentieth Century Fox.

Arledge, R., & Neufeld, V. (Executive Producers). (2005). *ABC 20/20* [Television series]. New York: ABC.

Aronowitz, G., Kalish, B., & Sakamoto, K. (Executive Producers). (2005). *Power rangers* [Television series]. Burbank, CA: Disney.

Barrymore, D., Goldberg, A., & Juvonen, N. (Producers), & Nichol, J.M. (Director). (2000). *Charlie's angels* [Motion picture]. Culver City, CA: Columbia/Tristar.

Bellisario, D.P. (Executive Producer). (2005). *JAG* [Television series]. Hollywood, CA: Paramount Pictures.

Biddle, A., & Lima, K. (Directors). (2000). *102 Dalmations* [DVD (animated)]. Burbank, CA: Disney.

Bird, B. (Director). (2004). *The Incredibles* [Motion picture (animated)]. Emeryville, CA: Pixar Animation Studio.

Bright, K., Goldberg-Meehan, S., Kaufman, M., Silveri, S., & Crane, D. (Executive Producers). (1994–2004). *Friends* [Television series]. Burbank, CA: Warner Bros.

Burnett, M. (Executive Producer). (2005). *Survivor* [Television series]. Washington, DC: Viacom International.

Burton, L., & Liggett, T. (Executive Producers). (2005). *Reading rainbow* [Television series]. New York: Public Broadcasting Service (PBS).

Cadiff, A. (Director). (1997). *Leave it to Beaver* [DVD]. Hollywood, CA: Universal Studios.

Carter, C. (Executive Producer). (1993–2002). *X-Files* [Television series]. Los Angeles: Twentieth Century Fox.

Casey, P., & Lee, D. (Executive Producers). (1993–2004). *Frasier* [Television series]. Hollywood, CA: Paramount Pictures.

CBS Broadcasting. (2005). *CBS News* [Television series]. Washington, DC: Viacom International.

Cerf, C., Hartman, D., Frith , M.K., Stiles, N., Stoia, J., & Sullivan, B. (Executive Producers). (2005). *Between the lions* [Television series (animated)]. New York: PBS.

Charest, M., Taylor, T., & Greenwald, C. (Executive Producers). (2005). *Arthur* [Television series (animated)]. New York: PBS.

Chulack, C., Crichton, M., Orman, J., Wells, J., Flint, C., Baer, N., et al. (Executive Producers). (2005). *ER* [Television series]. Burbank, CA: Warner Bros.

Clements, R., & Musker, J. (Directors). (1992). *Aladdin* [Motion picture (animated)]. Burbank, CA: Disney.

Collier, J. (Writer), & Anderson, M.B. (Director). (1996). Lisa the iconclast. In M. Groening, J. Brooks, & A. Jean (Executive Producers), *The Simpsons* [Television series (animated)]. New York: Fox Broadcasting Company.

Csupo, G., & Klasky, A. (Executive Producers). (1991–2003). *Rugrats* [Television series (animated)]. Washington, DC: Viacom International.

Davis, A. (Director). (2003). *Holes* [Motion picture]. Burbank, CA: Disney Entertainment.

Davola, J., Hamilton, A.L., Robbins, B., Tollin, M., & Perry, M. (Executive Producers). (2005). *One tree hill* [Television series]. Burbank, CA: Warner Bros.

Farrelly, B., & Farrelly, P. (Directors). (1994). *Dumb and dumber* [DVD]. Los Angeles: New Line Home Entertainment.

Fleming, V. (Director). (1939). *Gone with the wind* [DVD]. Burbank, CA: Warner Home Video.

Fottrell, M., Melniker, B., & Uslan, M.E. (Executive Producers), & Pitof (Director). (2004). *Catwoman* [Motion picture]. Burbank, CA: Warner Bros.

Fukunga, G., Fukunga, C., Watson, B., & Fukengama, G. (Executive Producers). (1996–2003). *DragonBall Z* [Television series (animated)]. New York: Time Warner.

Gendel, M., Ungar, R., Arad, A., Caracciolo, J.M., & Lee, S. (Executive Producers). (2004). *Spider-man* [Television series (animated)]. Santa Monica, CA: MTV Networks.

Greenwalt, D., & Noxon, M. (Producers). (1997–2003). *Buffy the vampire slayer* [Television series]. Hollywood, CA: United Paramount Network.

Groening, M., Brooks, J., & Jean, A. (Executive Producers). (1989–present). *The Simpsons* [Television series (animated)]. Hollywood, CA: Fox.

Grossfeld, N.J., Kahn, A.R., & Kenney, T. (Executive Producers). (2005). *Pokémon* [Television series (animated)]. Burbank, CA: Warner Bros.

Guthrie, B., & Duffield, R. (Directors). (1995). *Wishbone: Hot diggety dog* [DVD]. Richardson, TX: Hit Entertainment.

Hanna, W., & Barbera, J. (Executive Producers). (1978). *Scooby-Doo* [Television series (animated)]. Burbank, CA: Warner Bros.

Hartman, B., & Seibert , F. (Executive Producers). (2005). *Fairly odd parents* [Television series (animated)]. Washington, DC: Viacom International.

Hewitt, P. (Director). (2004). *Garfield* [DVD (animated)]. Los Angeles: Fox Home Entertainment.

Hillenburg, S. (Director). (2004). *SpongeBob Squarepants: The movie* [Motion picture (animated)]. Hollywood, CA: Paramount Pictures.

Hillenburg, S. (Executive Producer). (2005). *SpongeBob SquarePants* [Television series (animated)]. Washington, DC: Viacom International.

Jenson, V., & Adamson, A. (Directors). (2001). *Shrek* [DVD (animated)]. Glendale, CA: Dreamworks.

Kenney, T. (Executive Producer). (2005). *Yu-Gi-Oh!* [Television series (animated)]. Burbank, CA: Warner Bros.

Kessler, T., Twomey, J., Johnson, T.P., & Santomero, A. (Executive Producers). (1996–2004). *Blue's clues* [Television series (animated)]. Washington, DC: Viacom International.

Lehrer, J. (2005). *Online newshour with Jim Lehrer* [Television series]. New York: MacNeil/Lehrer Productions.

Loubert, P., Startz, J., Hirsh, M., Martin, K.L., Blank, A., Smith, C., et al. (Executive Producers). (1994–1997). *The magic school bus* [Television series (animated)]. New York: PBS.

Luske, H., & Johnson, W. (Directors). (1950). *Cinderella* [DVD]. Burbank, CA: Disney.

MacNeil/Lehrer Productions. (2005). *PBS online newshour*. Arlington, VA: Author.

McCracken, C., Miller, B.A., & Potamkin, B. (Executive Producers). (2005). *Powerpuff girls* [Television series (animated)]. New York: Time Warner.

Nelson, G. (Director). (1987). *Allan Quatermain and the last city of gold* [DVD]. Santa Monica, CA: Metro-Goldwyn-Mayer Pictures.

Nintendo. (1988). *Super Mario 2* [Video game]. Redmond, WA: Author.

Nintendo. (2004). *Mario vs. Donkey Kong* [Video game]. Redmond, WA: Author.

Patton, C. (Director). (2001). *Inspector Gadget saves Christmas* [VHS]. New York: Vidmark/Trimark.

Raimi, S. (Director). (2002). *Spider-man* [Motion picture]. Culver City, CA: Columbia/Tri-Star.

Raimi, S. (Director). (2004). *Spider-man 2* [DVD]. Culver City, CA: Columbia/Tri-Star.

Rollman, E.S., & Tufoya-Booton, D. (Executive Producers). (1999–2003). *Digimon* [Television series (animated)]. Burbank, CA: Disney.

Rosman, M. (Director). (2004). *A Cinderella story* [Motion picture]. Burbank, CA: Warner Bros.

Ross, H. (Director). (1989). *Steel magnolias* [VHS]. Culver City, CA: Columbia/Tri-Star.

Soria, M., Trench, T., (Producers), & Tennant, A. (Director). (1998). *Ever after* [DVD]. Los Angeles, CA: Fox Home Entertainment.

Spicer, B. (Director). (1997). *McHale's navy* [VHS]. Hollywood, CA: Universal Studios.

Thirteen/WNET. (Producer). (2005). *Nature* [Television series]. New York: Author.

Vernon, C., & Adamson, A. (Directors). (2004). *Shrek 2* [DVD]. Glendale, CA: Dreamworks.

Walsh, V., Gifford, C., & Johnson, B. (Executive Producers). (2005). *Dora the explorer* [Television series (animated)]. Washington, DC: Viacom International.

Yuyama, K. (2000). *Pokémon the movie* [Motion picture]. Burbank, CA: Warner Bros.

Zemeckis, R. (Director). (2000). *Cast away* [Motion picture]. Los Angeles: Twentieth Century Fox.

Zemeckis, R. (Director). (2004). *The polar express* [Motion picture (animated)]. Burbank, CA: Warner Bros.

INDEX

Note: Page numbers followed by *f*, *t*, and *r* indicate figures, tables, and reproducibles, respectively.